Energy Policy
and Public
Administration

Energy Policy and Public Administration

Edited by
Gregory A. Daneke
University of Michigan

George K. Lagassa
University of New Hampshire

LexingtonBooks
D.C. Heath and Company
Lexington, Massachusetts
Toronto

Library of Congress Cataloging in Publication Data

Main entry under title:
Energy policy and public administration.

    1. Energy policy—United States—Addresses, essays, lectures. I. Daneke,
Gregory A II. Lagassa, George K
HD9502.U52E5174   333.79'0973   79-3182
ISBN 0-669-03395-2

Copyright © 1980 by D.C. Heath and Company

Published simultaneously in Canada

Printed in the United States of America

International Standard Book Number: 0-669-03395-2

Library of Congress Catalog Card Number: 79-3182

Contents

Preface

The spark that ignited this joint enterprise came from the 1979 National Conference of the American Society for Public Administration, at which the editors chaired separate panels on the administrative dimensions of energy policy. Daneke's panel, "Administering Alternative Energy Systems," and Lagassa's panel, "The Role of the States in Energy Policy," both revealed the importance of involvement in energy decision making by all levels of government. Subsequent discussions between the editors led to the conclusion that the administrative balance that results from affording a key role to all levels of government was a major prerequisite to a desirable policy balance.

The need for such policy balance is made abundantly clear by the stalemate that has brought academic discourse on energy policy to a grinding halt. The nature of this stalemate may be easily discerned from a brief analysis of the energy policy literature that has emerged since the 1973 Arab oil embargo. According to this literature, it would appear that energy policymakers are confronted with an unrealistic and therefore paralyzing choice between two rather extreme sets of energy strategies and futures. On the one hand, there is the choice of large-scale, centralized technologies (such as nuclear power and synthetic fuels) which grant a disproportionate decision-making role to technical experts in large government and corporate bureaucracies. On the other hand, there is the choice of small-scale, decentralized, "appropriate" technologies, which rely on renewable resources, match energy quality to end-use needs, and are expected to lead to more democratic and humanistic decision-making styles. In developing this book, our objective has been not only to examine the nature of this choice but, more importantly, to move beyond it by showing that the best *possible* energy future will be not exclusively one path or the other but a balanced mix of both.

To this end, we have attempted to include points of view that clarify the advantages and disadvantages of both paths, display the successes and failures of actual energy policy innovations at various levels of government, outline the constraints and opportunities in emergent public policies, and specify realistic strategies for achieving a balanced energy future.

While our enterprise has not permitted an exhaustive examination of all possible energy resources and technologies, the chapters selected represent the basic policy issues and administrative questions that must be confronted along whichever path we choose to follow to our energy future.

1

The Defunct Energy Dichotomy

George K. Lagassa and
Gregory A. Daneke

With the publication in 1976 of Amory B. Lovins's article "Energy Strategy: The Road not Taken?"[1] a new dimension was added to the energy debate. For the first time a comprehensive vision of alternative energy goals, based on an integrated understanding of the technological, economic, environmental, social, and political aspects of energy strategy, was lucidly articulated. Lovins's criticism of present-day "centralized high technology" and his advocacy of a decentralized, diverse, and renewable energy future found ready supporters in those who had already been persuaded by similar arguments made previously by E.F. Schumacher,[2] Barry Commoner,[3] and Wilson Clark;[4] but it found equally ardent critics in the energy industry, particularly the electric utility industry, whose representatives castigated Lovins's position as a utopian vision which was based on inaccurate facts and overly romantic values.[5]

The debate between the advocates of the hard and soft paths continues, and by its very intensity it renders reasonable judgment difficult at best. This difficulty stems from the fact that a "zero sum game" mentality prevails between the competing camps, as a gain by one is viewed as a loss by the other. In other words, the soft and hard paths are viewed as mutually exclusive and incompatible. This, of course, need not be the case. While Lovins may be correct that limits upon fluid capital and slavish devotion to high technology greatly constrain the mix of hard and soft ingredients, some sort of mix will be required by existing sociopolitical realities.

Discovering the appropriate mix of energy ingredients is the task which lies ahead. This task is made more arduous not only by the bipolarity of the energy debate, but also by the existing systems of policy formulation and institutional change. Energy policy is, as Lovins suggests, a result of "incremental adhocracy." Energy perhaps more than any other policy domain is a paradigm case of what Theodore Lowi calls "interest group liberalism,"[6] or a situation in which competing interest groups (although not equally competitive) and fragmented institutional arrangements converge to disaggregate and diffuse the policymaking process. The result of this diffusion is a lack of comprehensive goals and lack of accompanying strategies for their achievement. While one might argue (as some of our authors do) that such a diffusion is the essence of democratic government, the confusion over goals and objectives allows powerful interests to make energy policy by default. Even a goal of letting market forces prevail would be difficult to assemble under the current structure of institutional arrangements. Moreover, it is unlikely that the delicate mixture of energy ingredients required to sustain our way of life will emerge spontaneously from the existing energy management morass.

The potential for ameliorating these difficulties is not great. Public confidence in institutional solutions seems to be decreasing in exact proportion to the increased time spent in gas lines. Meanwhile, the Department of Energy (DOE) blithely administers its Rube Goldberg mechanisms for increasing domestic production and decreasing consumption, without any appreciable success, and holds forth visions of nuclear utopia just around the breeder bend.

While it is true that the DOE, as structured by the Carter administration, does have a modestly funded Office of Small Scale Technology and an Office of Conservation and Solar Applications (with the major mission of commercializing solar technologies) and that the 1978 National Energy Act does provide tax incentives for residential, commercial, and industrial conservation efforts and solar installations, these increments of apparently soft path strategy are relatively small. The emphasis of current energy policy is not on the comprehensive development of the so-called alternative technologies—wind, geothermal, photovoltaics, low head hydropower, biomass, and other solar. Rather such technologies are treated as minor supplements to an energy system fundamentally based on "centralized high technology." Indeed, the most significant single funding program for solar research and development is earmarked for solar bulk power generation by earth-based mirror farms, huge orbiting satellites, and ocean thermal technologies (OTEC).

As several of our contributors demonstrate, the really exciting innovations in energy policy and administration are occurring at the state and local levels. The federal government, however, has had little role in stimulating or orchesrating these activities. Thus, potential for fostering soft path developments and then mixing them with the hard path remains unrealized.

The administration's myopia with regard to both alternative technologies and alternative institutional arrangements is highly unfortunate. Yet in making this point, we do not wish to magnify the hard versus soft path debate. Rather, we concur with the preliminary report of the Energy Project at the Harvard Business School[7] that the hard path-soft path debate involves "competing romanticisms" which have the consequence of clouding the more fundamental issue at stake. The fact is that the nations of the world are increasingly competing for international energy sources which grow scarcer with time. Even based on moderately optimistic predictions about the development of new technologies for the recovery of fossil fuels and the ability of American energy consumers to conserve, this nation will not be able to meet its future energy needs without relying to a considerably greater extent than it does now on soft path technologies—improved energy conservation techniques, more efficient end-use, and smaller scale processes using renewable energy sources. Certainly the virtual bankruptcy of Project Independence supports this conclusion. Its dedication to energy independence by 1980 (and subsequently, by 1985) through almost exclusive reliance on hard path strategies—encouraging further domestic production of fossil fuels with higher prices and accelerated leasing, expediting nuclear licensing procedures, increasing the generation of electrical energy using nonpetroleum primary fuel resources—emerges, in retrospect, as a miserable failure.

Increased reliance on dispersed and diversified energy technologies will, of course, encounter numerous constraints. Initially, there is the inertia of prior institutional commitments. These commitments are particularly evident in the electric utility field, where strong financial incentives have prevailed on the behalf of huge multi-state bulk power generation and transmission networks since the early 1950s.

These electric power systems, because they waste about three-fifths of the energy potential of primary energy sources at end-use, epitomize what is wrong with "centralized high technology" and have been a popular target for the wrath of soft path advocates. Yet we cannot realistically expect the electric utility industry to roll over and play dead simply to facilitate realization of a new life-style. A similar point can be made about commercial nuclear power, which has the weight of over two decades of government support behind it. Despite its various environmental, economic, and public image problems, it still looms large on many agendas for the energy future. In general, the centralized posture represented by the electric power industry has lost little vitality in the wake of the energy crisis, and it may indeed by solidifying its position through the impending introduction of integrated grids and power wheeling.

Another major constraint upon diversified systems is the American public and its immovable energy attitudes. Many people still do not accept that we have an energy problem, and even more are unwilling to make sacrifices to alleviate it. Whole cloth adoption of the soft path would be impossible without extensive public support, and, at this point in time, that support is not overwhelmingly evident. Moreover, low income groups and minorities have come out strongly in opposition to the low growth economy associated with the soft path.[8] It has yet to be shown (with the exception of isolated instances) how dispersed technologies and community self-reliance will serve the urban poor. While there may be many more unskilled jobs in diversified energy systems, until the infrastructure of full scale low technology industries is in place, minorities continue to suffer the disproportional impact of the energy transition.[9]

Nevertheless, some communities and sets of individuals are demonstrating a new energy ethos. On a piecemeal basis citizen groups around the country are developing more of an end-users perspective. Community-level experiments in conservation and alternative energy technologies are gradually becoming commonplace, and eventually, perhaps, this ground-swell will have a significant impact on energy developments.

In summary, then, since we cannot expect to continue to blindly follow the conventional or hard path to the exclusion of other technologies, and since the full-fledged adoption of the soft path is very severely constrained by the nature of the American policy process, prior commitments, and public attitudes, the soft path-hard path question becomes moot. The real issue is the degree to which the future is open to movement along the continuum between the hard and soft paths. To more fully comprehend the nature and configuration of that continuum in practical policy terms, the following set of original papers have been drawn together. Some of our authors approach the soft path in a pragmatic fashion, by describing and assessing steps that are already being taken at all levels of government (local and state as well as federal) to encourage alternative technologies, community and individual energy self-reliance, and the efficient use of renewable resources. Others illustrate the complex texture of energy and government systems and the resulting national dependency on the hard path. Collectively they display the institutional obstacles and opportunities which shape the nation's energy future.

Notes

1. Amory B. Lovins, "Energy Strategy: The Road Not Taken?" *Foreign Affairs* (Fall 1976):65-69.

2. E.F. Schumacher, Small Is Beautiful (New York: Harper and Row, 1973).

3. Barry Commoner, The Poverty of Power (New York: Knopf, 1976).

4. Wilson Clark, Energy for Survival: The Alternative to Extinction (New York: Anchor/Doubleday, 1974).

5. See Edison Electric Institute, "A Series of Critical Essays on Amory Lovins' 'Energy Strategy: The Road Not Taken?'" *Electric Perspective* No. 7713 (New York: E.E.I., 1977).

6. Theodore J. Lowi, The End of Liberalism: The Second Republic of the United States, 2nd edition (New York: W.W. Norton and Company, 1979).

7. Robert Stobaugh and Daniel Yergin, "After the Second Shock: Pragmatic Energy Strategies," *Foreign Affairs* (Spring 1979):836-871.

8. "Report of the NAACP National Energy Conference," December 21, 1977; Donnamarie M. Cronin, "Women's Place in a No-Growth Society," Public Utilities Fortnightly (January 4, 1979):21-23.

9. See Lenneal Henderson, "Energy and Social Equity," in Robert Lawrence, ed., New Dimension to Energy Policy (Lexington, Mass.: LexingtonBooks, D.C. Heath and Company, 1979).

**Part I
Managing the
Energy Problem**

Whichever energy path we follow, it is obvious that at some point some institution must be developed for making authoritative policy decisions. The chapters in part I address this issue from a variety of perspectives: chapter 2, by Gregory A. Daneke, questions the competence of the federal government to manage effectively the complexity and diversity of our energy problem and calls for more institutional innovation at the grass roots. Chapter 3, by Walter J. Mead, is founded on a similar critique of federal government management of the energy problem but concludes that government intervention in the energy marketplace is usually counterproductive. Chapter 4, by Richard Worthington, deals with the management problem from a more sociological perspective by contrasting previous styles of elite management with illustrations of the principle of self-reliance. The final selection, by Andy Lawrence and Gregory A. Daneke, specifies those energy goals which are best achieved on a decentralized basis and examines the interface between energy technology systems and decentralized social systems.

2
The Poverty of National Energy Policy and Administration

Gregory A. Daneke

Introduction

In a very fundamental sense, the energy crisis really is not an energy crisis at all; rather, it is an institutional crisis. The root problem, of course, is that demand for oil is increasing faster than production. Whether the apparent leveling off of production stems from absolute scarcity or from political decisions among producer nations is really immaterial—the effect is the same; the era of cheap and dependable (not subject to capricious interruption) oil resources is nearing an end. Equally uninteresting, from a practical policy standpoint, are the various arguments regarding the pros and cons of allowing market forces to adjust for any energy shortfalls (assuming they are slight). A free market has rarely prevailed in the energy realm, and given the various nonmarket factors associated with energy policy (for example, defense) it is unlikely that market signals (to the extent that they exist) will suffice. Moreover, whether on grounds of national security or a host of other nebulous reasons, the federal government is likely to pursue some sort of transition policy aimed at reducing dependence upon oil and ultimately developing more sustainable and/or renewable energy resources. Such a transition might involve a vast array of potential resources. The critical issue facing the nation is which resources offer the best chances for a smooth, cheap (both financially and in terms of thermodynamic match) and environmentally sound transition. It is not, however, the purpose of this discussion to explicitly identify these resources, for the mechanisms of analysis required to discover this delicate mix are not presently in place either within or without government. Rather, the purpose here is to explore briefly the unlikelihood of a smooth transition, given the various institutional arrangements and assumptions which now shape national energy policy. This institutional crisis, driven by the energy crisis mentality, is likely to lead to the development of several inefficient, environmentally destructive, and ultimately ineffective policies and programs. It is impossi-

These ideas stem from an effort to understand the nature of national energy planning and policy development which was sponsored by the U.S. General Accounting Office. The author, therefore, would like to acknowledge the contributions to his thinking by all of the members of the NEP Taskforce. He would like to thank his colleague Gunter Schramm for his helpful comments. None of these individuals nor the GAO, is responsible, however, for the opinions expressed here.

9

ble to capture all of the nuances of this energy management morass in a brief set of statements; yet the following list provides a starting point. Basically, the present situation reflects

1. A failure on the part of Congress and the executive branch to develop a comprehensive and coherent national energy policy.
2. A failure to provide a well-orchestrated approach to energy policy by the various federal agencies.
3. A failure to coordinate state and local responses and to capitalize upon grassroots initiatives.

These are, of course, complex issues. Thus, what is provided here must be regarded as merely an agenda for future inquiry.

The National Management Myth

As Howard and Elisabeth Odum vividly point out, energy is a fundamental element in all human and natural systems.[1] Energy is the all-pervasive exchange medium. Those cultures which have been able to capture large stores of energy and/or wisely manage limited supplies prospered. This, however, does not necessarily imply that an abundant supply of energy guarantees a high quality of life, for, abundant or otherwise, cheap energy encourages its substitution for other inputs into production such as capital and labor and generally a high-waste society. In other words, energy brings both affluence and effluents.

    Given the central role of energy in a highly technological culture, uncertainty regarding major sources of energy (in this case oil and nuclear) poses serious threats to the general welfare. This nation has certainly made transitions between energy sources in the past (for example, wood to coal and coal to oil); yet, even when aided by governmental interventions, these transitions took twenty to thirty years. Furthermore, these transitions were engendered, for the most part, by quasi-natural market forces, and primary sources were not necessarily subject to catastrophic disruptions. In an energy intensive society, the lack of a smooth and, therefore, gradual transition can have devastating effects upon the entire economy and the national security. Initially, a prudent strategy would involve reductions in the energy intensiveness or wastefulness of the society. In the long run, a diversification of supply would probably prove wise, for just as with natural systems, a diversified energy system would be more stable.

The National Policy Problem

While growing, this concern has yet to penetrate traditional approaches and institutions. In some respects energy has become a goal in and of itself, and many policymakers ignore the fundamental issue of "energy for what?" To the extent that goals for energy have emerged, there is still very little consensus upon them. In general, energy policy at the federal level is plagued by the following problems:[2]

1. *Lack of basic road map* for a suitable energy transition. In essence, even if the nation knew where it was going, it would not know how to get there from here.
2. A perpetuation of the general bureaucratic tendency toward *institutional proliferation*. Rather than challenging outmoded institutional constraints (designed to promote particular energy resources and therefore limit competition) the federal government is content to merely pile on additional institutional arrangements.
3. A general *neglect of the social and environmental factors associated with energy use*. Energy policymakers have been particularly eager to pursue life-quality trade-offs without a fundamental understanding of the value of either energy or the environment.
4. An overall reliance upon "ad-hocracy," or the tendency to respond to changes rather than facilitate collective choices and create changes.

Attempts at ameliorating these difficulties become quickly hung up on the pikes of the perpetual controversy over the appropriate role of the federal government. This controversy, while important, need not forestall energy policy indefinitely. Clear market signals may find it difficult to emerge from the labyrinth of incentives and subsidies currently in place. Through a number of highly convoluted institutional arrangements, certain resources with substantial impacts upon the environment have become artificially cheap (for example, oil, nuclear, and soon, perhaps, coal and synfuels). This "Gordian Knot" of artificial economies implicitly recognizes a number of nonmarket forces (public goods, allowable monopolies, and so on), while ignoring certain others (environmental values, community self-reliance, and so on). These observations do not deny the value of the "market concept," and of neoclassical economic theory generally, as heuristic policy tools. But the point that must be made is that even if one wanted to reinstate a semblance of competitive market forces for energy, it would require careful planning and intricate national policymaking.

However, a national policy must indeed be national and thus draw upon state and local perspectives and peculiarities. The notion that rational planning flows from the federal government downward is, at best, pernicious. Moreover, despite the establishment of a Department of Energy (DOE), federal energy policy is not monolithic. Agencies in Washington provide a widely divided front on energy issues. For example, numerous directives emerging from the Environmental Protection Agency and the Department of the Interior are in direct conflict with DOE initiatives. Even if executive agencies and Congress could get their act together, subnational energy policy would remain a crazy-quilt of selective responses.

The source of this lacuna is twofold. Initially, it is unlikely that exercises of central authority such as auto efficiency requirements and natural gas or even oil decontrols alone will guarantee the required transition. Second, federal initiatives designed to stimulate state and local responses may require a greater level of monitoring and control than is presently available in the structure of intergovernmental relationships and thus ultimately be unsuccessful. Besides largely determining the level of impact of major federal initiatives,[3] state and local governments as well as community interest groups can and have served as both vanguards and vetoes to national energy policy. National policy must, therefore, accept the fact that on occasion, state and local governments should be allowed to lead as well as follow.

The Vagaries of the National Energy Posture

To begin to address the divergency of subnational responses to the need for an energy transition, one must understand the national energy posture. This, however, is easier said than done. Numerous proposals have come and gone, and still most analysts would agree that there is no national energy policy. Nevertheless, a few basic themes have arisen out of the various national energy plans and policy initiatives.[4] These themes have included such items as economic growth (for example, increased productivity), economic stability (for example, lower levels of inflation), national security for the United States and its allies, and a reasonably sound relationship with the natural environment. In general, the vague objective of national energy policy since the oil embargo of 1973 has been to reduce the level of oil imports. This posture, of course, resulted form the realization that the United States was virtually helpless in the event of a long-term interruption of supplies from the Persian Gulf.

However, the desire to pursue the objective of reduced oil dependence was mixed, and strategies ranged from complete "Energy Independence" to slight import reductions. The idea of independence itself was sufficiently ill-understood as to foster a vast array of panic proposals. Whether viable or not, few of these proposals were very carefully conceived or adequately analyzed in terms of long-range societal objectives. From this hastily formulated energy agenda, the following batch of proposals continue to influence policy:

1. Oil and natural gas prices should immediately be increased to reflect actual replacement costs.
2. The nation should shift as much and as soon as possible to the use of its abundant coal reserves.
3. Nuclear development should be accelerated.
4. Inexhaustible resource technologies should be brought into the marketplace as rapidly as is feasible.

The Administrative Morass

The general lack of coherence exhibited in national energy policy is, of course, partially the result of the fact that Congress has abdicated policymaking to the fledgling Department of Energy. As its first director, Dr. James Schlesinger, once explained, "the main business of this department is the development of national energy policies and the national consensus behind them, to the extent that that is possible." This usurpation of congressional policy prerogative is fairly indicative of the growth of the administrative state, growth which occurs with a legislative blessing. When confronted with either a complex problem and/or issue which requires the clarification of national goals and objectives, Congress is more willing to create a new agency than to deal with the problem at hand in any coherent or comprehensive way. However, the creation of the Department of Energy from an amorphous collection of conflicting missions and mandates (previously housed over the years in the Federal Power Commission, the Atomic Energy Commission, the Energy Research and Development Administration, the Federal Energy Office, and the Federal Energy Administration) raises the problem of administrative policymaking to new heights of absurdity. Moreover, the creation of an agency which depends upon the energy crisis has led to a stream of policies which have actually exacerbated the energy situation. As William Rodgers has so cogently pointed out, ". . . the energy crisis is a bureaucrat's dream, so much to ponder, so much to analyze and coordinate. So much expertise required. So much paperwork."[5]

The trauma of bringing together the remnants of several misbegotten agencies (all with unique management styles) has been exacerbated by the leadership style which seems to have prevailed in DOE. In short, upper-level managers demonstrated a general lack of appreciation for basic communication and organizational dynamics. DOE's own internal management study, conducted by the firm of Coopers and Lybrand, while not exactly earthshaking, alluded to the following problems:[6]

1. Planning and policy development are practically nonexistent, or merely "ad-hoc," and have not been linked to program budgeting.
2. Personnel, whether holdovers or new hires, are generally ill-suited to the administrative tasks of the new agency.
3. Managerial and accountability systems for finance, procurement, and project oversight are rare.
4. Sophisticated modeling and analysis are misused to either justify or accept the blame for decisions made without the aid of analysis.

Like all closed systems, DOE has exhibited a high level of entropy and a general unwillingness to tap outside ideas and energies. A major Common Cause study identified DOE as the least open agency in the federal government, less open even than the Department of Defense. Its record on public involvement and access has been dismal, and these tendencies are particularly deadly when one considers, as Common Cause did, the narrow and homogeneous makeup of DOE employees.[7] Meanwhile, its support for university and nonestablishment research (outside the major think tanks and national labs) has been appallingly low for an agency with a broad research mission. This, of course, may explain why much of the innovation in terms of the energy transition has occurred beyond the federal government's purview.

Generally speaking, DOE has exhibited little of the foresight which Congress may have hoped for. Examples of DOE initiatives with unforeseen negative consequences abound (the glut of natural gas, the gas line-producing distribution scheme, and so on). Moreover, its one piece of forward-looking policy, the "Strategic Petroleum Reserve," is years behind schedule, and, if ever completed, will be billions over its budget. Another, and perhaps more telling example of a lack of long-range policy development capability within the Department of Energy can be found in the Iranian incident. DOE's principal policy formulation arm, the Office of Planning and Evaluation (P&E), literally went down for over six weeks to develop an "Iranian Response Plan." By the time this office was prepared to make its recommendations to Congress, impacts of the Iranian shortfall had been manifest at the nation's gasoline pumps for months. Certainly if P&E were in the business of developing contingency plans for the Department of Energy, it would have had something on the shelf to deal with such a situation as the Iranian Revolution. However, as its former director, Al Alm, so often remarked, "ours is principally a fire-fighting operation."

This notion of fire-fighting not only characterizes the capabilities of DOE but, perhaps, of the entire federal energy establishment. Given the prevalence of this approach, specific resource development strategies have come out of the federal oven somewhat half-baked. It is to these strategies which this discussion now turns.

The Cloud over Conventional Resources

A major thrust of national energy policy has been the substitution of domestic supplies of conventional resources for foreign supplies. Here "conventional" implies oil and natural gas (produced in the traditional ways), nuclear, and the direct burning of coal. More recently, certain unconventional production processes and alternative sources of traditional fuels (for example, synfuels) have been drawn into the emotional battle for energy self-sufficiency. Despite this virtual onslaught on domestic supply potential, "Energy Independence" remains as elusive today as when the notion was coined during the Nixon administration. Moreover, the rush for independence of supply without serious attention to reductions in demand (that is, conservation) is likely to produce a number of energy/environment dysfunctions.

Oil: The Big Uncertainty

No matter which projection of oil reserves one subscribes to, oil is becoming less plentiful, which is to say less cheap. As all economists know, the extent of remaining supplies is more a function of price than projected reserves, anyhow. Eventually, oil may prove far too precious an ingredient of petrochemicals and plastics to remain a primary fuel source; however, at present, its versatility and relative ease of transportation, marketing, and environmental control continue to make it the most attractive energy form. The problem is not in using oil, but in using it unwisely, or in ways that do not reflect its true value.

    For a number of years and a number of reasons (mostly political) federal policies have made oil (especially domestic oil) artificially cheap. The impacts of these policies have been complex; however, the following emerge as the most profound:

1. *Cheap oil and cheap energy generally encouraged waste* in terms of direct use, in extending the trend of producing nondurable goods, and in promoting a settlement pattern dependent upon extensive use of the automobile.[8]
2. Holding prices below market value discouraged the development of new sources, *engendering scarcity*.[9]

3. Lower domestic productivity, in turn, *increased dependence on foreign oil* (primarily from what are now OPEC nations), thus creating the potential for economically devastating disruptions of supply.

Essentially, federal policymakers have only and only very recently concerned themselves with the third problem listed above. The immediate solution appears to be the rapid decontrol of domestic oil. However, policymakers have vacillated on the level and time table of decontrol, as well as who will reap the profits when currently owned domestic oil jumps to world (OPEC) price. Given the amount of time (perhaps ten years) required for Americans to adjust to higher oil prices, gradual decontrol merely prolongs the agony and makes the ultimate transition more difficult. However, elected decision-makers have not been willing to suffer the political ramifications which will follow in the wake of the initial economic shock of decontrol. For example, the clandestinely formulated White House decontrol schedule, known to insiders as the "Eisenstadt-Shermer Plan," was designed primarily (and modeled explicitly) to put off the major economic impacts of decontrol until after the next presidential election.

Even if policymakers are willing to "bite the bullet" and decontrol oil immediately, there is no guarantee that it will have all of the desired effects, in particular the reduction of imports. Initially, decontrol strengthens the cartel which may continue to drag all oil prices up. Some groups of citizens (that is, the poor) will simply be priced out of the energy market entirely. Yet, many other Americans may be slow to adjust their consumption patterns if conscious conservation programs are not spelled out. Meanwhile, domestic production may not immediately rise to policymakers' expectations, given lagging price differentials and perhaps the realization of the ultimate limits of domestic supply.

Finally, major oil companies may not necessarily reinvest their newly found profits in producing more oil; they may (as some have already done) seek to diversify (that is, buy stock in nonoil and even nonenergy industries). Given the constant threat of nationalization, this is not an unwarranted strategy. The "Windfall Profits Tax" and "Energy Security Fund" have, of course, been proposed to rechannel a portion of the enormous profits gained through decontrol to the poor and to new energy projects, but there is virtually no way to determine the real rent gained by the vertically integrated majors.

For years a proposed strategy for reducing dependence was merely to limit oil imports, or tax them the way the West Germans do, and therefore return some of the potential profits to the public while discouraging waste. While simple and potentially effective, such a strategy was politically impossible. Enacted now, along with decontrol, it would merely serve to exacerbate short-run scarcity; however, ultimately some form of import quota may be the only way to insure a reduction in dependence upon foreign oil. Neither decontrol nor import restrictions deal with the equity problems of higher oil prices, but these issues might be just as well left up to welfare policies to resolve.

Government performance at all levels has merely served to make oil policy more complex, confusing, and ultimately more uncertain. A more efficacious path might be for government bodies (especially local government) to encourage reduced consumption. Auto efficiency standards and gas price increases alone will probably not be sufficient to cut the wasteful use of oil in the United States. A better strategy might involve the federal government in cooperative efforts to develop rigorous conservation measures in industry and localities (to be discussed at length later). Several states as well as numerous localities have already begun preparing for a less oily future.[10] But oil saving should be a vital consideration in all community infrastructure and capital facilities planning as well as state level management. A GAO survey of state energy offices suggests that availability of liquid fuels is rapidly emerging as a major concern among state governments.[11] Without federal coordination this concern is likely to yield to interregional competition, hording, and other dysfunctional manifestations.[12]

The Coal Chaos

The federal government continues to bank on coal as its energy "ace in the hole," and in recent years the hue and cry for greater coal utilization has again arisen in Washington. But increased utilization remains stalled due to the ambiguities of government policies. For example, while preaching coal conversion, DOE lifted its ban on natural gas as a utility fuel in order to reduce the glut created by its gas deregulation. Meanwhile, the Department of the Interior's new leasing and reclamation programs have made western low-sulfur coal a last resort,[13] and EPA's Air Quality Standards make burning high-sulfur eastern coal highly expensive. Surface mining provisions, exorbitant railroad rates, and declining ratios of electrical demand further cloud the coal transition. At present, a sizable coal surplus is ready for transport, but investments in coal generation have not been forthcoming largely because of the climate of uncertainty.

Aside from granting variances, which merely put off the air pollution problem, states have done little to ameliorate the coal conversion problem. If anything, state and local governments as well as Indian tribes have made the coal transition more remote.[14] Federal programs to revise railroad rates and to have EPA adjust New Source Performance Standards for low-sulfur coal plants may ease the coal malaise somewhat. Higher oil prices may also bring more coal utilization on line. But a full-scale transition will require internalizing of the negative externalities associated with coal. Coal is dirty stuff, and consumers of coal-generated energy will have to pay the cost of clean-up sooner or later. Paying these costs at the front end is far cheaper than when they are deposited in the environment. Scrubbers and bag houses, while expensive, are considerably less expensive than using human lungs as a filtering device. Moreover, rolling in the cost of reclaimed land may be more equitable and ultimately more efficient than leaving the residuals of strip-mining for the local communities, the watershed area, and/or future generations to deal with.

If there remains little willingness to pay for these associated costs of coal, it is probably just as well to leave it in the ground. Since electrical demand is not increasing at the rate predicted a few years ago, little added electrical capacity may actually be required. The Council on Environmental Quality contends that with serious conservation (increased energy efficiency) neither new coal-fired nor nuclear plants will be needed.[15] Nonetheless, if coal is truly to serve as an ace in the hole, productive capacity might be developed to absorb shortfalls in electricity which might result from the unkept nuclear promise. Futhermore, coal liquefaction may provide a valuable hedge against oil supply disruptions, especially if environmental as well as economic difficulties can be resolved.

The Synfuels Insanity

Along with coal liquefaction or merely gasification, a variety of other hybrid conventional fuel options have been grouped under the label "synthetic fuels" or simply "synfuels," which include such things as oil shale, unconventional natural gas, tar sands, and other heavy oils. Technologies for extracting these resources have existed for some time, but until recently they were viewed as uneconomical and/or environmentally unsound. In the "gas line summer of 1979," concern for synfuels was resurrected in a new wave of enthusiasm. What has been so perplexing about this new interest in synfuels is not so much that they are back on the policy agenda, but that they have been linked to various proposals for an entirely new policy process (for example, the Energy Mobilization Board). In essence, synfuels are now being forwarded in an atmosphere of haste in which their benefits in terms of national security, for example, are supposed to obscure the fact that they are still not economically or environmentally viable. In this scenario, synfuels will somehow be swept along in the movement for a more expeditious energy development strategy, and thus be exempt from NEPA (The National Environmental Policy Act) and other safeguards of administrative due process, as well as receiving massive subsidies. Such a process would not only be tremendously wasteful, and therefore inflationary, but it might produce severe environmental degradation.

This does not imply that mitigation is impossible, or that certain technologies may become highly economical. It merely suggests that appropriate trade-offs could well be ignored via these new strategies. Consider, for example, the current front runner among synfuels, oil shale. Some above-ground retorting processes for oil shale produce nearly a ton of solid waste and twenty-two barrels of polluted water per barrel of oil produced, not to mention various air pollutants.[16] The "in situ" or below-ground process (firing the oil in the rock) produces considerably less pollution, yet is far from pollution-free and still uses a good deal of the water from the arid regions where oil shale is located (for example, Utah, Colorado). In situ, of course, is also more expensive than the strip-mining used for above-ground retorting.

In sum, various environmental costs associated with synfuels have yet to be fully accounted for. Moreover, proposed "crash programs" for synfuels are likely to buy very little oil displacement at a very high environmental cost. A recent RAND study suggested that an accelerated synfuels program would "cause both higher cost and poor system performance," with projected cost overruns of 100 percent.[17]

State governments have exhibited a mixed set of responses to the synfuels push, but by and large they are all eager at least to experiment with the development of synthetic fuels. Through elected representatives in Washington, however, some states have expressed a general lack of enthusiasm regarding the various "fast track" procedures and their implications for state sovereignty. In particular, the prospect of a federal board forcing states to expedite their review process, or in some cases circumventing state reviews entirely has been viewed dimly by some potential producer states.

Giving Up the Nuclear Ghost

If additional reasons are needed for the government avoiding direct and massive energy investment, one need simply look to nuclear energy. While the myth of a cheap energy source in nuclear died some time ago, the corpse has been kept on display by a vast array of government incentives, subsidies, and liability guarantees as well as direct funding, under the guise of research, development, and demonstration (RD&D).[18] Despite the near disaster at Three Mile Island, and the growing recognition that electricity cannot effectively or efficiently meet the nation's energy needs, the administration still holds out hope that some fifteen quads of nuclear power will be available in the late 1990s. To realize this hope, they have been calling for a fast-track licensing procedure. Yet even with such a procedure and the administration's vote of confidence, it is highly unlikely that nuclear energy will fulfill these expectations. At present, nuclear energy is little more significant in terms of its total energy contribution than wood, developing somewhere around three quads. A five-fold increase would entail the construction of at least 100 new 1,000 megawatt power units in the next twenty years. Given that only seventy-two plants are currently licensed to operate (producing less than 50,000 megawatts) and that new orders have averaged less than two per year over the past few years, this type of increase would be monumental, to say the least.

However, the more fundamental question is not how much nuclear energy the nation will have; rather, it is how much it will need. Electricity is only essential for lighting and a handful of industrial processes. These demand sectors are probably less than 10 percent of the total energy demand. The real energy crunch is in transportation and low-grade heat (for example, home heating), where electricity is extremely inefficient. Even if the electric pie expands, it is probable that coal rather than nuclear will be experiencing the growth.[19]

State and local governments have not been nearly as tranquil on the nuclear issue as the federal government. While antinuclear initiatives failed in nearly all of the states which introduced them, de facto moratoriums have prevailed in some states. Community-level as well as national interest groups have carried on a fairly effective holding action against nuclear expansion. No state or locality has been willing to aid in the nuclear waste disposal dilemma, and uranium-producing states have yet to figure out what is to be done with radioactive debris.

In the light of these emerging realities and the growing concern over social and environmental costs, it would seem that optimism regarding a nuclear future is somewhat misplaced, the once artifically favorable investment structure notwithstanding.

Prospects and Problems of a Sustainable Energy Future

Sources largely agree that, at some point in the future, the United States will rely heavily upon sustainable or what have been labeled as inexhaustible resources. At what point remains unknown. However, more troublesome than the time schedule (which is obviously highly policy-sensitive) is the exact path that will take us from here to there. All that is evident at present is that this end of the path is cluttered with a number of institutional obstacles. Furthermore, all of the thinking about alternative energy has failed to shed much light on the role of conservation in shaping a sustainable future. To the extent that innovative approaches to these issues have begun to emerge, they have done so at the state and local level of government.

Solar Energy: A Case of Arrested Development

Solar energy is a nebulous concept encompassing such diverse resources as biomass, hydroelectric, ocean thermal, and numerous forms of direct and indirect solar collection and conversion (for example, photovoltaics for electricity). Until very recently most government sources were placing a substantial solar contribution as far off as the next century. The business-as-usual or "base case" of the Domestic Policy Review projects a solar potential of only 9.9 quads (or approximately 8 percent of supply) for the year 2000.[20] While this scenario is probably correct, the remoteness of solar energy is more a function of institutional arrangements than of the state of the technology.[21] Quite obviously, solar will not replace all of the various end-uses of oil in the foreseeable future; yet its potential contribution in residential and industrial applications could be greatly enhanced by more conscientious planning and management efforts.

Like coal, solar energy is forced to compete in an economic environment which was explicitly designed to promote oil and, more recently, nuclear development. Despite the unfair advantages given to other energy sources, commercial and residential solar applications for water and space heating are now economically competitive.[22] Following an era of cheap energy, however, consumers are not prepared to think in terms of long payback periods (or the number of years until recovery of their down payment). Moreover, a number of specific institutional barriers still inhibit consumers from readily investing in solar energy. These might include[23]

1. *Sun rights* or guarantees to solar access.
2. *Building codes* which prohibit aspects of solar design.
3. *Loan and financing problems*, given the conservative investment posture of local banks.
4. *Consumer protection* or the lack of insurance, warranties, and general performance standards.

Federal programs have yet to address most of these issues. While the "tax credit" is a start, it is too low to provide much assistance, particularly to primary investors and contractors. The federal government has been dragging its feet on basic performance standards and warranties, and these items are certainly holding up the solar parade.

With the exception of the power tower, ocean thermal, and satellite systems, solar energy is highly decentralized. Thus it stands to reason that institutional innovation would have to emerge at the grass-roots level. Examples of these innovations are myriad, but the best and most well-known example of rigorous solar policy comes from the state of California. California already has the highest tax credit available on solar equipment

(55 percent) and provisions for consumer protection (for example, the Cal-Seal Program), and, in addition, the SolarCal Council (a state agency) has included the following elements in its "action program":[24]

1. Liberal financing plans.
2. Greater consumer assurances.
3. Broader public information and participation.
4. Job training and development for solar applications.
5. Greater use of solar energy in public facilities.
6. Incentives for commercial uses of solar.

Through this program, California hopes to have "1.5 million solar equipped homes and businesses by the late 1980's."

State and local inventiveness is not limited to solar collection systems. End-user groups across the country are "voting with their feet," so to speak, for alternative management strategies, designed to enhance community self-reliance, and developing low head-hydro, biomass, and other local resources.[25] Federal and regional institutions are primarily designed to deal with producers of energy and are, therefore, ill-equipped to tap the resources of this emerging end-users' revolution.

Solar energy, however, is not without its negative aspects, and it would be well for local advocates to temper their enthusiasm with careful analysis. Low head-hydro development and extensive wood use can have devastating effects on the natural environment. Moreover, Kacser and Bingham point out that solar industries may produce serious pollution loads.[26] Nevertheless, given certain bounds, solar presents a much cleaner energy option than any of the conventional or unconventional fuel sources. Thus, lower environmental cost, coupled with favorable employment impacts, may eventually make it a highly economical (in the macro sense) energy alternative.

Conservation: The Forgotten Fundamentals

Conservation provides the key to any type of energy transition. Higher oil prices will, of course, initiate the search for this key, but some Americans may continue to expect a "technological fix" which will allow them to maintain their wasteful ways, and thus will be slow to adjust. The U.S. motto has been "a barrel earned is a barrel burned," yet as energy saving technologies enable consumers to buy a barrel of oil (displace it) for five dollars of initial investment, saving oil or energy generally should become a growth industry. Moreover, the once assumed inexorable ratio of energy input to GNP will have been debunked. Each American consumes (in all the goods and services used) about 90,000 calories of energy per day. Compare this with Third World nations, where per capita consumption is approximately 900 calories per day. The level of waste in U.S. energy consumption is even more apparent when one compares figures for various Western European nations; Sweden, for example, uses only about half the energy of the United States per individual to produce a similar standard of living and a superior quality of life. Given the high level of waste in this country's use of energy, the potential for conservation is considerable (nearly 5 million barrels of oil per day).

Current national conservation policy, however, is unlikely to achieve these levels in the very near future. The administration has continued to focus on minor behavioral changes (emphasizing sacrifice), such as driving less and lowering thermostats, rather than pushing for greater end-use efficiencies. More importantly, perhaps, policymakers have failed to emphasize the various benefits which a comprehensive conservation program could bring. These might include the following:[27]

1. A rigorous conservation program might bring a greater reduction in oil imports at a lower cost than various exotic energy development schemes (for example, synfuels).
2. Conservation technologies pose less of a threat to environmental integrity than most other energy investments.
3. Conservation strategies might aid in the stimulation of more competitive energy markets.
4. Conservation produces many more jobs than many other energy technologies, and these jobs are fairly widely distributed across geographic regions.

In sum, conservation would be a sound economic policy, bringing less inflation, more jobs, and a more equitable distribution of resources. Moreover, conservation technologies are fairly well proven, and therefore are less subject to the tremendous uncertainty costs which attend several other energy technologies. These uncertainty costs inevitably manifest themselves in RD&D cost overruns, for example.

The basic conservation strategies to be pursued are fairly straightforward and simple. They include such things as

1. Stimulating the retrofitting of existing buildings and houses to achieve greater energy efficiency, with required efficiency for all new buildings.
2. Enforcing fuel efficiency in automobiles, agricultural machinery, and so on, and providing programs to accelerate the turnover of inefficient equipment.
3. Encouraging investments in energy-saving production processes, and fostering industrial cogeneration.

4.   Allowing for nonautomotive transportation (from bike paths to rapid transit) to evolve in urban areas, and ultimately to foster less dispersed settlement patterns.

While simple, all of these items have encountered a certain level of institutional resistance. Given that most Americans relocate every five years, few are willing to retrofit their homes; the same is true of buildings which are often resold. Turnover in automobiles has been slowed considerably by the fact that gas-guzzlers are bringing less and less trade-in value. Most industries only invest in something with a swift 50 percent return on investment (30 percent after taxes). Compare this with utilities which operate on a 15 percent return rate. Meanwhile, bike paths and rapid transit compete with a strong urban highway lobby for limited funds.

Nevertheless, the conservation picture is bright. Here again, states and localities are trailblazing the conservation path. Davis, California, has cut its total energy use nearly in half through transportation and retrofit programs. The states of Oregon and Minnesota have established mandatory retrofits with a presale standard. However, some augmenting of subnational efforts may be required. For example, the federal government could provide larger tax breaks for industrial investments in energy-saving technologies. They could also buy up old gas-guzzlers with coupons applicable to the purchase of a fuel-efficient car (30-plus mpg). If the provision were added that it must be a U.S.-built car, such a program would provide a shot in the arm for ailing auto manufacturers. These federal programs would, of course, cost a good deal of money, yet they would probably cost less and be more cost-effective than proposed energy development programs.

Conclusions

In the final analysis the upcoming energy transition is actually a societal evolution. At present, our society is based on cheap energy resources, but this era is nearing its end. Fostering institutions compatible with the emerging epoch of more expensive and dispersed energy resources is the challenge at hand. Since public institutions at all levels of government have had a major role in diverting or hiding natural transition forces for a number of years, they must now accept responsibility for the loss of vital time, and must interject themselves so as to accelerate social change. In short, a national energy policy is more an instrument of social evolution than most government officials wish to admit. However, it offers an opportunity for gradual and planned change, while the current energy management morass may only offer the potential for catastrophic change.

As suggested, planned change is not merely a federal enterprise. Rather, it should be a mobilization of worthy aspirations at all levels of government and community activity. The federal government's most essential role will come with the orchestration of state and local innovations and in the interpretation of end-user demands. Seeking harmony amid the cacophony of energy crisis responses is the basis of sound energy policy.

Notes

1. Howard T. and Elisabeth Odum, *The Energy Basis of Man and Nature* (New York: McGraw-Hill, 1976).

2. For a more detailed discussion of these problems see Gregory A. Daneke, *The Poverty of Energy Planning* (Unpublished Manuscript).

3. See Ronald D. Brunner, "Energy Conservation and Renewable Resources: A Decentralized Approach" (Ann Arbor, Mich.: Institute of Public Policy Studies, University of Michigan, Discussion Paper NO. 135, December 1978).

4. See Executive Office of the President, *The National Energy Plan* (Washington, D.C.: Government Printing Office, April 1977); U.S. Department of Energy, *The National Energy Act* (Washington, D.C.: DOE, November 1978); DOE, *A Preliminary Outline and Approach: National Energy Plan II* (Washington, D.C.: DOE, October 1978): DOE, *Public Meetings on NEP II* (Washington, D.C.: DOE, 1979). Also note Office of Technology Assessment, *Analysis of the Proposed National Energy Plan* (Washington, D.C.: OTA, August 1979).

5. William Rodgers, *Energy and Natural Resources Law* (St. Paul, Minn.: West Publishing Co., 1979), p. 14.

6. Coopers and Lybrand, Inc., *Management Audit of Selected Areas of the Department of Energy* (Washington, D.C.: U.S. Department of Energy, Draft, March 1979).

7. Common Cause, *Open for Business Only? A Common Cause Study of the Department of Energy* (Washington, D.C.: Common Cause, February 1979).

8. For an overview of these phenomena see Wilson Clark, *Energy for Survival* (New York: Anchor, 1975), pp. 25-58.

9. This result is explained in depth in Edward J. Mitchell, *U.S. Energy Policy: A Primer* (Washington, D.C.: American Enterprise Institute, 1974), especially pp. 1-16.

10. Note examples in Richard Dorf, *Energy, Resources, and Policy* (Menlo Park: Addison-Wesley, 1978), pp. 440-441.

11. Discussions with John B. Noble, state-level survey coordinator and consultant, Energy and Minerals Division, GAO, March 27, 1979.

12. See U.S. General Accounting Office, *Better Planning Needed to Deal with Regional Energy Demand* (Washington, D.C.: GAO, February 22, 1978).

13. See GAO, *Federal Coal Leasing: Issues Facing a New System* (Washington, D.C.: GAO, September, 1979).

14. Note Kenyon N. Griffin and Robert B. Shelton, "Coal Severance Tax Problems in the Rocky Mountain States" and David A. Schaller, "An Energy Policy for Indian Lands," in *Policy Studies Journal* 7 (Autumn 1978):29-48; also note Mark A. Boroush et al., "An Integrated Technology Assessment of a Coal Based Energy System" (paper presented at the 1978 meeting of Systems, Man, and Cybernetic Society, Tokyo, Japan, 1978); Alfred Light, "From the Declaration of Independence to Valley Forge: Intergovernmental Relations and the Energy Crisis 1976-" (paper presented at the National Meeting of the American Society for Public Administration, Atlanta, Georgia, April 1, 1977); and Hanna J. Cortner, *Energy Policy Planning, Administration and Coordination in the Four Corner States* (report submitted to the Four Corners Regional Commission, Farmington, N.Mex., March 1977).

15. See Council on Environmental Quality, *The Good News about Energy* (Washington, D.C.: CEQ, 1979).

16. Figures calculated by using MITRE Corporation, *Environmental Data for Energy Technology Policy Analysis* Vol. I (McClean, Va.: Mitre Metrik Division, for DOE, 1979).

17. RAND Corporation, *A Review of Cost Estimation in New Technologies* (Santa Monica, Calif.: RAND, for DOE, 1979).

18. Note Gregory A. Daneke, "The Political Economy of Nuclear Development," *Policy Studies Journal*, 7 (Autumn 1978):84-90.

19. See Saunders Miller, *The Economics of Nuclear and Coal Power* (New York: Praeger, 1976).

20. Domestic Policy Council, *A Domestic Policy Review of Solar Energy: A Response Memorandum to the President of the United States* (Washington, D.C.: DPC, Draft Copy, December 3, 1978).

21. Note Gregory A. Daneke, "Toward a Solar Policy Agenda," in Michael Steinman, ed., *Environmental and Energy Policy* (Lexington, Mass.: LexingtonBooks, D.C. Heath and Company, 1979).

22. See Robert H. Bexdek et al., "Economic Feasibility of Solar Water and Space Heating," *Science*, March 1979, pp. 1214-1220.

23. Note Environmental Law Institute, *Legal Barriers to Solar Heating and Cooling* (Washington, D.C.: ELI, 1976); also note Office of Technology Assessment, *Applications of Solar Technology to Today's Energy Needs* (Washington, D.C.: U.S. Congress, OTA, 1977).

24. SolarCal Council, *Toward a Solar California* (Sacramento, Calif.: State of California, January 1979), pp. 25-53.

25. See Anita Gunn, *A Survey of Model Programs: State and Local Solar/Conservation Projects* (Washington, D.C.: Center for Renewable Resources, 1977); also note Philip Sharp and Ronald Brunner, *Local Energy Policies* (Ann Arbor: Institute of Public Policy Studies, University of Michigan, Discussion Paper No. 127, July 1978.

26. Pamela H. Kacser and R. Bingham, "The Sun in Our Future: Social Impacts of Two Projected Energy Scenarios" (paper presented at the Conference of Allied Social Sciences, Chicago, 1978).

27. For a broader discussion of conservation and its various benefits see Marc Ross and Robert Williams, *Energy and the Invisible Hand* (New York: McGraw Hill Book Co., 1980); also see Clark Bullard, "Energy and Jobs" (paper presented at the Conference on Energy Conservation, University of Michigan, November 1977).

3 The Performance of Government in Energy Regulations

Walter J. Mead

Introduction

An evaluation of government performance in energy regulation requires specification of a standard. Here the record of regulation will be evaluated in terms of optimum resource conservation, defined as the process of maximizing the present value of all resources at any point of time.

It is possible to distinguish two general paths by which resource conservation may be attained: free market allocation: or allocation by direct government regulations, the use of taxation, or the use of subsidies. There is wide agreement among economists that the existence of net externalities creates market failures and suboptimal resource allocation. The presence of externalities therefore has been used to rationalize government intervention in order to correct for market failures. The implicit assumption is that such regulation will in turn be economically efficient.

An influential body of opinion argues that the power of government should be used to enforce energy conservation as a means of resolving the "energy crisis." However, most of these arguments are based on naive definitions of conservation, meaning "use less" or "save energy," as if all other resources were of zero value. Concepts of this kind are found repeatedly in the Energy Policy Project report of the Ford Foundation.[1]

The Carter "National Energy Plan"[2] proposes a major expansion of government regulation, taxation, and subsidies. Before Congress legislates new government intervention in the energy sector, would it not be wise to evaluate the extensive record of past government intervention? In this chapter five major areas of government intervention over the past half-century will be briefly reviewed.

A Review of U.S. Energy Policy

More than a half-century ago Congress introduced percentage depletion allowance tax treatment for oil and gas production. Subsequently, provision was made for expensing of intangible drilling costs. The initial effect of

Walter J. Mead, "The Performance of Government in Energy Regulation," *American Economic Review* 69:2 (May 1979):5.

these two policies was to increase the after-tax rate of return on investments in oil and gas exploration and production. These tax subsidies led to increased capital flows into exploration. Consequently, new reserves were found and production was stimulated. But increased production led to lower oil prices and established the historic U.S. low-price policy for energy. This in turn led consumers to treat oil and gas as cheap commodities and to consume these nonrenewable resources excessively.

Legislation in 1975 removed the benefits of percentage depletion allowances for integrated oil companies only. For the nearly 10,000 independent oil and gas producers, the depletion allowance has been retained but the tax benefits have been reduced. The benefits of expensing intangible costs have been retained in total.

These two tax policies have probably been the most important items of government interference in the petroleum industry. In the absence of these artificial stimulants the market would have delayed production. Thus they contributed directly to the energy crisis of the 1970s and in general are counterproductive of a conservation goal.

Prorationing was authorized by the federal government in the 1930s and implemented subsequently by state governments. Stephen McDonald has shown that prorationing rules, with their depth-acreage allowable schedules and well spacing regulations, are purely arbitrary and are economically inefficient as a solution to the common property resource externality. He has proposed an efficient solution in the form of mandatory unitization.[3] Prorationing also included market-demand restrictions. This form of government intervention has been inoperative since 1972. For nearly four decades it created idle capacity and hence resource waste in the form of excessive investment in oil exploration and production. Thus, both MER and market-demand types of prorationing are inefficient and are counter-productive of a conservation goal.

Import quotas, introduced by President Eisenhower in 1959, were partly a consequence of market-demand prorationing. A protected domestic market is inconsistent with free trade. The effects of import quotas were to rstrict the supply of imported oil, to increase domestic prices, and to artifically stimulate additional domestic production of this nonrenewable resource. Thus, U.S. import quotas distorted the pattern of oil production worldwide and led to excessive production from rapidly declining U.S. resources, contributing directly to the energy crisis of the 1970s. An efficient solution to the dependence problem was not introduced until 1975 when the Strategic Petroleum Reserve was authorized by Congress.

Price controls on natural gas were introduced in 1954 and those on crude oil in 1971. In both cases, controls were administered in favor of artifically low prices. In the case of natural gas, low prices led to high demand

and low supply thus creating the usual shortage. Consumers who received natural gas allocations consumed it lavishly as a cheap commodity. In this respect the conservation objective has been thwarted. Part of the supply-demand gap has been filled by a close substitute, oil. This has led to increased imports and consequent dependence and balance-of-payments problems.

The effects of oil price controls are not as clear as in natural gas. Charles Phelps and Rodney Smith studied price controls and other regulations in the oil industry and concluded that "the controls have not reduced the prices

Deacon and myself tested two hypotheses involving comparisons of domestic and foreign whole-sale gasoline prices between 1971 and 1977. Both tests indicated that U.S. price controls effectively lowered the price of gasoline through mid-1976. However, from that point through 1977, the evidence failed to support the hypothesis that price controls lowered gasoline prices.[5]

If gasoline prices are not currently below levels which would be attained in the absence of price controls, then demand is unaffected by price controls. However, producers of crude oil receive artifically low prices under the price control system. Phelps and Smith pointed out that, "While the price controls on crude oil did not influence product prices, they did transfer profits within the petroleum industry."[6] Wealth was transferred from crude oil producers to refiners, and from one refiner class to another. If domestic crude oil supply elasticity is greater than zero, then domestic suppliers are artifically restrained by the control system and imports are artifically stimulated, again leading to higher imports, balance of payments, and dependency problems.

Clearly, natural gas price controls have set prices below equilibrium levels. Further, evidence supports the point that oil price controls had similar effects through mid-1976. At lower prices consumers demand more. In the case of petroleum, there is an open-ended supply in the form of imports. If consumption is artifically stimulated, then conservation goals are not attained. In the case of oil and gas price controls there is further resource misallocation in the high cost of price control administration, both within the government and on the part of complying industry.

Arguments against eliminating price controls and allowing the market to allocate scarce oil and gas resources take three forms: (1) world oil prices are alleged to be monopoly prices set by an Organization of Petroleum Exporting Countries (OPEC) cartel. Supporters of price control argue that U.S. oil and gas prices should not be permitted to rise to such monopoly price levels; (2) market-clearing prices would unfairly impact on the poor; (3) market-determined prices would confer windfall profits on oil and gas producers.

The cartel rationale in support of price controls was recently articulated by Paul Davidson.[7] But the evidence for the cartel thesis is mixed. On the one hand, the dominant "firm" in the alleged cartel is clearly Saudi Arabia. In the years from the strong crude oil market in 1973, to the relatively weak markets in 1975-1977, Saudi Arabia expanded its market share from 24.2 to 30.4 percent of OPEC production. This evidence is inconsistent with either a fixed market shares or a dominant-firm price-leadership model of oligopoly behavior. On the other hand, OPEC output, in the aggregate, is consistent with cartel behavior. The OPEC share of world crude production declined from 55.5 to 52.5 percent during the increasingly weak markets from 1973 to 1977.

Some new research by Ali D. Johany has shown that crude oil price movements from approximately $3 per barrel in the early 1970s to approximately $12.50 per barrel in 1974 are rational in terms of individual oil producing countries maximizing the present value of their resources.[8] By joining property rights theory to capital theory, Johany has carried our understanding of optimal crude oil prices beyond recent work by William Nordhaus and Robert Pindyck.[9]

Johany pointed out that during the 1950s and 1960s there was a progressive awareness on the part of international oil companies holding oil concessions in the Middle East that their property rights were in jeopardy. Nationalization, or its euphemism, "participation," was the wave of the future. Fear of loss of property rights caused international oil companies to accelerate their foreign production. From 1950 through 1970 the compound annual growth rate in oil production from the Middle East was 10.9 percent. From 1970 through 1973, the growth rate was 15.0 percent.

Reflecting these output increases, world crude oil prices were relatively stable during the two decades from 1950 through 1970. Output increases were matched by worldwide growth in demand with only modest increases in nominal prices.

By the end of 1973, however, host countries were in complete control of output within their borders. Given firmly established property rights and lower discount rates, one would expect reduced output growth rates and sharply higher prices. The record shows that from 1973 to 1977 Middle Eastern oil output increased at a compound annual rate of only 0.7 percent. As a consequence, crude oil prices in world markets rose sharply from 1970 to date, a fact which can be explained without the aid of a cartel theory.

Johany examined the opportunity cost of capital for Saudi Arabia and concluded that for large sums of money, the U.S. government Treasury Bill market yielding 8 percent appeared to represent the most attractive alternative to leaving oil in the ground. Adjusting for inflation, the real opportunity cost was judged to be 1 percent. If one believes that the real price of oil fifty years hence will be approximately $21 per barrel, as determined by the cost of oil substitutes, then present values are rational. If so, the U.S. crude oil price controls cannot be justified in terms of a cartel theory.

Oil and natural gas price controls as methods of subsidizing the poor are haphazard tools. If additional public subsidies to the poor are warranted, then a direct approach through the negative income tax device would be a more efficient means.

Finally, decontrol would confer windfall profits on oil and gas resource owners and lease holders. But federal and state governments own most of the known and probable future productive oil and gas resources. That part of the windfall accruing to lease holders would be subject to income taxes. In 1975, the percentage depletion allowance was totally removed for all integrated oil companies. Therefore, combined federal and state income taxes would capture close to half of any windfall gains which accrue to integrated producers. For future leases issued after decontrol, the auction bidding system would totally eliminate windfalls due to decontrol.

A final element of government policy toward energy is the process used in auctioning leases. In 1978, Congress enacted a major overhaul in legislation governing outer continental shelf (OCS) oil and gas leasing. Under prior leasing procedures, tracts were leased after oral auction cash bonus bidding. The winning bidder obtained the right to explore for oil and gas resources. If production were undertaken, a one-sixth royalty had to be paid. However, motivated by a belief that competition under the present system is inadequate and government is not receiving "fair market value" for its resources. Congress mandated the use of bidding systems other than cash bonus bidding.

However, recent research has shown that competition for OCS oil and gas leases is intense and as a result the government has received more than a fair market value for its leases.[10]

Preliminary findings indicate that the nominal internal rate of return generated by lessees on 839 leases issued between 1954 and 1962 was 9.5 percent *before* taxes. This is a subnormal profit level and indicates that the winning bidders bid too much for their leases. Economic theory, supported by this analysis of the bonus bidding record, indicates that under the proposed bidding systems, the goals of resource conservation will be sacrificed.

The Political Economy of Public Policy

This short and necessarily superficial review of major past and emerging energy policies indicates that government intervention has been counterproductive with respect to resource conservation. The reasons are to be found in that ancient discipline known as political economy.

The main concerns of a politician are to get elected and to continue in office. These concerns require that politicians individually and collectively respond to dominant organized pressures brought to bear on them. Pressures from the oil industry obtained and then sustained tax subsidies and market-demand prorationing. The coal industry joined with the domestic oil industry to obtain import quotas. The political power of the oil industry has declined since the early 1970s, to be replaced by environmentalists and consumerists. These groups, together with organized labor, appear to sustain price controls. Concerns for optimum resource allocation are not primary concerns of politicians.

Second, economists advanced the externalities (market failure) concept. Informed laymen and politicians have embraced the concept. But political scientists have been slow to point out its counterpart in the political framework. If congressmen do not bear the full cost of the positions which they take and the consequent legislation which is enacted, then political market failure occurs. Where benefits of legislation are concentrated (the beneficial interests know who they are and are grateful!) and costs are dispersed (those who bear the costs are not well informed and the cost per person is low) the net political externality may be significant.

Third, the legislative process is a compromising process. Economists may agree on the character and the extent of a tax subsidy or regulation necessary to correct an externality. But any agreed upon correction must pass through the political process where hearings are held and interest groups have a right to bring pressure to bear on their elected representatives. Political scientist Daniel Ogden pointed out that ". . . national policy is made through a system of power clusters," and, further, "administrative agencies jealously guard their subject matter 'turf.' They yield jurisdiction only after a major struggle and only in the face of overwhelming political force." Individual congressmen will approve only what is acceptable by the dominant pressure groups to which they must be responsive. What economists believe to be an appropriate correction for an externality is not what is likely to emerge from the political process.[11]

Fourth, whatever emerges in legislation must then be administered. Another political scientist, Marver Bernstein, wrote that "the history of [regulatory] commissions indicates that they may have survived to the extent that they have served the interests of the regulated groups."[12]

Finally, the presence of a net externality is not a sufficient justification for government intervention. The costs of correction, including the costs added in the legislative compromise process and actual administration accommodations referred to above, must be less than the cost of the net externality to be corrected. Failure to meet this test will lead to even greater resource misallocation.

One might assume that with the declining political power of the oil industry in the last decade, future energy policy will be legislated in the national interest. However, the only change is that the power of one interest group has been displaced by others. The structure of public policy formation as outlined above is unchanged.

President Carter has called for a "comprehensive national energy policy," and his "first principle" asserts that "we can have an effective and comprehensive energy policy only if the Federal government takes responsibility for it. . . ."[13] The record of past energy policy does not lead one to be confident that more intervention will improve resource allocation. An alternative national energy policy would be to let the market allocate scarce resources.

Notes

1. David Freeman et al., *A Time to Choose* (Boston, Mass.: Ballinger, 1974).

2. Office of the President, "Detailed Fact Sheet, the President's Energy Program" (Washington, D.C.: Executive Office, 1977).

3. Stephen L. McDonald, *Petroleum Conservation in the United States* (Baltimore: Johns Hopkins, 1971).

4. Charles E. Phelps and Rodney T. Smith, "Petroleum Regulation: The False Dilemma of Decontrol" (Santa Monica, Calif.: Rand Corp. R-1951-RC, 1977). p. v.

5. Robert Deacon and Walter Mead, "Price Controls and International Petroleum Product Prices" (Report to the Federal Energy Administration, June 1978).

6. Phelps and Smith, *Petroleum Regulation*, p. vii.

7. Paul Davidson, "Beware the Modern Tripoli Pirates of Natural Gas," *Los Angeles Times*, August 6, 1978, p. .

8. Ali D. Johany, *OPEC Is Not a Cartel: A Property Rights Explanation of the Rise in Crude Oil Prices* (Santa Barbara, Calif.: Unpublished Ph.D. dissertation, Univ. of Calif. Dept. of Economics, 1978).

9. See William D. Nordhaus, "The Allocation of Energy Resources," *Brooking Papers* (Washington, D.C.: The Brooking Institution, No. 3, 1973); also note Robert S. Pindyck, "Gains of Producers from Cartelization of Exhaustible Resources," *Review of Economic Statistics* 60 (May 1978):238-251.

10. R.O. Jones, Walter Mead, and P.E. Sorensen, "Economic Issues in Oil Shale Leasing Policy" *Oil Shale Symposium* (forthcoming).

11. Daniel M. Ogden, Jr., "Protecting the Energy Turf: The Department of Energy Organization Act," *National Resources Journal* 18 (October 1978).

12. Marver Bernstein, *Regulating Business by Independent Commission* (Princeton, N.J.: Princeton University Press, 1975).

13. President's Energy Program, p. 1.

4 The Politics of Energy Self-Sufficiency in American States and Regions

Richard Worthington

The modern history of American energy development was until recently a one-sided story of the exploitation of people and natural resources by big corporations and their governmental allies. The scarred landscapes and pervasive poverty of Appalachia serve as a grim reminder of this asymmetry in the domestic development of energy resources. Similarly, tax and other revenues earned from the leasing of public and Indian lands in the western United States for fuels and minerals development through 1975 were not even sufficient to cover the administrative costs borne by state and local governments as a result of these programs, let alone social and environmental costs. Overseas, the growing American appetite for oil during the third quarter of the century was abetted by national elites in the oil producing nations, who enjoyed the favor of the foreign corporations and governments at the cost of declining real prices for oil on international markets for much of the period.[1]

Things have changed during the 1970s. The OPEC countries have followed their dramatic quadrupling of prices in 1974 with a second round of large increases in 1979, Indian tribes have won landmark litigation limiting the corporate exploitation of coal on their lands, the state of Montana has imposed a large 30 percent severance tax on all coal mined within its boundaries, environmentalists have developed legislation at all governmental levels to tighten controls on the polluting effects of energy production, and the nuclear industry is in disarray. Just who (if anyone) shall be the beneficiaries of this emerging pluralism remains to be seen, but it is clear that the days are gone when a small circle of corporate and government elites could expect the public passively to absorb the "external costs" of exponential growth, and leaders in the OPEC countries are similarly disinclined to see their primary source of export earnings clear the market at fire-sale prices.

The Era of Self-Sufficiency

One of the key symbols to enter into the mainstream of policy concerns in the wake of these events is that of energy self-sufficiency. President Nixon's

37

(and subsequently President Ford's) Project Independence was the earliest post-oil embargo embodiment of this symbol. While neither man was successful in his stated goal of implementing policies that would break the American dependency on foreign oil, the spate of studies and legislative proposals that constituted Project Independence did a great deal to promote the idea that it was necessary for America to become more self-sufficient in its energy use.

Yet despite the fanfare that accompanied Project Independence, its continuity with the past was at least as striking as any departures, as the Nixon-Ford policies basically sought to replace the exploitation of foreign people and resources with the exploitation of American people and resources. Scarcely a word was uttered in the pronouncements of the Republican administrations on conservation or more environmentally attuned life-styles: American energy self-sufficiency would be achieved by stepping up the nuclear power program alongside the increased exploitation of domestic sources of fossil fuels (especially offshore oil and western coal). Citizen concerns about nuclear safety, air pollution, strip-mining, and offshore oil blowouts did not seem an obstacle from this side of the problem, and the militant United Mine Workers could be left to the declining Appalachian fields with the move to western coal. The traditional array of incentives to produce energy—totaling $217 billion since 1917, according to one study[2]—would have been supplemented by a $100 billion government energy corporation to help the private companies in the financial end of things, had the fondest hopes of Vice-President Nelson A. Rockefeller come to pass (they did not).[3]

If anything has become clear in subsequent years, however, it is that the energy problem will not yield to the traditional alternatives proffered by the American political process. President Carter has been scarcely more successful than his predecessors in developing a coherent energy policy, despite the advantage of working with a Congress dominated by his own political party. But while the goal of self-sufficiency has encountered a stalemate at the national level, it has clearly filtered down to many states and regions in the country which are sponsoring studies and developing programs designed to bring energy production within their boundaries more closely into line with energy consumption.

An early traveler of this road was the Oregon Office of Energy Research and Planning, which published a report in 1974 entitled *Transition* suggesting that 75 percent of the state's energy needs could be met from internally produced renewable resources by the year 2000. While not as distinctly environmentalist in approach as Oregon, nearly all the remaining states have examined their prospects for greater self-sufficiency in recent years, primarily reflecting a pragmatic concern that repeated shortages in externally produced supplies (especially foreign oil) would have serious effects on their economies as well as the health and welfare of their citizens.

An important milestone in the concern for regional and state energy self-sufficiency was marked by the publication in 1976 of Amory B. Lovins's article "Energy Strategy: The Road Not Taken?" which was part of his subsequent *Soft Energy Paths* (1977). Lovins turned the energy world topsy-turvy with his compelling argument that the nation could and should embark on a sustained effort to develop renewable, simple, decentralized energy technologies (principally solar energy), abandoning nuclear power altogether, and using fossil fuels as the bridge to a future all-renewable energy supply system. To the technical and economic merits of the soft path, Lovins added the appeal of a more intimate and locally controlled life-style than is likely in a world dominated by the large organizations required to manage centralized technologies. In the wake of the interest stirred by Lovins, California, Hawaii, Montana, and New England have conducted or are conducting studies exploring soft path scenarios, while the soft path cast of thought has appeared in policy debate around the country.[4]

A basic issue that has arisen amidst the increasing concern for energy self-sufficiency is that one person's solar utopia is another person's parochialism. To many outside the region, the hefty coal severance taxes enacted in Montana, North Dakota, and Wyoming have created an image of "blue-eyed Arabs" who value their own gain above the welfare of the nation.[5] The reactive nature of energy localism was also brought to light when the city of Los Angeles, which had been instrumental in organizing the Southern California Council of Local Governments to fight offshore oil development, dropped out of the organization when the federal Department of the Interior removed Santa Monica Bay from its list of potential drilling sites.[6] And the nuclear industry never tires of observing that vociferous local opposition to nuclear power plant siting is rarely matched in intensity by support for reduced electricity consumption: people want the electricity, nuclear advocates say; they just don't want the nuclear power plant in their back yard.

It is not my purpose here to issue a judgment on whether energy self-sufficiency in the states and regions is a reactive or progressive movement, for clearly the kinds of events reviewed above have elements of both. Nor am I interested in joining the debate on the relative merits of the soft path and the more traditional centralized approach to energy development. Rather, given my sympathies for the soft path approach, I will examine in the rest of this chapter the problem of how soft path policies can become more progressive and less reactive. This will involve (1) a discussion of the ideological underpinnings of the energy debate, (2) a review of several cases which show the political conflicts involved in the issue of state and regional energy self-sufficiency, and (3) an examination of the kinds of strategies that might enable the soft path approach to be more widely accepted and implemented.

Elite Management and Self-Reliance

Underlying the politics of energy in the United States is a broad ideological conflict that affects many other policy issues as well. In this section, I will use the terms elite management and self-reliance to refer to the principal approaches to public policy that are involved.

At the outset, some definitions are needed, which are provided in table 4-1. An important point to elucidate is the manner in which energy self-sufficiency, self-reliance, and elite management are related. The essence of the matter is that energy self-sufficiency is a narrow goal of matching energy production and consumption *within* a given political entity. This is often confused with energy self-reliance, but as used here both this term and elite management refer to broader approaches to problem solving in general that are particularly salient in their applications to energy issues. Drawing on our previous discussion, energy self-sufficiency theoretically can be achieved through either elite management (Project Independence) or self-reliance (the soft path).

While the basic factors which impel us toward energy self-sufficiency have already been reviewed, the ideas of elite management and self-reliance and their relevance to energy self-sufficiency deserve further examination. The basic point to be made here is that elite management has the weight of industrial development to commend it, although its viability for the future is under increasing scrutiny.

Viewed historically, the trend toward large-scale, hierarchical organization is striking. As Stephen Hymer has observed in a perceptive article on the multinational corporation,[7] the emerging capitalist system of the early

Table 4-1
Definitions for an Energy Debate

Energy self-sufficiency   Maximum use of internally produced energy supplies by a locality, state, region, or nation.

Self-reliance   Individual or group problem solving that places chief responsibility on the affected persons. All interactions among groups and individuals are made on the basis of reciprocity, so as to maximize individual autonomy without sacrificing community welfare. In short, self-reliance means maximum responsibility for and control over the decisions affecting one's life. Energy self-reliance implies involving people actively in the solution of their energy problems at a local level.

Elite management   Problem solving based on hierarchical organization, specialization of tasks, and coordination of these sub-components from higher authority, thereby relieving most people of responsibility for addressing the whole of a problem and leaving them to concentrate on a part or have no involvement in problem solving at all. Elite management of energy policy implies having the experts in business and government develop programs and solutions with the majority of the population being passive objects in the process.

industrialization period turned the organizational premises of its predecessor upside down. In the precapitalist order, labor was divided hierarchically in the system at large through the agency of classes, castes, and guilds which enforced a rigid and authoritarian social structure, but within these various groupings individuals functioned as relatively indepen-dent equals. Laissez-faire capitalism, on the other hand, banished the social organization of labor in favor of the principles of a competitive marketplace, but developed a hierarchical organization of labor within pro-duction units in its stead. This hierarchical organization of work life was ad-vanced to the status of a sicence by the writing of Frederick Winslow Taylor at the beginning of the twentieth century.[8] Accompanying this rationaliza-tion of the productive sphere has been a similar increase in the typical size of production units. Since the Industrial Revolution, Hymer tells us, the size of the typical firm has increased progressively: the workshop, then the fac-tory, the multi-divisional corporation, and presently the multinational cor-poration have all in turn represented the predominant organizational unit in the economy. Each new form has also required a more complex ad-ministrative apparatus to coordinate the actions of the subunits, while also requiring more centralized control to plan for survival and growth.[9]

Elite management remains the most widely used means of presiding over this system. The primary concern of elite management is the efficient production of goods and services, from which human well-being is assumed to follow. It is important to note that marketplace criteria extend to the public sphere as well, where "public goods" are produced and distributed under the same organizational principles. As already indicated, the means by which this goal is achieved include the centralization of decision-making authority, hierarchical organization, the division of labor into specialized and simplified tasks, and, consequently, the standardization of producers and products.

Now it should come as no surprise that political elites in America tend to focus their attention on the development of centralized technologies that would supply a growing demand for energy. Although per capita growth as the distinguishing feature in a society's energy use is a relatively recent phenomenon, it has been essential in maintaining the hierarchical structure of industrialized societies just discussed. Prior to industrialization, those who controlled the land (and hence the stable supply of photosynthetic energy) controlled society. When societies broke away from the steady rate of energy use that characterized previous dependence on converting sunlight to plant growth, a more dynamic set of power relationships accompanied the more dynamic energy conversion propensities of industrializing societies. The radical expansion in conversion through the exploitation of nonrenewable fossil fuels led to growth in energy use and growth in the number of political claimants.[10]

The core political conflict between capital and labor in these societies has been mitigated to a great extent by their ability to expand production through the ever more intensive conversion of energy. It is not likely that this fundamental conflict could have been as successfully suppressed had not these societies borrowed extensively on stored energy capital (fossil fuels) and had they not freely visited the pollutants from these activities on society at large, especially as the more oppressed groups (minorities, women, and so on) successfully organized to claim a piece of the action. It should be clear that growth in energy conversion is not the brainchild solely of the capitalist class, however much it benefits them. The NAACP is every bit as willing as Exxon to continue the trend of centralization and increased energy conversion. Continued expansion would help to hold this shaky alliance intact both by sustaining the traditional payoff of expanded material output and by keeping control of the energy producing technologies in politically safe hands. That labor is a junior partner in this scheme has for the most part not prevented its acquiescence.

But the debt accumulated through past borrowing of energy capital is now coming due, as an ever greater proportion of energy production has to be devoted to producing energy, and as various interest groups resist the myriad costs of this growth. The physical basis of Western industrialization is thus rather shaky, and the politics has not been long in following. In addition to all its other problems, nuclear fission, excepting the dangerous breeder reactor, is not exempt from the need to use progressively more energy input per output. It builds a larger artifice on a weaker foundation.[11]

While the bureaucrat charged with administering a state energy program is understandably likely to despair that alternatives to elite management are unrealistic—historical vision is generally not the province of those enmeshed in the realm of day-to-day affairs—credulity is stretched by the claim that continued centralization can long be sustained. Enter self-reliance.

If our society is to exchange increasing conversion of nonrenewable fuels for a steady conversion of renewable sources, it will have to abandon the politics of growth that elite management inevitably produces. Decision-making will have to be collective rather than hierarchical, and implementation will have to be self-directed rather than other-directed. Elites can not maintain their privilege without distributing patronage, which means energy growth; and they can not coordinate the affairs of others without commanding concentrated supplies of energy, which means a worsening energy input/output ratio and a primary role for non-renewable fuels.

A society of equals would be much more likely to recognize its interest in a steady rate of energy conversion, and a society of self-directed persons can turn off the lights, build solar collectors locally, grow more of its own food, and otherwise reduce its dependency on concentrated forms of energy. Self-reliance is increasingly held to be efficient in the narrow economic sense of the term as well. As Charles E. Lindblom has noted, the traditional emphasis of social scientists and managers on coordination as the key to efficiency is increasingly being challenged by innovators who proclaim the superiority of tapping the latent energies and inventiveness of the rank and file worker. While in the not-too-distant past this perspective was held largely by Maoist ideologues, Western managers, too, are now beginning to emphasize resourcefulness over ever more precise coordination.[12]

The self-reliance approach is thus fundamentally opposite to elite management: where elite management sees efficiency as instrumental to individual well-being the primary concern of the self-reliance approach is the well-being and development of the individual, from which efficient production is assumed to follow. While this argument takes many forms and appears in diverse places, it has probably been most eloquently advocated by E.F. Schumacher.[13] A second important characteristic of the modern Western variant of self-reliance is an aversion to bigness, which is the larger theme of Schumacher's book and strikes a responsive chord in a worldwide revulsion with bureaucracy. In policy terms, then, one of the major consequences of a renewed interest in self-reliance has been the demand for decentralization of decision-making in modern society, whether this means reducing the size of economic and governmental organizations (for example, smaller enterprises) or providing more equitable control over them (for example, worker management). In the United States self-reliance thinking has tended to reflect an individualistic concern for reducing the size of organizations. However, decentralization more broadly defined as expanded human competence and control over the decisions affecting one's life also includes collective, egalitarian management of large scale organizations. In both of these cases it is *power* that is decentralized.

These emphases on human development, participation, and decentralization displace material growth as a primary organizational goal, relegating it to the status of a means to human ends that may or may not be appropriate in various contexts. Indeed, "less is more" as a slogan focuses attention on the abilities of people to provide for themselves as a means of breaking the alienating cycle of hierarchical production and standardized consumption which are the results of the prevailing concern with expanded material output.

Whether it is a trend for the future or a passing fancy, the current resurgence of political interest in self-reliance and decentralization is undeniable. While the rhetoric fosters visions of a back-to-the-land movement and a return to simpler life-styles in many minds, in actuality the self-reliance movement has included mainstream social groups as well, appearing in the nation's population centers in forms as diverse as neighborhood organizing, consumer and producer co-ops, and self-help health care.

In the energy field, self-reliance advocates are generally concerned with reducing local dependence on fossil fuels and nuclear power by increasing conservation efforts and promoting the development of solar energy. Furthermore, they are suspicious of high-technology approaches to conservation and solar: the struggle over solar commercialization, for example, has already pitted the decentralists against the aerospace industry and other high-technology advocates who envision orbiting solar space stations that relay energy to earth.[14] Decentralists prefer simpler technologies because these can be understood at a popular level, are held to be more environmentally benign, and promote social equity by relying relatively more on labor and less on capital than other alternatives.

While there no doubt is a relationship between the expanding popularity of decentralization politics and recent energy policies, by and large the policies enacted at national, state, and local levels to encourage solar and conservation commercialization have relied on traditional incentives and inducements such as tax credits and property tax exemptions.

It is here that the distinction between self-sufficiency and self-reliance has become clear. For example, the recent objections of minority groups to a solar tax deduction scheme pending before the San Francisco County Board of Supervisors (on grounds that it favored the middle- and upper-income groups who would be the most likely to avail themselves of the policy) was an indication that solar advocates were either unwilling or unable to deliver on the progressive claims of energy self-reliance in that case.[15]

A similar controversy has emerged over energy conservation through cogeneration in New York City. Cogeneration involves using the waste heat from electricity production for low-grade applications such as space heating. This heat is normally dissipated into the atmosphere at centralized utility generating stations, but an industrial or commercial user who generates electricity on site can more easily recycle the low-grade energy. The economic attractions of cogeneration have been sufficient to warrant installation in a number of New York office buildings and commercial facilities in recent years. Yet a controversy has emerged because the reduced demand for electricity from Con Edison has reduced its revenues, and hence its tax payments to the city. In the present institutional environment the benefits of cogeneration are private and the costs are public.[16] While neither of the cases cited presents insurmountable obstacles, they do draw attention to the distinction between policies which strictly promote self-sufficiency via the pecuniary motivation of the marketplace and those which complement this concern with a broader view of equity and self-reliance.

The Politics of Self-Sufficiency

Four cases in which self-sufficiency has been a significant policy issue in the United States are the development of the SolarCal program in California, the congressional consideration of new legislation for the Bonneville Power Administration in the Pacific Northwest, the politics of coal exploitation in the Northern Plains (especially Montana and North Dakota), and the controversy over the development of offshore energy technologies (oil and floating nuclear power plants) adjacent to the mid-Atlantic states of New Jersey and Delaware. While the cases are complex and diverse, in the first two the development of a self-reliance model is at issue, while in the last two resistance to the consequences of centralized energy development is at the center of the controversy.

The Decentralist Approach

An obvious problem confronting state and regional policymakers in these cases and others is the lack of administrative coherence which afflicts the policy apparatus at all levels. This is to be expected since energy policy has only recently achieved high salience among the many troublesome issue facing the nation, but the problem is no less significant for the clarity of its origins. In the mid-Atlantic case, for example, the federal agencies with primary responsibility for developing the offshore technologies found that the lack of established channels for interfacing with state and local authorities led to miscommunication, confrontation, and political opposition.[17]

In other cases—especially that of northern plains coal development—confrontation has evolved not so much from a lack of coordination as from effective resistance to federal and corporate coordination at state and regional levels. Whether the origins of these conflicts are administrative or political, they have occasioned a concern among policy makers and academics that the energy policy arena would suffer the crippling effects of "Balkanization." This Balkanization is held to be evident in the fact that the domestic development of uranium, coal, and offshore oil resources have all been slowed by local concerns over the negative impacts of development, leading to increased dependency on foreign oil.[18]

Yet, to put the issue this way is to overlook the obvious structural characteristics of centralized control over technology, and the possibility of changing that structure itself, rather than forcing localities to conform to its imperatives. Harold P. Green, an early student of the politics of technology assessment, has grasped the essence of this issue in his observation that new technologies usually have powerful vested interests promoting them. The propensity of the promoters to highlight positive aspects of the technology and overlook the negative ones is abetted by the likelihood that most experts will be protechnology. Opponents will often have to state their case without full access to all pertinent information and without expert assistance. Their incomplete and inaccurate claims can then be easily discredited by the promoters, who can even cast doubt on the very idea of opposition as well as on specific arguments. The opposition must then take an even more extreme position, which in turn is an easier target for the proponents. The end result of this process is to increase the centralized control of technology by experts and their institutional backers (typically the federal government and large corporations).[19]

Distributing the burdens imposed by centralized energy technologies is of course a legitimate concern, but shifting to decentralized systems is, too, and the latter issue tends to escape scrutiny in the kind of atmosphere just described. Just what happens when the decentralist concept is introduced into the political arena is a matter to which I now turn.

SolarCal and the New Age

Popular myth has it that California is a trend-setter for the rest of the nation. However valid this is as a general proposition, there is good evidence of its truth with respect to energy policy. Perhaps more than any other state California has put the brakes on centralized technologies and is moving toward a soft path, although dependence on liquid fuels for automobile transport in southern California will represent a difficult problem to overcome. Significant opposition to the myriad negative consequences of fossil fuel development dates at least to the Santa Barbara channel oil blowout of 1969, and even previously to struggles over air quality in the Los Angeles basin. In a state highly dependent on natural gas for home heating and cooling, there is mounting opposition to the importation of liquefied natural gas. Furthermore, the state legislature passed very strict nuclear safeguards legislation in 1976 just prior to the vote on a citizen initiative measure proposing even stricter safeguards. The two proposed nuclear projects to come before the State Energy Commission for approval since 1976 (San Diego Gas and Electric's Sundesert proposal and Pacific Gas and Electric's Stanislaus County proposal) have been rejected because they could not meet the requirements of the new legislation.[20]

California has also been a leader in the move toward a soft path future. A soft path study conducted at the University of California in 1978 has held forth the prospect that virtually all of the state's energy requirements could come from such sources by the year 2025.[21] A much more conservative study by researchers at the California Institute of Technology's Jet Propulsion Laboratory claimed that solar energy could potentially account for two-thirds of the energy used in space and hot water heating by 1995.[22] Among the many soft path legislative initiatives taken in California is a 55 percent solar energy tax credit for homeowners, passed by the state legislature in 1977.

One of the most significant models for self-reliant development of solar energy is provided by the SolarCal program currently being implemented in California, which basically calls for maximum development of solar energy, under the tutelage of a state-level SolarCal authority. This legislation was developed by the California Public Policy Center in Los Angeles, one of a number of grass-roots political action-public interest organizations in California associated with the names of Tom Hayden and Jane Fonda. Despite its left-of-center tone, much of the original SolarCal legislation was passed by the state assembly in 1978. The basic goals of SolarCal have been expressed by its sponsors as follows:

> SolarCal's mandate is to foster a democratic decentralized solar energy in-
> dustry in California. SolarCal's goals are to (1) stimulate local economic
> development, (2) conserve energy and (3) create jobs.[23]

To these ends, the original legislation included policies which banned utility and energy monopoly representation on the SolarCal board of directors and specified labor, consumer, and low-income representation; encouraged small business participation in solar manufacturing, distribution, and installation; provided financing to small businesses and consumers at low interest rates; and encouraged the hiring of unemployed and underemployed persons in the solar industry. The SolarCal authority was also mandated to speed the commercialization of decentralized solar electricity applications.

The clear strategy of SolarCal is to assure democratic control of solar energy commercialization by limiting the influence of concentrated private interests, that is, the private utilities and energy companies which have promoted fossil fuels (especially liquified natural gas) and nuclear power as California's future energy sources. Significantly, SolarCal's sponsors have focused attention on the economic development aspect of their legislation, arguing that a solar energy industry will provide consumers a hedge against inflating fossil fuel and nuclear prices, reduce unemployment because of its job-intensity, and keep energy expenditures within the state rather than sending money overseas or to distant corporate headquarters.

Veteran observers of the policy process are, of course, not surprised that what comes out of the legislative pipeline often bears scant resemblance to what went in. An early change in the SolarCal program was made by the sponsors themselves, whose prescient pre-Proposition 13 observation was that California's voters were not likely to approve the bonding authority to finance solar commercialization called for in the original legislation. In an ingenious inversion of the common scenario where privately owned utilities raise capital from public and consumer sources to finance their expansion, the SolarCal sponsors proposed having California's utilities, which are chartered by the state as public service companies, raise the capital for SolarCal on private markets as a public service.

Predictably, what emerged from Sacramento was an executive order establishing a SolarCal office within the state Department of Business and Transportation, but lacking at the outset the kind of financial and political authority necessary to seriously promote solar commercialization in a manner envisioned by SolarCal's sponsors.[24] Yet, while the outcome at this point invites the cynical observation that the soft path was thrown a bone, SolarCal's sponsors have vowed to press their case. While the political power required for serious implementation still eludes SolarCal's proponents, the general popularity of soft path technologies and the restraints placed upon centralized technologies in California both augur well for eventual success. More germane to our purpose in this chapter, the SolarCal experience focuses attention on two key aspects of transition to a soft path future often overlooked by advocates obsessed with the more technical aspects of energy self-sufficiency: the struggle over the control of governmental institutions and, more broadly, the struggle over the use of society's capital.

Bonneville Power and Political Power

The Bonneville Power Administration (BPA) was created in 1937 to distribute the vast hydroelectric power generated by the Grand Coulee Dam and other federal projects in the Pacific Northwest's Columbia River basin. The political battles at that time between private electric companies and public power advocates were intense, but the legislation establishing BPA clearly gave preference to the interests of consumers and public utilities. With time, corporate interests were able to guide BPA along paths more amenable to their concerns, to the point that in recent years BPA management has exhibited a proindustry orientation in many of its policies, particularly in the area of increasing energy supply. As the electricity surplus of past years has declined due to increasing demand a zero-sum conflict has ensued, with industry forces and their BPA allies lobbying for abolition of the "preference clause" which mandates first priority in the sale of electricity to public utilities and rural cooperatives. The BPA role as a distributor must change as it moves from a situation of surplus to scarcity of supplies, and the question is whether the course taken will encourage elite control or self-reliance.

Two bills to reorganize BPA were introduced into Congress during 1977 which quite clearly reflect these different principles. While both bills died in committee, and a successor compromise bill during the 1978 session suffered a similar fate, their contents are rather instructive in disclosing the policy implications of elite management and self-reliance approaches to energy issues.

The Pacific Northwest Electric Power Supply and Conservation Act, authored by the Pacific Northwest Utilities Conference Committee (PNUCC) and introduced by Senator Henry Jackson of Washington, is the industry version of a desirable future for BPA. The Columbia Basin Energy Commission (CBEC) Act, introduced by Congressman Jim Weaver of Oregon, places a much greater emphasis on energy self-reliance. Both acts are similar in that they go beyond BPA's current legislative mandate to distribute power by giving it a more active role in balancing energy supply and demand. Basically the PNUCC legislation provides the statutory and administrative means for rapid growth in thermal plant construction; the merging of public and private capital for these purposes; the continued access of private industry to public hydropower which was previously available only as a surplus not used by public customers; and the averaging of rates paid by public and private utilities for BPA power, again a departure from the previous preference for public customers. The CBEC bill, on the other hand, is strongly committed to conservation and solar energy, citizen participation, and continued preferred access of public utilities to cheap BPA hydropower. In particular, citizens in localities would have much greater direct control over their energy futures than in the PNUCC bill.

These fundamental differences are clear throughout the specific sections of the two bills. For starters, the PNUCC legislation calls for the BPA board of directors to be comprised of half public and half private utility representatives, while under CBEC two board members would be appointed by the president and the other three would be elected by citizens of the member states. Accountability to local constituencies is thus facilitated through the elective process. The CBEC bill contains articles which encourage both responsiveness and conservation by making forecasting and long-range planning open to public scrutiny through hearings. Under PNUCC these functions remain the prerogative of the BPA and the utilities, who have traditionally issued high-growth predictions.

Other articles of the two proposed bills have a more direct impact on conservation. The PNUCC bill encourages increased demand by averaging rates for BPA customers in all areas, thus forcing customers in conserving areas to pay the same rate as customers in high consumption areas. The price incentive to conserve is thus very indirect: the benefits are moderated for conservers, as are the costs for wasters. Similarly, the PNUCC scheme makes it difficult to assign the costs of new thermal facilities to those areas and customer classes requiring them, since the costs of new plants are averaged by selling power to BPA, which then distributes it to all customers at an average rate. CBEC, on the other hand, stresses that new centralized plants are to be built only after local options, including conservation and solar, have been examined and proven noncompetitive. Finally, it provides a means by which decentralized production and conservation are likely to occur. The first means is to establish a Rate I class of low-cost electricity available to all public customers for basic needs, calculated on the assumption of strict conservation. To assure this conservation, CBEC requires (and provides financing for) weatherization of all residences within ten years of enactment. Second, CBEC requires examination of and provides financing and other incentives for local production options including solar before new centralized plants are built. This financing would be available to utilities and their users, which could include neighborhood groups as well as individuals. PNUCC gives no provisions for alternative energy, and only mild incentives for conservation.[25]

An important difference, then, is between an approach that gives citizens a role in pursuing conservation and solar at a local level, and rewards them for this, and one which excludes citizens from decision making while leaving elite interests to preside over a high growth energy future which entails high economic and environmental costs for consumers. The latter scheme aggrandizes vested interests while the former gives citizens a concrete and constructive role in change which benefits the public at large as well as specific individuals.

One of the key sections of the PNUCC bill was a requirement that BPA purchase up to one-fourth of its electric power from private utilities at their full production costs. The privates could thus build expensive new fossil fuel and nuclear generating plants and have a guaranteed market for a substantial portion of their capacities at premium rates. This clause was sufficiently objectionable to merit taking a new tack in the "compromise" legislation introduced by Senator Jackson in 1978. Under the new bill BPA was only required to purchase electricity generated from waste heat, cogeneration, and renewable resources. But BPA's role in subsidizing private utilities was essentially reversed under the new legislation, as it would be required to *sell* electricity to private utilities for use in supplying their residential customers, and would be authorized to issue bonds to finance construction of nuclear and fossil fuel facilities to meet the requirements of its customers. Under both bills, the private utilities would gain access to the cheap hydro-power, and they would be able to use public money to essentially finance their new construction, albeit through the circuitous means outlined above. It is also worth noting that the compromise bill is riddled with loopholes and vests nearly all powers in the BPA administrator, who is appointed by the president. The elaborate participation scheme outlined in the bill limits citizens to a strictly advisory role.[26]

In summary, this review of recent BPA politics suggest three important points. First, the CBEC bill demonstrates that sensible policies which use public institutions and resources for the promotion of a soft path future need not fragment energy policy or impose unwieldy bureaucratic structures. Indeed, the CBEC bill would provide a well-integrated, coherent, fiscally sound, and democratic approach to regional energy policy. Second, however, the industry bills clearly convey the point that public institutions can just as readily be put at the disposal of elite management as they can be used to further self-reliance. Third, we once again see that the use of society's capital is a crucial variable in energy policy considerations.

Central Planning and Local Control

The rancorous conflict over national energy policy in the last several years has left many Americans with the impression that the essential line in this battle is the one which divides "government" from "private enterprise." In the fall of 1977 President Carter called oil industry attempts to subvert his crude oil equalization tax "the biggest ripoff in history," and more recently he has termed proposed congressional schemes to tax windfall oil profits a "charade" that would instead turn billions of dollars over to the industry.[27]

Behind these attention-grabbing events lies a more basic interest that allies corporate and governmental elites in their outlook on energy policy: their shared perception that the nation's energy future will require ever more centralized control of ever more centralized technologies. The fact that industry and corporate elites are in conflict over their respective roles in exercising that centralized control should not obscure a fundamental consensus. Notwithstanding President Carter's claims that conservation would be the "cornerstone" of his approach to energy policy, it should be recalled that his proposed National Energy Plan of 1977 called for supplying the forecast energy growth through 1985 with a 50 percent contribution from coal, 23 percent from nuclear, and 16 percent from conservation measures. Moreover, 53 percent of the increment in energy use during the period would be used to generate electricity, which is thermodynamically inefficient for most uses (in 1976 28.4 percent of the nation's energy was used to generate electricity). The National Energy Act ultimately signed into law by Carter at the end of 1978 contained weakened and deleted conservation provisions, such as the standby gasoline tax and the gas guzzler tax. With an oil import crisis again looming over the nation in 1979, Carter renewed the rhetoric of conservation with a dramatic speech calling upon Americans to conserve, but his policy proposals called for expanded production of domestic supplies (especially synthetic fuels) to account for about 90 percent of the oil imports to be displaced under the program, with conservation measures accounting for 10 percent of the displacement.[28]

Given its requirements for large amounts of capital, sophisticated technology, and environmental regulation, it would be impossible for this production-oriented scenario to take place without increased centralized planning and coordination of the activities of the major energy corporations, utilities, financial institutions, and governing institutions from the federal down to the local level. These are precisely the roles that would be played by Carter's proposed Energy Security Corporation (finance) and Energy Mobilization Board (planning). Whatever the final balance among the various sectors, the leaders in this effort would clearly be the highly integrated corporate institutions and the federal government, especially the regulatory and cabinet agencies in the executive branch.[29] The common citizen and local government institutions (state governments, utility districts, and so on) would be followers, essentially responding to the directives from the top. This scenario, however, is beginning to founder on a fundamental contradiction: there are too many interests at the subnational level that want to be part of the planning. This participatory urge is not quite the same thing as a strong commitment to a soft path energy future, but it does have important political implications for soft path prospects, as the cases of coal in the Northern Plains and offshore technologies in the Mid-Atlantic demonstrate.

Northern Plains Coal

More than half of America's recoverable coal deposits are west of the Mississippi River, and as much as 80 to 95 percent of the nation's low-sulfur coal is in the West. Most of that coal, including the world's largest low-sulfur deposit (the Fort Union Basin), is located in the northern plains states of Montana, Wyoming, North Dakota, and South Dakota. In the eyes of most federal and corporate energy planners, these deposits will be crucial in achieving national energy self sufficiency.

The impact of developing these resources on the northern plains states would be enormous, and is indicated in the results of an environmental impact statement prepared by the Energy Research and Development Administration. Under a high development scenario, as many as 367 coal conversion facilities (coal-fired generators, coal gasification plants, and so on) would be developed over the next fifty years. These facilities would be concentrated in the Powder River and the Fort Union Basins. About 1.6 million permanent workers would be required for these facilities, plus their families and additional population for support services. Up to 3.8 million people would be required for short-term construction purposes, about twice the aggregate 1976 population of Montana, Wyoming, and North Dakota. Under such a scenario, 25 percent of the nation's energy would be provided by these northern plains states, including an amount of electricity equal to 90 percent of 1976 output.[30] A National Academy of Sciences report on the impacts of this coal development used the term "national sacrifice area" to describe the northern plains role in America's energy future.[31]

Sentiments run high in the region against large corporations and the federal government, and are rooted in a history of resource policies, often coordinated by the federal government, that have returned high profits to companies headquartered outside the region, while leaving ghost towns and environmental degradation in their wake. The case of copper mining in Butte, Montana, is particularly instructive, where a huge open-pit mine, high lung-cancer rates, economic stagnation, a population less than one-fourth that of 1917, the destruction of more than one-fourth of the city's homes to make way for the expanding mine, and the stunted plant growth in the area around Butte all testify to the negative public impacts of past resource exploitation. With the eyes of the nation once again set on northern plains resources, strong political support has emerged for taxes that would enable the various states to cover the costs of coal development and establish a fund for economic development after the coal reserves are exhausted. In the words of North Dakota's tax commissioner,

> we intend to be the first generation of planners who insist that development pays for its own costs—all of its costs. We won't accept the notion that the creation of environmental sacrifice areas represents industrial progress. For that reason, the states have insisted on coal severance taxes to cover all costs. . . .[32]

Despite this aggressive approach on the part of the states, their action is nonetheless reactive in an important sense: its main effect is to raise the cost of coal development, while spreading the burden more equitably. It does *not* fundamentally alter the fact of coal development. Montana, for example, is expected to have a coal output in 1979 four times that of 1973.[33] Montana has also taken some initiatives toward a renewable energy future, but it is worth noting that these efforts are largely supported by an allocation of 1.87 percent of the coal severance tax revenues for alternative energy development.[34]

This concern for the sustainable energy sources in turn reflects a compromise between advocates of elite management and self-reliance that is increasingly witnessed in regional and state legislation, under which planning authorities are directed (in very difficult-to-enforce terms) to examine alternatives to centralized technologies in the process of energy planning. Yet the relative size of the allocation to sustainable energy development again drives home the point that the soft path will continue to occupy a subordinate role without access to capital and without more specific statutory authorization.

Offshore Energy in the Mid-Atlantic

The Mid-Atlantic states of Delaware and New Jersey have been the scene of a relatively mild controversy concerning the development of offshore energy technologies in the 1970s. At issue have been oil drilling in the Baltimore Canyon Trough running parallel to the coastline approximately fifty miles offshore the two states, a deepwater oil tanker port, and floating nuclear power plants off the coast of southern New Jersey. For the present, the development of all three of these energy technologies has been virtually halted. The deepwater port has been dropped at the initiative of the oil industry due to factors such as inadequate refinery capacity, uncertainty of supplies, and environmental regulations. Exploratory drilling by the oil companies in the Baltimore Canyon has contradicted earlier predictions that the area would provide large quantities of economically viable oil. Finally, Public Service Gas and Electric Company (New Jersey) has been forced to cancel its contract for the floating nuclear power plants because of declining demand for electricity. Still, the local reaction to these proposed technologies is an instructive case in the politics of energy self-sufficiency.

My focus here will be on New Jersey, which is the larger of the two states and which would be more directly affected by the technologies. New Jersey is the most densely populated and the most heavily industrialized state in the union. The state produces no oil or natural gas, yet the petrochemical industry (supplied from foreign and Gulf of Mexico oil fields) is New Jersey's largest industry, accounting for $4 billion of an annual gross product of $50 billion. Manufacturing provides more than 40 percent of New Jersey's jobs. In short, the New Jersey economy is very energy intensive and the energy comes almost exclusively from outside the state. The attractions of greater energy self-sufficiency through the development of offshore oil and nuclear power are, in light of these statistics, rather obvious. But, in purely economic terms, there is a substantial basis for conflict over offshore technologies in New Jersey, since its second-largest industry is tourism ($3.5 billion), most of which is located in the same coastal areas that would be affected by the offshore technologies.[35]

Aside from citizens and state and local government officials, the Mid-Atlantic case involves various agencies of the federal government with responsibility for offshore leasing and nuclear licensing, and such energy giants as Exxon, Arco, Shell, and Offshore Power Systems (a General Electric subsidiary).

The most striking aspect of the reaction to the proposed technologies in New Jersey, as documented by a congressional Office of Technology Assessment (OTA) study, is the nearly unanimous sentiment that the federal government should be more sensitive to a need for local participation in development planning. What does this localism mean? The same study showed that public officials wanted a more substantive role in the management of the offshore technologies, but that they did not question their fundamental viability.[36] The study also showed that citizens who responded to a questionnaire saw more positive than negative effects stemming from the development of the Baltimore Canyon and floating nuclear power plants.[37] Finally, alternative energy leaders in New Jersey have recognized that they are far less powerful than similar groups in other areas, such as the Clamshell Alliance in New England.[38] In short, the desire for local control more likely stems from an interest in self-sufficiency than self-reliance, an interpretation that is consistent with the state's dependence on energy-intensive industry.

But despite this general support for centralized technologies, citizen comments in the OTA study were surprisingly skeptical of the long-term viability of centralization. Cited as typical of citizen attitudes was the following statement:

> Before these options are explored, the State and the Nation must develop a comprehensive energy conservation policy, including development of mass transit and recycling of all usable products. As a second step, all minimum polluting forms of energy—such as solar, wind, and geothermal—should be utilized wherever possible. If offshore facilities are eventually developed, legislation should spell out clearly that they must conform to all existing environmental legislation. This is especially important regarding onshore development which will definitely affect air quality maintenance planning.[39]

It is at this point that the perspectives of elite managers and common citizens part ways. It is not at all surprising that most officials and citizens in New Jersey support immediate policies that would continue the trend toward centralized technologies. The vulnerability of such policies, however, is underlined in this case by the fact that they have collapsed with virtually no opposition. Moreover, the citizens consulted in the OTA study exhibited a preference for soft path directions over a longer term. It would seem, then, that such support as there is for continued centralization derives largely from the political obstacles lying in the path of an alternative. The obvious need is to overcome the pathologies of the short run by developing institutions and a political movement that would make the soft path more practical.

Conclusion: A Postscript on Strategy

If the foregoing excursion through the topic of energy self-sufficiency shows anything, it is that politics is the crucial variable in determining the nation's energy future. There are no major technical obstacles to energy self-reliance, and the requisite economic infrastructure is substantially in place (especially in the ability of the economic system to generate capital and the high educational levels of the population). Moreover, there is widespread public support for energy self-reliance.

What is lacking is the kind of political movement that can take on centralized government and corporate power, and win. The self-reliance approach to energy will bear fruit less as the result of heroic individual actions than through the development of a broad political movement that puts people more directly in command of their lives. Individual inertia is only half of the problem; institutional inertia is the other half.

If politics is crucial to our energy future, then basic images of political economy will significantly shape the kinds of strategies to be pursued. My sense is that soft path advocates are excessively enamored of the laissez-faire market model of the economy and the liberal, interest-group politics that goes with it. Lovins, in particular, has promoted the notion that the smart money is already moving into soft technologies as the inherent failures of continued centralization become more evident, and that the financial basis for the pursuit of energy self-reliance will come through competitive capitalism.[40]

Yet, the sprinkling of energy corporations throughout the Fortune 500 (including four of the top six in 1977), combined with the hostile attitudes of the major banks, the energy corporations, and most utilities toward soft technologies, induces skepticism that these key actors are bound by competitive market forces.[41] Nor does the concentration of wealth and power characterizing our economic system in general banish concern that more is required than adjusting market mechanisms in order to make the soft path a reality.

The image that I think more accurately reflects the actual nature of our political economy is one of corporate predominance that is *historical* in its origins, that is, it is the logical outcome of an entire era in the development of industrial capitalism. As such, this corporate power will prove more deeply rooted, and more tenaciously wedded to continued centralization, than one would surmise by viewing the economy as essentially a sphere of competitive interactions, with inequalities being mitigated by benign government intervention. This image suggests two observations that seem crucial to the politics of energy self-sufficiency.

1. The role of governing institutions is to harmonize the various interest groups which enter the policy process, *assuming the essential distribution of power implicit in the prior organization of the political economy.* I have discussed above the shared interests of the federal government and the major corporations in a pyramidal power structure when it comes to energy policy. What can be added after examining the four cases of self-sufficiency politics is that decentralists will be bargained into the institutional structure

on clearly subordinate terms, with government leaders loudly proclaiming this as evidence of their commitment to renewable energy and participatory democracy.

2. Opposition to centralized energy technologies can only be reactive within this power structure, in the sense that the reformers simply do not command the resources with which to take bold development initiatives. Instead, they are mostly capable of throwing a wrench into the plans developed by corporate and government officials and engaging in piecemeal, case-by-case self-defense.

Paradoxically, then, self-reliance will require some measure of centralized power. To the extent that the self-reliance movement remains principally concerned with issues in a local context, it will only be able to react to initiatives coming from the center.

Localism will of course be crucial to energy self-reliance, for the best laid plans can turn bureaucratic and coercive if they are not held accountable by enlightened activism at the grass roots. But in addition to the kinds of initiatives being taken in states and regions reviewed in this chapter, some other general lines of action will be important.

First and foremost, energy issues should not be severed from the need for a more democratic economic system. The closure of major production facilities by distant corporate headquarters has inflicted severe economic hardship on communities like Youngstown, Ohio, Forest Grove, Oregon, and many others. After the fact, local leaders are painfully aware that they lack input into decisions affecting the welfare of their communities, whether these decisions concern energy per se or economic development in general. Holding corporate activity accountable to the public interest will be at the center of public issues in the 1980s, precisely because corporate planning decisions have serious public impacts in highly centralized societies. In the likely event that a new era of laissez-faire capitalism fails to emerge, input into corporate planning and decision-making will be crucial in energy and other policy areas. New schemes promoting public and worker representation on corporate boards are sure to receive more serious consideration as the traditional mechanisms of liberal capitalism encounter economic stagnation and policy stalemate.

For energy in particular, three issues involving the control of centralized technologies and power structures are important. First, government institutions can be used to compete with private enterprises in oligopoly situations. For example, a federal oil corporation, which would buy oil from producers and sell it to refiners could be used as a means of mitigating monopoly control in that industry. In Cleveland, the conflict over continued municipal ownership of the Cleveland Municipal Light Company (Muny Light) in part involves the ability of Muny Light to provide competition to Cleveland Electric Illuminating Company, a privately owned utility that supplies most of the city. Second, government institutions have to be used to help finance energy alternatives that serve a public good that will not be met by private enterprise. Solar energy is the primary case in point, and proposals for a national solar bank currently being introduced to Congress suggest an important possibility. Finally, research and development funds need to be directed away from the present emphasis on nuclear power, under which nuclear expenditures in the Department of Energy outstrip solar expenditures by a margin of approximately 4 to 1, despite recent increases in the latter.[42]

Taken together, the kinds of strategies briefly reviewed here constitute the minimum necessary to move the nation toward energy self-reliance. The energy path promoted by elite managers is riddled with its own contradictions and will likely become an increasing burden on the economy and the environment unless an effective movement built on the basis of present self-reliance initiatives can effectively take the lead in energy policy. This puts the decentralists in the ironic position of seeking centralized power, but there is no alternative. The real challenge lies in judiciously blending centralization and decentralization in a manner compatible with maximum self-reliance.

Notes

1. On western public lands policy see Council on Economic Priorities, *Leased and Lost: A Study of Public and Indian Coal Leasing in the West* (New York: CEP Report, 1975); on state and local government impact see Raymond B. Pratt and Dwayne Ward, "Corporations, The State and Energy Development in the Northern Rockies," presented to the American Political Science Association, New York, 1978, p. 9. International oil pricing is discussed in John M. Blair, *The Control of Oil* (New York: Vintage Press, 1978).

2. Battelle Memorial Institute, *An Analysis of Federal Incentives Used to Stimulate Energy Production*, (Springfield, VA: National Technical Information Service, 1978), p. 7.

3. Barry Commoner has discussed the Rockefeller proposal in *The Poverty of Power* (New York: Knopf, 1976), p. 68.

4. "Distributed Energy Systems in California's Future" in *Soft Energy Notes* 1 (1978); D.R. Neill and P.K. Takahashi, "Energy Self-Sufficiency for the State of Hawaii," in T. Nejat Veziroglu, ed., *Solar Energy and Conservation Symposium-Workshop: Conference Proceedings* (Coral Gables: University of Miami, 1978); Mitre Corporation, *New England Sustainable Energy Project*, 1978; Energy Research and Development Administration, *Choosing an Electrical Energy Future for the Pacific*

Northwest: An Alternate Scenario (Washington, D.C., 1977); Montana Department of Natural Resources and Conservation, *Design Study Outline of Montana Sustainable Energy Project: Blueprint for an Energy Future* (mimeo, 1979).

5. Byron L. Dorgan, "Taxing Coal," North Dakota Tax Department (mimeo, 1977).

6. Paul Krueger and Richard Louv, "The Offshore Oil Conflict: California Cities vs. Washington" in *California Journal* 5 (1978).

7. Stephen Hymer, "The Multinational Corporation and the Law of Uneven Development" in Jagdish N. Bhagwati, ed., *Economics and World Order* (New York: World Law Fund, 1971, prepublication copy).

8. Frederick Winslow Taylor, *The Principles of Scientific Management* (New York: Norton, 1967).

9. Hymer, "The Multinational Corporation and the Law of Uneven Development," p. 6.

10. For an excellent discussion of power structures and energy use from a historical perspective, see Fred Cottrell, "Energy and Sociology," *Humanity and Society* 4 (1978):237-249.

11. Amory B. Lovins and John H. Price, *Non-Nuclear Futures: The Case for an Ethical Energy Strategy* (Cambridge, Mass.: Ballinger Publishing Co., 1975).

12. Charles E. Lindblom, *Politics and Markets* (New York: Basic Books, 1977), p. 332.

13. See especially the chapter "Buddhist Economics," in E.F. Schumacher, *Small Is Beautiful* (New York: Harper & Row, 1973).

14. The politics of high-tech and low-tech approaches to solar energy are discussed in *Government R & D Report: Solar Energy Edition*, June 1, 1978.

15. "Preventing a Solar Backlash," in Lee Webb, *Public Policies for the 80's* (Washington, Conference/Alternative State and Local Policy, 1978).

16. *New York Times*, April 15, 1979.

17. Office of Technology Assessment, *Coastal Effects of Offshore Energy Systems* (Washington, D.C.: Congress of the United States, 1976).

18. Robert Lawrence, "Introduction—Symposium on Energy Policy," *Policy Studies Journal* 7 (1978):6-8.

19. Harold P. Green, "The Adversary Process in Technology Assessment," cited in Francois Hetman, *Society and the Assessment of Technology* (Paris: Organization of Economic Co-operation and Development, 1973), pp. 113-114.

20. Ron Roach, "Senator Frankenstein," *California Journal* 5 (1978).

21. "Distributed Energy Systems in California's Future."

22. Alan S. Hirshberg and E.S. Davis, *Solar Energy in Buildings: Implications for California Energy Policy* (Pasadena: Jet Propulsion Laboratory, California Institute of Technology, 1977).

23. California Public Policy Center, "SolarCal: Dawn of a New Age" (mimeo, 1977).

24. SolarCal Council, *Toward a Solar California* (Sacramento: SolarCal Office, 1978).

25. Information on the BPA legislative alternatives is presented in "The Columbia Basin Energy Commission Act of 1978," H.R. 5862 Revised; "The Pacific Northwest Electric Power Supply and Conservation Act," S. 2080; "The Pacific Northwest Electric Power Planning and Conservation Act," S. 3418, all 95th Congress; and Lane Council of Governments, "Expanded Background Paper on the Pacific Northwest Electric Energy Picture for the L-COG Board of Directors" (mimeo, 1977).

26. See S. 3418.

27. *New York Times*, October 13, 1977, and April 17, 1979.

28. The figures on the proposed National Energy Plan are presented in Barry Commoner, "The National Energy Plan: A Critique" (New York: Scientists Institute for Public Information, 1977). The figures on the 1979 proposals are calculated on the basis of information provided by the Carter administration to the press and reported in the *Wall Street Journal*, July 17, 1979.

29. On concentration in the energy industry see Robert Engler, *The Brotherhood of Oil* (Chicago: University of Chicago Press, 1977); and Pratt and Ward, "Corporations, The State, and Energy Development in the Northern Rockies," p. 10.

30. Energy Research and Development Administration, *Draft Environmental Impact Statement: Coal Research, Development and Demonstration Program*, cited in Pratt and Ward, "Corporations, The State and Energy Development in the Northern Rockies," p. 54.

31. National Academy of Sciences, *Rehabilitation Potential of Western Coal Lands*, cited in Pratt and Ward.

32. Byron L. Dorgan, "Taxing Coal," p. 1.

33. Ibid.

34. Kenyon N. Griffin and Robert B. Shelton, "Coal Severance Tax in the Rocky Mountain States," *Policy Studies Journal* 7 (1978):37.

35. Office of Technology Assessment, *Coastal Effects of Offshore Energy Systems*, pp. 119-122.

36. Ibid., pp. 138-140.

37. Ibid., pp. 259-260.

38. *New York Times*, July 13, 1977.

39. Office of Technology Assessment, *Coastal Effects of Offshore Energy Systems*, pp. 255-256.

40. See Amory B. Lovins, "The Soft Energy Path," *Center Magazine* 5 (1978):32-46.

41. For a more in-depth treatment of this issue, see Richard Worthington, "Public Policy in Capitalist Society: The Case of Solar Energy," presented to the Northeastern Political Science Association, 1978.

42. Lee Johnson, "Side-Stepping the Sun," *RAIN* 4 (1978):12-15.

5 Issues Affecting the Decentralization of Energy Supply

Andy Lawrence and
Gregory A. Daneke

Centralization versus decentralization is a classic theme in the annals of public policy and administration.[1] Nowhere, perhaps, are the implications of this debate more profound than in the area of energy policy. Amid the U.S. preoccupation with capital-intensive, centralized energy systems, the concept of decentralization appears somewhat mythical and much maligned. Proponents of the status quo see decentralization as a barefoot, "back to nature" movement, using energy as a vehicle for social change.[2] However, as Amory Lovins and others have so often pointed out, there may be a good deal more social change in store along the "hard path" than along the "soft."[3] Meanwhile, existing political and economic institutions tend to extol centralization and obscure the potential for decentralization. There are a number of fundamental problems (social, environmental, and economic) in present policies designed to substitute synfuels and nuclear energy for foreign oil. The president's commitment (at least symbolic) to provide 20 percent of the nation's energy through renewable resources by the year 2000 would make it seem that the time to consider decentralization seriously is at hand.

Why Decentralization?

The Arab oil embargo of 1973 introduced what has come to be known as the "energy crisis." The solidification of the OPEC cartel has had large impacts upon the U.S. economy. Moreover, it has served to underscore the basic dependence of the United States upon oil imports from the nations of the Middle East. More basic than this potential threat to our national security has been a recognition of the reliance of the American economy upon a nonrenewable energy supply. With the exception of hydroelectric power, virtually all energy in the United States is supplied by oil, natural gas, coal, and uranium—all depletable resources for which there has been accelerating demand.

In response to the lessons of the Arab oil embargo, the United States has embarked upon a national effort in energy planning. Today, the Department of Energy (DOE) is the focal point of this planning effort. But the task of energy planning has not been an easy one. There has been a general lack of national consensus with respect to energy goals. Congress dismantled the president's National Energy Plan (NEP-I) of 1977 and left the major issues of energy policy largely problemmatic. Economic shocks and "gas lines" which accompanied the temporary loss of Iran from the world oil market vividly illustrate that current energy planning still lacks the capability to deal with probable contingencies. The President's Second National Energy Plan (NEP-II) thus emerged as an ad hoc response to oil market fluctuations.[4] The focal point of NEP-II is the decontrol of domestic oil prices in the remote hope that it will encourage increased domestic production capacity. In addition to this stop-gap response, the president is now calling for a rigorous program to develop synthetic fuels (oil shale, coal liquefaction). By and large, this synfuels package ignores the great potential of heavy oils (tar sands) and unconventional natural gas, which are much more environmentally benign and therefore less costly in the long run. Meanwhile, the president has also endorsed the findings of another planning effort, known as the *Domestic Policy Review of Solar Energy*, or the Solar DPR. This review contends that an earnest commitment to solar technologies could yield almost twenty quads (quadrillion Btus) in the next century (about a quarter of the total U.S. energy supply, given reasonable conservation).[5] However, despite these efforts at energy planning, there is no detailed "road map" of the energy transition, and decentralization remains more a myth than a methodology.[6]

Centralization versus Decentralization

While the Arab oil embargo of 1973 and the return of the gas lines in 1979 sent us one message with regard to domestic energy patterns, other warnings have surfaced as well within the past two decades. In the fall of 1965, a failure of the electrical grid threw the entire notheastern United States into a now infamous blackout. More recently, other incidents have occurred. For example, in April 1973 more than 2 million people were affected by successive electrical blackouts on Florida's "Gold Coast," stretching from Palm Beach to the Florida Keys. The cause of the failure was the automatic shutdown of a nuclear power plant rated at 650,000 kilowatts of capacity, which triggered a series of failures in other power plants in the electric power network in southern Florida. The recent incident at the Three Mile Island nuclear facility further underscores the high energy-high technology nature of our domestic energy mix and the vulnerability of the U.S. supply network to impact beyond the whims of OPEC.

The current high energy-high technology nature of the American energy supply and demand network is supported by a regulatory framework which has held the price of energy below its replacement cost and encouraged the centralization of supply. In the face of this artificially inexpensive energy supply, energy use in the United States has been marked by waste and thermodynamic inefficiencies. However, the rising price of imported oil, coupled with dwindling natural gas supplies (over the long term) and increasing costs associated with the use of coal and nuclear energy, has put an end to the era of cheap energy. The energy policymaker is faced with planning for a future which may look very much different from the past. It is within this uncertain future that the possibilities of a decentralized energy system must be analyzed.

A great deal of effort has been expended within DOE to assess the technologies and fuel sources by which future energy demand can be met. Much less effort has been devoted to the development of an understanding of the nature of this energy demand itself. The issue which concerns us here is the feasibility of meeting energy demand through an appropriate mix of decentralized and centralized energy technologies. A key corollary to the concept of decentralization is the formulation of an energy policy responsive to the nature of the demand for energy and the needs of energy users and based upon an efficient use of resources.[7] Thus conservation and thermodynamic matching of energy types to energy needs are important factors.

The decentralization of energy supply need not be approached as an either/or proposition vis-à-vis high technology options. Decentralized technologies must be evaluated in the context of "economies of scale," investments in infrastructure, and issues of optimal deployment. The United States is comprised of many energy markets characterized by a wide variety of energy demands. In some settings, a centralized power source represents "overkill," fraught with thermodynamic inefficiencies. In others, centralized energy sources may be essential to meet the energy needs of a densely populated area. A decentralized energy policy must recognize these differences and adjust its goals and objectives accordingly.

Having outlined the framework in which an approach to decentralized energy systems can be taken, it is appropriate to set forth the research strategy by which a demand-oriented energy policy based on decentralization can emerge.

Toward a Decentralized Approach

The first step required is the establishment of goals for a decentralized energy program. As has been seen, the development of energy goals in the national arena has been difficult. Careful assessment needs to be directed toward the following questions:

1. What should be the role of decentralized energy sources in the national energy mix?
2. How much energy can be expected from decentralized sources over time?
3. What are their economic costs/benefits?
4. What are their environmental effects?
5. What are their impacts (both positive and negative) upon quality-of-life and social well-being?
6. What regional arrangement of decentralized technologies makes most sense?
7. What are the economic, technological, and institutional barriers to the introduction of decentralized supplies and how easily can they be reduced?

Through addressing these questions a set of goals and objectives for decentralized systems might begin to emerge. While DOE and its national laboratories have begun to raise these types of questions,[8] the answers remain elusive.

The second step of a research program geared toward developing a decentralized energy strategy is an evaluation of the full range of technological options for the decentralization of energy supply. A partial list of decentralized options is presented below:

1. District heating.
2. Solar heating and cooling of buildings.
3. Low-head hydroelectric power.
4. Biomass: use of agricultural and forestry wastes, silvicultural plantations, kelp farms, and so on.
5. Wind energy conversion systems.
6. Methane from coal seams.
7. Geothermal heat/geopressurized gas.
8. Photovoltaic/solar thermal electric power (small scale).
9. Fuel cells.
10. Magnetohydrodynamics (MHD).
11. Human and animal wastes.
12. Waste heat: combined cycle, cogeneration, cascading.

Given this list, it should be obvious that decentralized systems are not always synonomous with renewable systems. For example, there is some discussion among nuclear engineers of using small fission reactors (research and/or submarine scale) for industrial applications in which all of the heat woud be utilized and problems which plague the large utility reactors would be minimized. However, the distribution of the highly enriched (that is, weapons grade) fuels required for these small-scale reactors suggests numerous other problems, not the least of which is proliferation. Thus, in very broad terms, it is fair to think of decentralization as being closely aligned with renewable (largely solar) technologies.

A third step in approaching a decentralized energy strategy is an examination of regional factors relevant to each technology option. The U.S. currently has a scattered energy resource base, and frequently energy supplies are far from demand centers. For example, the vast supplies of sub-bituminous coal of the West are quite distant from midwestern and eastern markets. This means that the costs and benefits of conventional energy supplies do not necessarily accrue to the same parties and that transportation is a significant cost. With respect to decentralized energy supplies, regional availability is an important factor. Solar energy may favor areas in the South and West. Geothermal energy may only be appropriate to certain western areas. A 50 Mw wood-fired power plant may be more appropriate in Vermont than solar collectors. Thus, decentralized systems should be compared with one another as well as with conventional systems. This notion of regional comparison as well as end-use applicability form the underpinnings of a concept of "appropriate technology."

The fourth and perhaps most crucial step in the analysis of energy decentralization is how it will interface with existing systems. Vast utility networks are expensive to maintain and require advanced knowledge of demand to operate efficiently. Haphazard introduction of decentralized systems will accelerate the level of uncertainty costs associated with existing systems, and miscalculations may create serious economic dislocations. It is this need for adequate interface that necessitates some form of national planning for what will be essentially regional, state, and local energy systems.

On Getting from Here to There

Given the capital intensive-high technology nature of the energy supply and demand network, energy policy is generally framed within a centralized context. Traditional energy planning has been almost solely in terms of supply—how can we produce more energy? As suggested, policymakers have little experience with decentralized energy planning, nor do they approach energy from an end-user's perspective. The myopia of existing institutions will have to be altered if decentralized systems are to take hold. A more synoptic approach to energy policy might begin by asking:

1. What kinds of support are most appropriate to each of the decentralized energy options: R&D funding, subsidies, tax incentives, and so on.

2. How can federal policy reduce the economic, technological, and institutional barriers identified for each technology option?
3. What are the lead times for these technologies given appropriate federal support?
4. How much energy can these technologies supply by type (heat, steam, and so on) and region?
5. How can federal policy be coordinated with and/or supplemented by state and local programs?
6. How can private interests be stimulated to develop and/or make use of decentralized technology options?

A case study for a particular region or a particular decentralized technology may offer a model for a comprehensive approach to the numerous economic, institutional, technological, and social issues raised by the questions outlined above.

The Department of Energy has already incorporated a community-level case study approach into at least two of its major assessments of solar energy. The Technology Assessment of Solar Energy (TASE),[9] sponsored by the Office of Technology Impacts, Technology Assessment Division within DOE, uses generic case studies as part of its overall study plan. TASE addresses environmental and social questions related to solar energy development from both the national and community perspectives. In the community impact anslysis, the consequences of increased solar-based energy use on a typical community environment and infrastructure are being examined. In the TASE approach, three hypothetical communities (having residential, industrial and commercial areas, schools, public service facilities, labor forces, green space, transportation networks, and so on) are defined to examine the potential impacts of at least two postulated levels of solar energy use.

The Decentralized Solar Energy Technology Assessment Program (TAP),[10] conducted under the auspices of the Office of Solar, Geothermal, Electric and Storage Systems, Division of Planning and Technology Transfer, features a community-based decentralized solar energy technol-technology assessment. Five communities will be examined as part of the overall study to assess the social, economic, institutional, and life-style impacts of the widespread use of decentralized solar technologies. Unlike TASE, the Decentralized Solar Energy TAP focuses upon actual rather than hypothetical comunity settings. For the first phase of the study, three small communities have been funded to undertake their own TA: Corning, New York; Richmond, Kentucky; and Kent, Ohio. In the second phase of the TAP, Franklin County, Massachusetts, and another community to be determined later will be added to the list. Through studies such as these, answers to some of the questions posed above can begin to emerge.

Understanding Constraints

A decentralized energy approach essentially calls for a rethinking of energy supply-and-demand questions. "Corrective" actions need to be directed toward the high energy-high technology contributors to our supply-oriented energy outlook. Within the private sector, this target is comprised of the electric utility industry and the nuclear, oil, coal, and gas industries, which promote the "bigger-is-better" approach to energy supply. As mentioned, the decentralization of energy supply need not be viewed as a punitive action designed to penalize high-technology villains. Economies of scale and other factors will prolong the need for a continued use of centralized energy sources. The achievement of an optimal balance between energy from centralized and decentralized technologies is one of the biggest challenges of a demand-oriented energy policy. For example, it might be asked whether the energy park concept ought to be replaced with a more decentralized network of supply—one suitably matched to the energy needs of the demand sectors of a given region. If the latter seems more appropriate, we need then to determine what policy mechanisms are best designed to achieve this goal.

Further, the decentralized approach represents more than just an effort to introduce a demand orientation into the planning outlook of the Department of Energy. It calls for a regional perspective which does not attempt to apply a single solution to all geographic settings. A framework must be developed by which national energy policy can be based upon appropriate regional energy mixes so as to promote the most efficient use of energy resources throughout the nation. Areas of coordination with state and local governments, utilities and utility commissions, and decentralized energy suppliers need to be identified and strategies for cooperation planned. The role of reigonal energy offices requires explicit definition with respect to decentralized energy planning.

However, a national policy geared toward energy decentralization must be framed within the realities of the existing energy system. The institutional barriers to decentralized supplies posed by the high energy-high technology character of the existing energy supply network is a major area requiring careful study. The need for electric utilities to amortize their capital investment exists regardless of the use of residential solar devices. A reduction in the demand for electricity through increased use of residential solar systems does not reduce a utility's operating costs or its guaranteed return on investment. To offset a reduction in demand, a utility may seek a rate hike which, if approved, would offset any monetary savings a homeowner might accrue using a decentralized energy option individually. Such initial incompatibilities between centralized and decentralized energy supply systems must be addressed as part of a policy commitment to energy decentralization. In fact, once a goal of increased energy decentralization is established, the centralized supply industries should (and must) be invited into the planning for the kinds of transitions and adjustments which will take place as centralized and decentralized systems are made compatible.

In addition to the traditional systems of supply, a new energy supply industry will begin to appear. Manufacturers of photovoltaic, geothermal, wind, MHD, and other kinds of energy technology systems will begin to offer the energy consumer a wider range of options in energy supply. The nature of these industries must be assessed with respect to their ownership, size, resource requirements (labor, capital, materials, and so on), environmental impact, and other relevant parameters so that their economic and life-quality impact can be analyzed and planned for.

The energy-demanding sectors of the economy are important affected parties in the assessment of decentralized energy supply. Homeowners, business and commercial establishments, industries, and the transportation sector will be affected by the development of decentralized energy supplies. Assessment is required as to which of the decentralized technologies available is most thermodynamically suited to the energy needs of each demand category. In such an assessment, the following questions need to be addressed:

1. How are the energy demands of the residential, commercial, industrial, and transportation sectors currently met?
2. Where are the thermodynamic efficiencies highest? Lowest?
3. Which decentralized technologies are appropriate to those areas where the greatest inefficiencies exist? Are these technologies regionally available?
4. How much energy can decentralized technologies be expected to supply by need/region—at what cost? And at what life-quality impact?
5. What are the projections for energy use over time by region and demand category, under differing growth scenarios?

Finally, approaches must be developed to make the energy-planning apparatus of the federal, state, and local governments compatible with the new institutional arrangements that decentralized energy technologies will bring. This includes the subsidy-tax incentive-rate regulation decisions which must be made across all technology options to ensure an efficient and equitable energy supply network.

The Energy Future Awaits

National energy programs are the first policy area requiring assessment with regard to a decentralized approach to energy supply. As previously discussed, national energy policy is currently oriented toward capital intensive-high technology sources of supply. The budget categories for decentralized energy technologies need to be evaluated with an eye to the establishment of an *integrated* program of energy decentralization—one sensitive to the energy needs and supply capabilities of the different regions of the country. Such an approach will likely require the establishment of new budget categories and the redefinition of existing DOE program areas. Decentralized solar options must be assessed relative to one another as well as in relation to other decentralized energy technology candidates as part of integrated regional energy composites. A decentralization of energy supply cannot be planned for through separate and loosely coordinated programs. Efforts must be devoted to the development of a suitable approach to national planning for a decentralized energy system, an approach appropriate to the goals established for an optimal centralized/decentralized energy mix.

In addition, state and local energy planning capabilities must be assessed from the point of view of their ability to facilitate a centralized/decentralized supply network. Approaches by which states can take a more comprehensive view of the concept of decentralization and develop an institutional framework by which to promote sound energy planning consistent with national goals must be devised. Areas must develop an enlightened approach to growth which can assure that energy supply will be available in forms suitable to demand needs.

The Technology Assessment of Solar Enegy and the Decentralized Solar Energy Technology Assessment Program discussed previously will provide a framework in which these issues can be addressed. In TASE, solar energy use in each hypothetical community (in terms of a mix of technologies) is projected on at least two levels of penetration. The two principal aspects of this early phase of the study are (1) the spatial arrangement of the defined communities and the overall size (as measured in area, economic base, and energy demand) are held constant; and (2) the focus of the analysis is on the influence of community form(s) (spatial distribution) on a selected set of economic, social, and environmental indicators as appropriate mixes of solar technologies are introduced to satisfy an increasingly greater percentage of total energy demand.

Impact variables to be evaluated include air and water pollution, water consumption, noise, travel time, traffic accidents, land use, public services, streets and roads. The primary result of the study will be a matrix of impact indicators for percentages of solar energy penetration in each spatial form analyzed. This information will be used to assess problems that established communities may incur in assimilating larger shares of solar-derived energy.

The TASE study also includes a threshold analysis which looks at the ability of communities to progressively absorb social and economic changes. The goal of the threshold analysis is to determine which community forms are most adaptable, and at what point "nonadaptability" (the saturation point for solar transitions) is reached. The threshold states are to be examined for several possible indicators, including, but not limited to, land availability, transportation, support services, institutional arrangements, and life-style considerations. The communities selected are to be analyzed dynamically (based on assumed population, economic, and energy changes) at periodic intervals between now and the year 2025. A parametric analysis is also to be performed by varying the assumed solar energy technology mixes and the amount of solar-based energy in proportion to the total energy demand.

In the Decentralized Solar Energy (TAP) community-level technology assessments are designed to be responsive to community needs and goals. They will involve local citizens in discussions of their possible energy futures. Working teams will be formed within each community to develop a plausible scenario for local solar development and use. These scenarios are to be based upon perceived community energy needs, community goals and preferences, availability of solar resources, and other agreed-upon values. An assessment of the likely social, economic, institutional, and life-style impacts of the scenarios selected will be undertaken with a wide range of citizen involvement. Results from both the TASE and TAP studies will provide insights into the local policy and planning issues which will emerge as decentralized energy technologies become increasingly available.

Policy Variables

No single comprehensive energy policy can meet all domestic energy needs efficiently and reliably. Energy policy requires flexibility and the ability to accommodate change. Goals for the decentralization of energy sources must be formulated with such a flexibility in mind. If a commitment to decentralized energy supply is deemed to be in the national interest, an evaluation of the role of federal RD&D, tax incentives, rebates, and so forth will be needed with respect to overall goals. This requires a detailed understanding of the behavior and needs of energy consumers as input to the measures best suited to influence market behavior toward the decentralized concept. In essence, there are three kinds of innovations needed: (1) national policymaking to create a favorable climate for planning for decentralization, (2) technology in the area of decentralized supply systems, and (3) behavioral changes among consumers to adopt this new approach to energy supply. Successes in the first two areas may be rendered meaningless without success in the third. It is toward this demand orientation that much of the investigation of the possibilities must be directed.

Current long-range national energy goals call upon a reliance on abundant domestic coal resources as a bridge toward an energy future based upon renewable energy supplies. But many of the proposals for coal use—electrification, liquefaction, and gasification—are not only centralized, but may be environmentally unsound. Other uses of coal such as MHD and fluidized bed combustion could be used on a much smaller scale with a greater potential for supply decentralization and less likelihood of environmental degradation. Many of the renewable energy supplies upon which the energy economy of 2050 may be based are not suited (in a thermodynamic sense) for centralized approaches. A 1000 Mw wind utility or a 100,000 barrel per day methanol-from-biomass facility are highly unlikely in the foreseeable future. Thus current emphasis on the decentralization of supply offers an opportunity to gain some experience which will be useful in the transition to a renewable energy base. It may also prepare us for the economic, environmental, and quality-of-life aspects of the future energy supply and demand network.

Methods for Measuring the Utility
of Decentralized Systems

Throughout our discussion we have alluded to certain uncommon utility functions associated with decentralized systems. Such criteria as life-quality impact are not presently a part of the energy planning nomenclature. Generaly speaking, the level of performance of the energy supply system is based on a price of energy below the cost of replacement. While consumer preference may favor the cheapest energy prices possible, in terms of efficient use of available resources such as arrangement may not prove to be the wisest investment over time. Dispersed technologies, particularly those which provide renewable or inexhaustible energy supplies, should be priced in terms of "life-cycle costs." Moreover, there should be a way to roll in advantages of reduced environmental loadings.

To wit, a 1,000 Mw coal-fired electric utility,[11] operating in compliance with existing environmental law, can be expected to result in the following pollution levels annually:

Pollutant	*Amount (in tons)*
Total suspended particulates	1,200
Sulfur dioxide	13,400
Nitrogen dioxide	14,400
Total dissolved solids	2,200
Scrubber sludge	250,000
Boiler ash	36,000
Electrostatic precipitation ash	142,000

Despite the use of expensive pollution control equipment (which, of course, adds to the price of delivered electricity), a large centralized coal-fired utility will still release large amounts of pollution on an annual basis. These pollutants have hidden costs in their public health, ecological, and aesthetic impacts each year for the twenty- to thirty-year life of the utility. And the pollutant emission levels cited above do not even address the problems of acid rain, the release of respirable particulates, and the potential for carbon-dioxide build-up in the atmosphere also associated with the operation of coal-fired power plants. Further, additional environmental costs must be considered as part of a coal-fired utility's life-cycle costs. To supply the coal necessary to fuel an electric utility, the environmental impacts associated with underground- and strip-mining, coal-cleaning, and coal transportation will occur. Often these impacts are felt in a location far distant from the utility site itself. And secondary impacts, such as those associated with coal-mining, may well become more severe as our coal resources are depleted, and we move toward mining less accessible coal deposits with lower mine yields.

Were the same electricity that is generated from a 1,000 Mw coal utility to be supplied by decentralized solar applications, the resultant environmental loadings would be negligible compared to those associated with coal use. Further, solar energy represents an inexhaustible energy resource whose extraction costs will not increase over time. While the manufacture of solar equipment, chemicals, and other necessary components for decentralized energy sources will not be without environmental impact, the operating systems themselves will be virtually pollution free. In terms of life-cycle cost, decentralized solar energy use may become cost effective well before the price of solar-based energy is competitive with centralized fossil fuel and nuclear sources.

The thermodynamic matching of supply types to energy uses offers a third possible effectiveness measure for decentralized energy technologies. The measurement of energy supplies according to their second law efficiencies will give a clearer picture of the efficacy of various supply techniques as measured against a theoretical optimum. The overall mix of centralized and decentralized energy supplies can be rated with respect to a "system efficiency" to assess the benefits caused by the contributions of decentralized technologies and to identify where improvements can still be made.

Quality-of-life-social well-being indicators are as yet rudimentary measures of social utility; however, the systematization of these techniques would offer a comprehensive approach by which to measure the effectiveness of decentralized technologies against social, environmental, and economic goals. Methodologies to develop quality-of-life indicators should be investigated as part of assessing the effectiveness of the decentralized approach to energy supply.

Finally, regional considerations are important inputs as effectiveness measures to decentralized supplies. The regional contribution of locally appropriate supply technologies represents another possible measure of effectiveness. The reliability of geothermal contributions to northwestern regional energy mixes, solar contributions to the energy needs of the Sun Belt, and wind energy contributions to the Great Lakes region, with respect to the overall regional energy mix, indicates possible measures of the useful contributions to total energy supply that decentralized sources can represent.

A Systematic Approach

A "general systems" type of approach seems the most comprehensive and reasonable way to address the many energy, environmental, economic, social, and technical questions associated with the decentralization of energy supply. Through the use of normative forecasting, scenario simulation, and a regional approach, a technology assessment (TA) can be designed to systematically identify the various possible impacts that a decentralization of energy supplies will bring. Technology assessments have been powerful tools in other areas of comprehensive planning, and, as has been seen, already figure prominently in the DOE approach to understanding the range of impacts likely to be associated with decentralized solar applications.

The discipline of technology assessment, as it has evolved over the last decade, has risen to such importance in our national policymaking that the U.S. Congress established an Office of Technology Assessment as one of its four major sources of analytical support. Typically, a technology assessment is policy-oriented research designed to anticipate, identify, and evaluate the potential impacts of a new technology. A TA considers both primary (direct) and secondary (unplanned or indirect) impacts and consequences of technological development and deployment; it goes beyond mere questions of technical feasibility, direct or internalized costs, and safety considerations. A technology assessment has the following primary characteristics.[12]

1. TA focuses on long-range impacts or consequences of a technology; the impacts may be physical, biological, or social.
2. TA addresses a wide range of possible consequences (social, economic, environmental, legal, institutional, cultural, behavioral).
3. TA is oriented toward providing a broad information base for determining policy options and alternatives, that is, toward decision-making and policy formulation. Therefore, it integrates and illuminates trade-offs or issues that will arise in implementation or deployment of a technology.

4. TA identifies potentially affected parties and segments of society beyond those who would be investors, manufacturers, and customers—TA is not market research.
5. TA includes quantitative as well as qualitative data wherever this is appropriate and significant to potential decision-makers.

But while the technology assessment approach offers—in theory—a broad-based analytical framework by which the issues of energy decentralization can be addressed, it should be noted that the most widely used assessment models and methods were developed primarily with large, centralized activities in mind (for example, power plants, mines,). These analytical techniques may not be readily transferable to the study of the decentralization of energy supply.[13] Thus, not only do centralized technologies dominate the current energy market, but the analytical tools available to assess the potential for energy decentralization are tailored to the high energy-high technology system in existence. As the research plan for the Decentralized Solar Energy TAP points out, many aspects of distributed energy systems, and decentralized solar energy in particular, make it essential that nontraditional assessment techniques and methods be developed:[14]

1. Decentralized solar energy technologies may have significantly different environmental, social, and equity impacts from traditional, large-scale, centralized energy technologies.
2. Decentralized solar energy technologies have the potential for generating conflict with existing energy distribution and control systems.
3. Decentralized solar energy technologies are significantly adaptable to community energy needs and community goals.
4. Decentralized solar energy technologies may require technology utilization decisions by institutions (for example, communities) whose decision-making processes in such situations are not well understood.

Perhaps one of the most important contributions the technology assessment approach can offer is the involvement of communities in planning and evaluating their own decentralized futures. As previously discussed, the interface between the existing high energy-high technology network and an emerging decentralized energy system will be at the local level. The Decentralized Solar Energy TAP addresses this point in its research plan:[15]

> The nature of solar technologies and their adaptability to local situations and preferences makes site-specific community-based assessment a reasonable and needed approach. Allowing a wide range of citizen interests to be factored into the final assessment of decentralized solar energy, it

provides an approach to energy planning and technology development which is responsive to local needs and preferences. The dissemination of the results of the TAP will assist other communities in the planning and assessment of their energy futures, and it will assist DOE in prioritizing its research needs and programs.

Further, the TA process can provide a mechanism for diffusing technical information and planning and assessment methods for energy development at the local level. Assessments such as the TAP can provide DOE with a two-way communication link. First, they offer a method by which communities can do their own assessments of solar and other energy development, and provide a focus through which communities can gather the information and resources needed to carry out an assessment. Second, they can provide DOE with information about existing and perceived concerns and needs, at the local level, for use in policy development.

As has been seen, the TA approach is already well integrated into the DOE assessment of potential for solar energy systems. But the two studies cited do not exhaust the areas requiring assessment in the decentralization of energy supply. As noted earlier, energy decentralization does not necessarily imply solar technologies alone. Many other decentralized energy sources require extensive examination not only in relation to the existing energy system, but to each other. Further, the nature of the high energy-high technology supply mix in the United States will change over time. Coal liquefaction and gastification technologies will also begin to emerge just as increasing energy decentralization will become feasible. How will these new technologies affect the decentralization of energy supply? What technical, institutional, economic, and environmental issues will emerge at the new centralized/decentralized interface? The technology assessment approach can be used again and again to identify options for the national, regional, and local decision apparatuses responsible for energy policy.

A Final Look

America's preoccupation with capital-intensive, centralized energy systems has led to national energy production and consumption patterns which are characterized by thermodynamic inefficiencies and ever-increasing energy demand. At present, the nation's energy network lies precariously exposed to both the whims of OPEC and the potential for blackouts, brownouts, and other shortfalls of supply. As domestic energy policymakers attempt to wrest national energy dependence from the stranglehold of the OPEC cartel, the alternatives offered by the decentralization of energy supply merit attention. Decentralized energy sources depend solely on domestically available energy sources, many of them renewable. Some will argue that energy decentralization is a frivolous notion, and one which will not support the American way of life. But it has been the centralization of energy supply itself which has gone a long way toward shaping our life-style. And the spiraling rate of energy demand spawned by this centralization cannot be supported indefinitely by finite energy supplies. What is needed is an energy supply policy which is appropriate to the nature of energy demand. The degree to which decentralized energy sources make sense in such a matching must be carefully examined in the formation of national energy policy.

One of the main themes of this chapter has been that the interface between centralized and decentralized energy sources will occur at the local level. National energy policy which is not sensitive to the nature of energy use at the local level will continue to promote the waste and inefficiency endemic to our present energy system. But through studies such as TASE and the Decentralized Solar Energy TAP, the Department of Energy has recognized the importance of understanding the technical, institutional, economic, environmental, and social issues which must be addressed for any policy which promotes energy decentralization. It has also been a theme of this chapter that there is not an either/or choice between centralized and decentralized energy technologies. The real policy questions lie in making the two systems compatible in a cost-effective and environmentally sound manner. The time of the centralized electric utility has not yet passed, although the era of electric resistance space heating may well be gone. As emphasized previously, the thermodynamic matching of supply to demand is the standard for evaluating energy choices.

This chapter has not attempted to resolve the innumerable issues associated with the decentralization of energy supply, but has begun to identify both the energy potential and the policy options which exist for decentralized energy sources. The technology assessment has been suggested as a systematic approach appropriate to the analytical issues posed by energy decentralization. DOE, as noted, has already embarked upon the TA path in the solar area and has recognized the need for a local perspective in its analytical approach. But, as has been suggested throughout, energy decentralization requires a rethinking of traditional energy supply and demand patterns. Even the TA approach itself has evolved based upon centralized technology applications. New assessment techniques and methods will be required to evaluate the potential role of decentralized technologies in our national energy mix. Only through a reasoned, unbiased approach can we outline a role for energy decentralization in our energy future.

Notes

1. For a review of some of the major positions on this issue see Gregory A. Daneke, "The Metropolitan Miasma," *Bureaucrat*, October 1976.

2. See H. Peter Metzger, "The Coercive Utopians: Their Hidden Agenda," *Denver Post*, April 30, 1978.

3. See Armory Lovins, *How to Finance the Energy Transition* (San Francisco: Friends of the Earth, mimeo, 1979); also see Lovins, *Soft Energy Paths: Toward a Durable Peace* (Cambridge, Mass.: Ballinger, 1977).

4. See U.S. Department of Energy, *National Energy Plan II* (Washington, D.C.: DOE, May 7, 1979).

5. Domestic Policy Group, *Domestic Policy Review of Solar Energy: A Response Memorandum* (Washington, D.C.: DOE, February 1979); for a discussion of solar forecasting see Gregory A. Daneke, "Forecasting and Alternative Energy Futures," in Lewis Perelman et al., eds., *The Energy Transition* (Washington, D.C.: American Association for the Advancement of Science, 1980).

6. For a more elaborate discussion of problems in energy planning see Gregory A. Daneke, *The Poverty of Energy Planning* (Unpublished Manuscript).

7. Lovins, *How to Finance the Energy Transition*.

8. Note, for example, Benson H. Bronfman et al., *Decentralized Energy Technology Assessment Research Program* (Oak Ridge National Laboratory, May 1979).

9. Department of Energy, "A Technology Assessment of Solar Energy Systems, Project Summary for Fiscal Years 1978, 1979," Assistant Secretary for Environment, Office of Technology Impacts, Division of Technology Assessment (July 1978).

10. Bronfman, *Decentralized Energy*.

11. These pollution levels are adapted form "Environmental Data for Energy Technology Policy Analysis," prepared by the MITRE Corporation, Metrek Division for the Division of Environmental Impacts, Office of the Assistant Secretary for Environment, DOE (M78-74, Volume I, August 1979). Two 500 Mw utility boilers each with a heat rate of 10,000 Btu/KWh, a thermal efficiency of 34 percent, and a capacity factor of 55 percent are assumed. High sulfur eastern coal is assumed to be the utility feedstock. The utility is postulated to meet revised New Source Performance Standards (NSPS) through use of an electro-static precipitator for particulate control and a nonregenerable lime scrubber to control sulfur dioxide emissions.

12. This description of a technology assessment is adapted from the TASE Project Summary.

13. "Decentralized Solar Energy Technology Assessment Program: Resource Plan," p. 3.

14. Ibid., p. 4.

15. Ibid., p. 1.

Part II
Applications

A number of the more exciting developments in the energy field have already taken place at the local and state government levels. The chapters in part II illustrate the successes, failures, and potentials of these more decentralized energy policy efforts. In chapter 6, authors Philip Sharp and Ronald D. Brunner present a catalogue of local energy policy efforts and conclude that federal government policy should be remolded to more effectively encourage local energy enterprise. Chapter 7, by Henry V. Harman, also focuses on the relationships between the federal and local governments in establishing local energy programs. Harman calls for the development of new grantsmanship skills at the local level as a means of making optimum use of various previously existing federal grants-in-aid in order to improve municipal energy conservation. Chapter 8, by Elaine T. Hussey and George K. Lagassa, explains the intergovernmental dynamics of geothermal development in California and illustrates the need for new institutions which can integrate the various perspectives on energy development held at different levels of government. The case they examine also reveals the need to develop institutions which can manage the costs and benefits for local publics of energy developments with translocal significance.

The next two chapters in this section, chapter 9, by Jerry Yudelson, and chapter 10, by Sumner Myers, also examine transorganizational processes but focus primarily on private-public sector relations as a means to encourage innovative technologies. Yudelson limits his comments to solar technologies and argues that successful commercialization in this field will require the abandonment of old paradigms and preconceived notions about public administration. He further argues that the encouragement of solar applications is done least effectively at the federal level, and he holds out the experience of the SolarCal Office in California as a model for fostering the adoption of solar energy techniques. Dealing with commercialization more generally, Sumner Myers stresses the importance of government officials possessing business acumen in order to prod private-sector development of innovative technologies.

Finally, chapter 11, by Marc Ross, examines the very serious administrative problems associated with incentives and regulations designed to encourage energy conservation.

Local Energy Policies

Philip Sharp and
Ronald D. Brunner

On May 22 and June 5 and 9, 1978, the House Subcommittee on Energy and Power, under Chairman John D. Dingell, held hearings on local energy policies. The purpose was to consider energy policies made and implemented at the local level as means of accommodating the diversity of energy needs and options that exist across the country and contributing to the fulfillment of national energy goals, particularly conservation of nonrenewable energy resources and conversion to renewables.

After an overview, the subcommittee focused on energy policy processes in three communities, each of which was represented by at least three witnesses who participated in a major energy decision.

In 1975 the Davis, California, city council adopted an energy conservation ordinance that encouraged the use of passive solar heating and cooling processes in new residential buildings. The ordinance, one of a series of innovations in Davis, was opposed by builders and developers prior to adoption.

In 1976 the Seattle city council turned down an option to invest in two proposed nuclear power plants and adopted instead a vigorous electricity conservation policy that was implemented with more than thirty specific programs. This climaxed fourteen months of intensive analysis and debate in which the municipal utility, independent analysts, a "Citizens' Overview Committee," the mayor's office, and some 12,000 Seattle citizens also played an active role.

In 1977 the citizens of Springfield, Vermont, voted to condemn the local distribution facilities of Central Vermont Public Service Corporation and to issue $58 million in bonds to develop the hydroelectric potential of nearby low-head dams. This project to establish a municipal utility has been opposed by Central Vermont and has received initial, but not final, clearance from the Federal Energy Regulatory Commission (FERC).

The subcommittee then focused on federal and federally supported energy policies and programs as they affect local energy policies. Testimony was given by officials from Bridgeport, Texas; Virginia, Minnesota; Clearwater, Florida; Dade County, Florida; and Washington, D.C. While local officials often took the lead in these instances, individual citizens and community groups typically played important roles. To conclude the hearings, officials from the Department of Energy also appeared before the subcommittee.

This chapter is an initial attempt to summarize the findings of these hearings on local energy policies and to formulate legislative proposals for consideration by Congress and others. Its purpose is to raise suggestions and criticisms directed toward the possibility of draft legislation.

The Potential of Local Energy Policies

The subcommittee did not attempt to assess the overall, long-term costs and benefits of any particular local energy policy. Rather, it focused on the potential of local energy policies as indicated by selected results to date.

Local energy policies can effectively reduce the consumption of nonrenewable energy resources and expedite conversion to renewables. Davis claims an 18 percent reduction in electricity and natural gas consumption in the residential sector since the building ordinance was proposed in 1973. Seattle realized a 7.7 percent reduction in electricity consumption in 1977, the first year of its conservation programs, although an undetermined part of this reduction was attributed to drought-induced conservation. Whatever the eventual outcome of Springfield's project, it already appears to have encouraged Central Vermont to take an active interest in low-head hydroelectric potential at several sites in the state. Moreover, relatively non-controversial projects in a number of other communities have realized results. For example, the city of Clearwater has increased the miles-per-gallon average of its vehicle fleet by 31 percent in three years, and now saves about 10,300 barrels of oil annually.

Local energy policies can also accommodate local differences. One indication is the range of different policies evolved in these communities. The building ordinance for the passive use of solar energy is well adapted to Davis, a city of 38,000 located in a flat, hot interior valley near Sacramento. Equally well adapted are its extensive bikeway system, demonstration projects using solar collectors, and a proposed energy conservation zoning ordinance. Seattle's decision reflects in part an historical reliance on inexpensive hydroelectric power. Low rates have fostered inefficiencies that now make conservation a prominent option, and the marginal cost of thermal generation is unusually high compared to historical costs. Springfield's decision stems in part from New England's dependence on fuel oil, which has quadrupled in price since 1973. The price is expected to increase still further. Wood and low-head hydro are the main local resources available as substitutes, and the latter is the least expensive.

Another indication that local energy policies can accommodate local differences is the achievement of a working consensus on each policy, even though vigorous opposition arose in each case. Davis officials who shared the lead in the year-long campaign for approval of the building ordinance have been retained in office and continue to innovate. Seattle's Energy 1990 decision was a major issue in the mayoral and city council elections of

November 1976. The election of those identified with the policy of conservation was interpreted as an affirmation of the Energy 1990 decision. Springfield's project was approved twice at the polls, the second time by a 4 to 1 margin with high turnout. Such results on major issues openly studied and debated suggest that the major interests in each community—economic, environmental, social, ethical, political, and others—have been successfully integrated and traded off with each other, and with such material factors as resources and climate. What works in one community may not work in another because communities differ.

The communities represented in the hearings are among the leaders in local energy policy initiatives, if not results. The record indicates that many other communities and local governments have at least taken a first step toward addressing their own particular energy needs and options. In November 1976 the energy projects of the National Association of Counties, the National League of Cities, and the U.S. Conference of Mayors, under contract with the Federal Energy Administration, prepared *A Guide to Reducing Energy Use Budget Costs* for local governments. It provides technical information on energy conservation as well as examples, complete with the name, address, and phone number of the local official to contact for further information in each case. The guide is now in its fourth printing. Over 15,000 copies have been circulated. The three organizations that prepared the guide have attempted to update their records and to continue to respond to requests. The Institute for Local Self-Reliance and the Citizens' Energy Project, both headquartered in Washington, D.C., have performed similar functions for neighborhood groups. Moreover, Davis, Seattle, Bridgeport, and possibly other communities represented in the hearings have received hundreds or thousands of requests for information on their energy policies and programs, many from local governments and community groups. For example, the Office of the People's Counsel in Washington, D.C., has made inquiries about Seattle's Energy 1990 decision.

Factors Contributing to Successful Local Energy Policy

A number of specific factors were cited by individual witnesses to account for the results in each case. By inference from several cases, however, there do appear to be some general explanations. First, leadership is required to initiate an energy policy process at the local level, given the existence of local energy problems and opportunities. Interruptions in local supplies of gasoline, heating oil, natural gas, and electricity, as well as chronic energy price increases, are not in themselves sufficient. The assumption that energy is a national problem, and therefore a matter for national energy policy alone, inhibits rather than encourages local initiatives. So does the assumption that individual consumers can and will find effective means of dealing with their particular energy problems. In the cases examined by the subcommittee, it is possible to identify one or a few people who broke through these barriers by initiating action within the local government or the community as a whole.

Second, an open and informed policy process at the local level is required to develop effective policies adapted to local circumstances. In Davis, Seattle, and Springfield decisions traditionally dominated by individual builders, a municipal utility, and a regional investor-owned utility, respectively, were opened up to additional groups and viewpoints. And as different leaders attempted to mobilize public support in each case, technical analyses and expert testimony turned out to be competitive alternatives to more generalized and emotional appeals. Among these were appeals to pro- and antigrowth sentiments within the public. Relevant and dependable information is an antidote to the tendency to find emotionally satisfying, but unrealistic and ineffective policies. Openness in the development and circulation of proposals (with supporting analyses and justifications) reduces the chance that one interest will dominate the outcome to the exclusion of others.

Of course there are no guarantees. An open and informed policy process is only approximated to the extent that it is in the interest of those involved. Under favorable conditions, some local leaders see an advantage in openly searching for answers rather than imposing a single solution, and citizens with diverse interests insist on an informed and effective role. This tends to encourage other leaders and other citizens to participate in similar ways, or else find support for their positions undermined. Among the favorable conditions are human resources, particularly competent and responsible leaders and citizens. But information resources, quickly and easily available to all participants, can be important. As inferred from the system of information transfer described above, and indicated in direct testimony by local officials, relevant and dependable information includes information on technologies, what has happened elsewhere (cases), and the energy situation in the community itself. Local information needs were also emphasized by a Princeton statistician who testified in the opening session of the hearings. Cases help clarify what is technically and politically feasible, suggest analytical and political models that might be adapted, and help identify legal and regulatory considerations as well as additional sources of funds and information. Modest financial resources, not monopolized by any one interest, are required to adapt this information to local circumstances and to develop energy planning information on the community itself.

Third, the consequences of local energy policies are relatively obvious, immediate, and direct for participants at the local level. This strengthens motivations required for responsible and effective implementation. During the resolution of a major energy issue, proponents of the policy eventually adopted tend to develop a commitment to making the policy work and a public obligation to do so. Majorities in Davis, Seattle, and Springfield were not simply making policies for others. They were making them for themselves, and therefore assumed the risks and costs as well as the projected payoffs. Similarly, opponents of the policy adopted tend to develop an interest in effective oversight. In Davis, a builder compared room temperatures between old units and units built under the new code, in an effort to prove the building code ineffective. (Having seen the results, he now endorses the building code and implements its principles outside Davis.) In Seattle, the advocates of new nuclear generating capacity are monitoring electricity consumption in the expectation that reductions to date are transitory, and that new capacity is needed to accommodate growth. An open and informed policy process also leaves citizens with a degree of understanding and involvement in the issue. These are important assets for broad-based oversight.

Moreover, controversy and the resulting publicity generated during the resolution of a major local energy issue can result in energy conservation, in addition to conservation resulting from the policy adopted. Witnesses from Davis attributed most of the 18 percent reduction in residential energy consumption to publicity arising from controversy over the building ordinance. Only a very small percentage of Davis's housing stock has been built under the new code in the few years since the ordinance was adopted. The importance of motivational and psychological factors was underscored by a Davis builder, who testified that energy bills in physically identical units can vary by a ratio of 3:1 depending on the occupants. Psychological factors are more difficult to isolate in the case of Seattle, but may have played an important role in the 7.7 percent reduction in electricity consumption in 1977. Seattle's conservation programs rely on voluntary compliance.

The Federal Role

Because federal attention in energy policy has been focused on the national and international levels, it is not surprising that the federal government has so far played a relatively minor role in assisting these local initiatives. The Department of Energy (DOE) has been a useful source of information on energy technologies, particularly for the planner-coordinator of the city of Virginia. However, the department apparently has not addressed the other information needs identified by local witnesses. The chairman of Seattle's Citizens' Overview Committee illuminated this situation in his comment on the response of a DOE regional office to a contact by Seattle consultants during the Energy 1990 controversy: "The regional office, of course, would not touch the policy questions that we were discussing with a ten-foot pole." More generally, the state energy offices supported by the federal government appear to be bypassed by local governments. According to a statement supplied for the record by the U.S. Conference of Mayors, only eight of the fifty cities most active in municipal conservation developed plans in conjunction with the state. To meet their energy information needs, local governments appear to rely on local experts, paid consultants, and each other, through the system of information transfer described above.

State and federal agencies may receive more information about local energy policies than they distribute, but there is no systematic program. On the one hand, Seattle, Clearwater, Dade County, and possibly others have provided information and advice to state or federal governments. On the other hand, a Davis official testified that the DOE and its predecessors had not yet requested information about Davis's energy programs or asked to study them.

To fund their energy programs, local governments have tapped a variety of sources, including a number of federal sources. Development of the Davis building ordinance was financed with a grant from private sources, city appropriations, and a grant from the Department of Housing and Urban Development. Seattle, Springfield, and Clearwater apparently relied on local rather than federal sources of funds in policy development and implementation, although Seattle has used a few DOE grants and Clearwater has used some CETA funds to support conservation programs. The Washington, D.C., Office of the People's Counsel has received funds from DOE to assist consumers and community groups in utility regulatory decisions. Those funds were authorized in the Energy Conservation and Production Act of 1976 (ECPA). However, there is no indication in the record that funds for energy conservation allocated to the states by the federal government under the Energy Policy and Conservation Act of 1975 and ECPA have played a role in these eight communities.

Without state or federal funding, Dade County is about to begin construction of a $138 million solid waste facility that (among other things) will use combustible waste to generate seventy megawatts of electricity, enough for about 41,000 families. A county commissioner testified that the federal government has construction grants for sewage treatment plants but not for solid waste plants like this one. Bridgeport, Texas has been seeking federal support for a five megawatt solar thermal generating facility, and the city of Virginia, Minnesota has been seeking federal support to repair and upgrade an existing district heating system. According to testimony, these projects are not within the scope of existing programs. Capital projects such as these are much more expensive than policy planning and development; but, as the Dade County project indicates, some capital projects are within the means of local communities.

Federal programs have handicapped local initiatives in some instances. Several witnesses claimed that their time and effort had been wasted in filing documents with the federal government and waiting months for a response. The consequences were perhaps more serious in Springfield. The manager testified that overlapping jurisdictions among agencies at both the state and federal levels have resulted in large amounts of unnecessary paperwork, unnecessary expenditures, and expensive delays. Regulatory approval of the hydroelectric plans has been the most difficult aspect of Springfield's project.

Prospects and Proposals

The record indicates that local energy policies can effectively contribute to the achievement of both national energy goals and diverse local energy goals. What are the prospects for realizing this potential on a broader scale, with many more communities taking an active and productive role? No doubt a number of additional communities will take the initiative, relying largely on local resources, the system of information transfer, and a variety of funding sources including the federal government. This is merely a continuation of the present pattern. On the basis of the hearing record, however, the prospects are good that a larger number of communities can become involved, and involved in a productive way, if the federal government invests modest amounts of attention and other resources in local energy policies. Proposals for this purpose are outlined in the next section.

In any case, it is clear that energy problems as experienced by individuals and groups at the local level will intensify. Under existing and nearly completed laws, the prices of oil and natural gas are scheduled to increase and eventually to be decontrolled and deregulated. The prices of coal and nuclear generation are also expected to increase; and many communities will be subjected to further disruptions, economic and otherwise, by energy shortages. The question is the extent to which local communities will be involved in the development and implementation of policies to deal with these problems.

The following proposals are an initial attempt to define a federal policy for encouraging local energy policies as a means of realizing national energy goals and of accommodating the diversity of energy circumstances at the local level. The package of proposals provides resources to support local initiatives as well as federal evaluation and planning.

Focus Attention on Local Initiatives

1. *Goals.* Require the DOE to disaggregate existing national energy goals for conservation and for the utilization of renewable resources by community size and region, and to make whatever revisions appear necessary as a result.

2. *Performance Indicators.* Require the DOE to develop indicators of local community performance with respect to energy conservation and the utilization of renewable energy resources, taking into account the indicators already developed for these purposes at the local level.

As we have seen, the assumption that energy is a problem requiring only federal and individual responses tends to inhibit local initiatives. These proposals would focus attention on the potential and the results of local energy policies, and thereby encourage more local governments to act. Moreover, according to a witness from the Institute for Local Self-Reliance, community-level goals are more effective means of motivating citizens and consumers than national goals; and disaggregation would reveal the need to revise national energy goals upward. Data based on performance indicators would be essential in evaluating local energy policies as an instrument of national energy policy and in implementing other parts of this package (see proposals 4, 7, and 9).

Transfer Information Among Local Leaders

3. *Clearinghouse.* Authorize the DOE to fund a national organization or consortium of national organizations to

a. Match requests for energy policy information from local governments and community groups with the existing energy programs (local, state, and federal).
b. Maintain and update files on both requests received and energy programs in place.
c. Report periodically to the Energy Information Administration (EIA) on the number of requests received and programs documented, by request and program types.

4. *Documentation and Distribution.* Authorize the DOE to fund each of a small number of local governments (perhaps five to fifteen) with outstanding performance records in energy conservation or conversion to renewable energy resources to

a. Document and update their own individual policies and performance records, including

History and descriptions of local energy policies.

Methods and sources of funding, local, state, and federal.

Institutional barriers identified, including local, state and federal laws and regulations.

Trends in the local consumption of nonrenewable energy resources and electricity.

Trends in the use of technologies based on renewable energy resources.

b. Distribute information on their own individual policies and performance records to other local governments and community groups on request.

c. Report periodically to a national clearinghouse and to the EIA on policies and performance, and on requests received.

Quick and convenient access to relevant policy information encourages local initiatives and reduces the cost of resolving major issues on an open and informed basis. These proposals would support the existing system of information transfer and extend its scope. Organizations now functioning as national clearinghouses are handicapped by insufficient resources, even at the present level of local energy policy activity. Communities with outstanding performance records have tended to document and distribute some information on their experience, but this turns out to be a drain on local resources. Improving and increasing the number of documented cases would increase the range of options for communities just getting started in energy policy. These proposals would also generate useful information for evaluation and planning at the federal level.

Inform Consumers and Citizens

5. *Utility Bill History*. Require each gas and electric utility above a minimum size to provide a summary of bill history in the monthly bill sent to each ratepayer. A summary of bill history might be consumption, rate, and amount due in the corresponding month of the previous year.

6. *Community Energy Indexes*. Require each gas and electric utility to make available to the local government and news media, on a timely basis, aggregate data for each community it serves. The aggregate data would include consumption, rate, revenues, and number of ratepayers for each major rate class.

An effective energy policy process at the local level depends in part on informed participation by citizens and consumers. These proposals would encourage broad-based and informed participation. The point is not to tell people what they should think and do about energy, but to provide easy access to existing data that individuals can use to clarify their own interests. According to political and economic theory, informed citizens and consumers are necessary to realize the benefits of democratic and market processes.

There is some experience to draw upon, apart from the hearing record. Bill history in some form has been implemented by Seattle City Light, Atlantic City (New Jersey) Electric, and perhaps other utilities to provide individualized and recurrent feedback for conservation purposes.[1] Community energy indexes have been used in a number of places, including Seattle and Allegheny County in Pennsylvania, as an emergency measure to encourage voluntary conservation. So far we have not been able to find a detailed evaluation. An important consideration is the cost to utilities of providing such information. The larger utilities already tend to collect the necessary data and store it in computerized form.[2] Monthly statements and local newspapers are some of the existing means of distributing the data.

Fund Local Energy Initiatives

7. *Small Grants.* Authorize the DOE to establish a program of small grants for local governments to support energy policy planning and development in the areas of conservation and conversion to renewables.

a. Eligibility would be restricted to local governments with above average performance records in conservation and/or conversion to renewables.
b. Selection would be by expected success of the proposal in terms of these objectives, taking into account local circumstances, and by regional diversity, but not by the type of technology or method proposed.
c. Recipients would be required to report performance periodically to the national clearinghouse and the EIA.

Communities are not equally willing and able to tackle their own local energy problems, particularly in view of the range of other problems that may have higher local priorities. Those communities that have already taken such inexpensive but effective steps as reducing energy use and budget costs within the local government have already demonstrated a degree of willingness and capability. Seed money provided through a small grants program would help such communities plan the next steps to sustain momentum, and would provide an incentive for other communities to take a first step. Innovation can be encouraged by using performance criteria rather than method or technology in selection. The intent is to match federal funds with promising local programs, rather than vice versa.

Federal Policy Evaluation and Planning

8. *Validation.* Require the EIA to validate data and information received from the national clearinghouse(s), the outstanding local governments, and

the recipients of small grants (proposals 3, 4, and 7, respectively) on a continuous but selective basis.

9. *Publication and Documentation.* Require the EIA to publish and distribute an annual energy review that coordinates information on

a. The number of requests received and programs documented, by request and program type, as submitted by the national clearinghouse(s).
b. The policies and performances of the local governments funded to document their own cases or to develop particular energy programs under the small grants program.
c. Institutional barriers and program opportunities collectively identified by the national clearinghouse(s), the outstanding local governments, and the recipients of small grants.
d. The results of the EIA's data validation program.

Congress, the administration, and other participants need timely and dependable data to evaluate local energy policies as an instrument of national energy policy, and to make adjustments accordingly. Such data do not now exist, and the proposals are intended to fill the gap. An EIA role in validation would encourage suppliers of data and other information to emphasize dependability and it would assist users in estimating dependability. An EIA role in coordinating, but not substantively modifying or selecting from the data submitted would make timely publication feasible. In addition, the information listed in proposal 9.a would identify gaps between the mix of local energy needs and the mix of programs intended to meet these needs, as both change through time. The information in 9.b would track experience at the local level. To suggest the diversity of local energy experiences and to encourage inclusion of institutional and other important but unquantified factors, the information could be organized and presented by cases rather than by variables. The information in 9.c would clarify what laws, regulations, practices, and organized activities have made a difference across many communities, and clarify in a preliminary way whether the difference is in the direction of goals. It would amount to a shopping list, updated annually, of topics for congressional oversight and executive evaluation, as well as policy planning at the federal level.

Underlying Assumptions

Certain assumptions of this package are worth underlining. First, it can be considered an experiment to surface policy-relevant information on local energy policies as an instrument of national policy. As indicated above, it is designed to generate dependable and timely information for policy evaluation and planning at the federal level. Initial costs could be scaled down to the range of a major study, perhaps $2 to $3 million per year, and would be expected to produce payoffs in terms of national energy goals as well as policy-relevant information. The package is relatively inexpensive because the primary constraints on local energy policies at this point, according to the findings, are informational rather than fiscal. Costs of the package can be scaled up or down because they depend primarily on the number of communities funded directly. Finally, the package is experimental in the sense that it would be feasible to terminate it if results fall short of expectations, for it would not create a new infrastructure but would utilize existing ones.

Second, the package assumes that local communities differ in their willingness and capability to deal with their own particular energy problems. Some communities have already demonstrated their willingness and capability, and some have not. The latter are provided with an incentive to demonstrate what they can do as a condition of eligibility for modest financial support. And all communities could benefit from information from the practical experience of those that already have outstanding performance records. For example, the analytical and political barriers to the design, adoption, and implementation of an energy conservation building code are considerably reduced since Davis has shown what can be accomplished and how to do it. The wheel does not have to be reinvented for each new application.

Third, the package recognizes the limitations of the federal government with respect to such national goals as energy conservation and conversion to renewable resources. Differences in energy circumstances among the thousands of local communities across the country tend to be averaged out at the federal level. A policy "optimized" for the nation as a whole is suboptimal for all communities that depart significantly from the national averages, and is likely to be perceived as such. In addition, psychological and human factors are extremely important in broadening and strengthening voluntary efforts to conserve and to convert to renewables, and these factors are best addressed at the local level. The incentives for effective participation in the policy process and for effective implementation of the policy adopted are much higher when the decisions are made locally than when they are made in Washington. As noted in the National Energy Plan,

> . . . this society can function at its best only when citizens voluntarily work together toward a commonly accepted goal. Washington can and must lead, but the nation's real energy policy will be made in every city, town, and village in the country.[3]

Notes

1. See Kurt W. Riegel and Suzanne E. Salomon, "Getting Individual Customers Involved in Energy Conservation: A Printed Comparative

Energy Use Indicator on Customer Bills?'' *Public Utilities Fortnightly*, November 7, 1974, pp. 29-32; and Fred D. Baldwin, ''Meters, Bills, and the Bathroom Scale,'' *Public Utilities Fortnightly*, February 3, 1977, pp. 11-17.

2. See Customer Activities Committee of the American Gas Association and Edison Electric Institute, *1975 Directory of Customer Accounting Methods and Equipment* (New York, 1975).

3. *National Energy Plan* (Washington, D.C.: U.S. Government Printing Office, 1977), p. 26.

7 Creative Grantsmanship for Municipal Energy Conservation

Henry V. Harman

One of the seeming tragedies of the current energy crisis is that it is occurring at a time when financially strapped municipalities are least able to respond with effective energy conservation programs. Because such programs may require a significant capital investment (retrofitting of existing public buildings, solar installations, solid waste recycling programs), cities may simply be unable to afford their immediate dollar costs. Moreover, energy conservation investments may not fare well in the budgetary process when considered together with competing needs and demands for other community services. Never mind that a city may, in the long run, save money by more thoroughly insulating public buildings, the short-run costs of such programs are more visible and immediately felt and, therefore, less popular with taxpayers and their elected representatives. There are, in any event, acute needs for other more direct human services which cannot and should not be foregone in the interests of energy conservation.

Yet, as this country's oil imports reach their all-time high, it is obvious that every contribution to the conservation of scarce energy resources is significant and that local governments have an important role to play in achieving national energy goals. There is no need to wait for clearer directions from the federal government to recognize this fact and to take appropriate action at the local level.

In the previously described context of limited municipal budgets, city grants administrators can and will play a key role in facilitating effective local energy programs without foregoing other needed human services. To this end, a creative style of grantsmanship wil be required to combine federal grants for community and human resource development with federal and state funds for energy and/or environmental conservation. Such creative grantsmanship can provide benefits to targeted low-income groups and also allow communities to undertake energy conservation programs which would otherwise be too costly.

In order to show how municipalities can meet some of the costs of energy conservation by means of creative grantsmanship, the major part of this chapter reviews examples of various municipal projects that have combined grants-in-aid for those purposes with federal funding for community and human resource development. In the field of community development, the Community Development Block Grant (CDBG) was the most important program reviewed, as was the CETA (Comprehensive Employment and Training Act) program in the human resources development field. One important criterion for selecting the projects reviewed was that they provide benefits to either or both a low-income target area of a city or low-income residents. For this reason, some projects of more general scope were not considered.

**Combining Community Development and
Energy Conservation in Public Buildings
and Public Housing**

In Richmond, Virginia, the city is building a new branch library equipped with a solar system which will provide approximately 75 percent of the space heating and cooling and hotwater requirements for the building. The new library is located on the edge of a Community Development Block Grant "transitional neighborhood" in which the city is investing $300,000 of CDBG funds in public improvement and the Housing Authority will make at least 200 housing rehabilitation loans. As such, the new building qualifies both for CDBG funds and ERDA demonstration project funds (see table 7-1).

Because this particular branch library is the first of several branch libraries to be built to serve various neighborhoods in Richmond, the design of this building is being viewed as a prototype for maximum energy efficiency in subsequent library construction projects. The solar system for the library is also being viewed as an effective tool for educating the public in the advantages of solar installations. "Since it is expected that this building will have a

**Table 7-1
North Avenue Branch Library Costs and Funding Sources**

Description	Cost	Funding Sources
Conventional building costs	$364,000	
Land acquisition costs	64,000	
Architectural, engineering, and administration costs	88,000	
Subtotal	516,000	$516,000 (CDBG)
Additional costs for solar energy system	83,000	62,000 (ERDA)
		21,000 (CDBG match)
Subtotal	83,000	83,000
Total	$599,000	$599,000

great deal of public exposure, both through the city education system, local colleges and other interested groups, we feel it is wise to have a solar system which is a major work horse in terms of energy in this building."[1]

A final significant aspect of this branch library's solar system is that it has been designed to have a relatively flat electric power demand curve. The solar cooling system is backed up by natural gas (which is available during the summer) and permits the library to have a stable electric power demand limiting program. As such it adds no appreciable peak load burden to Virginia Electric and Power Company, the summer peaking utility which will serve the building.

A similar prototypical approach was taken in St. Petersburg, Florida, where, in January 1976, the city's Department of Housing and Redevelopment was successful in obtaining a grant of $9,428 from the U.S. Department of Housing and Urban Development (HUD). The grant was awarded pursuant to a Solar Technology Demonstration program formulated by ERDA and administered by HUD and was used to finance the installation of solar water heating systems in four of seventeen recently renovated public housing units (the Jamestown Apartments). Four other units with standard hotwater systems will be monitored so that a comparative evaluation can be made of the relative costs and benefits of the solar hot water systems. Significantly, this project not only benefits the residents of the four subject housing units, but it also provides a model for similar installations in municipal buildings and all other housing in the city of St. Petersburg.[2]

**Combining Energy Conservation and
Environmental Improvements with
Community Development Needs**

The city of Richmond, Virginia, is installing methane gas migration control systems in three landfills and paying for one with CDBG funds. This, the Fells Street landfill, is within the city's CDBG target area, adjacent to a large public housing project. The Gilpin Court Housing Project, 1,250 feet south of the landfill area, is currently heated with hot water from a natural gas boiler. The methane gas control system will recover approximately 650 cubic feet of landfill gas per minute over the next twenty years. It is estimated that this gas could deliver approximately 325,000 Btu/minute. Utilizing this gas in the central boiler facility of the Gilpin Court Housing Project will result in an annual fuel savings of $45,000. Based on a ten-year life for the installed control system, the estimated amortized cost is $36,000, realizing a 26 percent return on investment.[3]

While this project was deemed feasible by the U.S. Department of

Energy, DOE did not contribute funds to the project, arguing that their limited funds are going to projects they consider even more cost effective.

Combining Community Development and/or Human Resource Development Funds with Energy Conservation Programs

Appropriate Technology

One approach to energy conservation which is particularly amenable to being blended with other programs which are targeted for low-income groups is that of appropriate technology (AT). Because AT tries to match technologies with end use needs, its inherent efficiencies can save money for low-income energy consumers, and it is particularly well suited to alleviate the disproportionate burden imposed on lower- and fixed-income groups by accelerating energy prices. Indeed, a consortium of community action agencies and regional appropriate technology centers now exists under the title "Energy Advocacy Project" with the express purpose of bringing appropriate technology to the aid of hard-pressed low-income consumers.[4]

One particularly interesting application of appropriate technology in Laramie County, Wyoming, successfully combined several elements: training for low-income youth, food for the low-income elderly, employment for the low-income elderly, and energy conservation. Specifically, Community Action of Laramie County (CALC) is engaged in a solar greenhouse project, the principal purpose of which is to raise vegetables for low-income senior citizens.[5]

As originally planned, the greenhouse system was to have two key components. The first component, the greenhouse itself, was built during the summer of 1977 by a group of teenagers working in a federal youth program. The construction was entirely paid for by a combination of funds for CETA employees and $60,000 from the Community Services Administration (CSA) under a Community Food and Nutrition program grant. The second component, a methane digester to be capable of converting cow droppings into combustible biogas to fire the backup furnace for the greenhouse, proved to be economically unfeasible and was thus scrapped. Regardless, installed backup wood stoves have never been used during the two winters of greenhouse operations, and energy costs for the 1978-1979 winter amounted to a mere $18.

Greenhouse operations employ a variety of underemployed and needy persons including two full-time CSA staff, one CETA worker, and some seventy senior citizen volunteers who work one four-hour shift per week on a rotating basis and receive free vegetables in return. In addition, the greenhouse program involves many youths through local high-school work experience programs and a summer program for economically disadvantaged youths. More recently, the greenhouse has begun to employ physically and mentally handicapped persons and juvenile delinquents who are ordered to work at the greenhouse as an alternative to court fines.

One-third of the greenhouse is run on a commercial basis, including a store, and is entirely staffed by volunteers. The commercial operation allows the project to be self-sustaining and also provides additional business training for participants.

Residential Installations

Two of the most common residential energy conservation programs, solar energy and weatherization, may use various combinations of resources from Community Development Block Grants, the Community Services Administration, the Department of Energy, and the programs of the Department of Health, Education and Welfare pursuant to the Older Americans Act.

An excellent example of this type of funding combination is the Ettrick, Virginia, Home Improvement Program. Initiated at the request of Chesterfield County, the Richmond Community Action Agency submitted a proposal for a three-part home improvement program. In Ettrick the program consists of three activities: a survey to assess home improvement needs in Ettrick, weatherization of twenty-five homes of low-income residents, and safety-related home repairs for twenty-five low-income elderly homeowners. More importantly for our purposes, the program is being funded by combining $40,000 of Chesterfield County CDBG monies with CSA and DOE monies channeled through the Virginia Association of Community Action Agencies and HEW funding from the Capital Area Agency on Aging.[6]

**Combining Employment Programs
with Energy Conservation**

The "Solar Utilization/Economic Development and Employment Program" (SUEDE) is jointly funded by the U.S. Department of Labor (CETA), the Department of Energy, and the Community Services Administration. The dual objectives of the program—to demonstrate the feasibility of solar water heating systems and to provide training and employment for low-income individuals—fit extremely well with the theme of this chapter. Primarily because this program is designed to combine different program goals at the federal level, it substantially simplifies the grantsmanship skills required at the local level. Nevertheless, the detailed example given (Richmond, Virginia's, proposal for SUEDE funds) was not funded. But this fact is quite edifying, because the Richmond proposal was very similar to one funded for the Lehigh Valley (Pennsylvania) Manpower Consortium. We have concluded that the Richmond proposal was not funded because of Richmond's lower unemployment rate and the Lehigh Valley Consortium's admirable track record in participant placement. Brief descriptions of other SUEDE projects are provided in table 7-2.

Table 7-2
Some Successfully Funded SUEDE Projects

Prime Sponsor	Funding	Description
Southern New Hampshire Services (with cooperation of Massachusetts balance of State), working with Total Environmental Action, the Univ. of Mass. Extension Service, and the Center for Ecological Technology	$582,100	Approx. 28 trainees will be enrolled, installing 105 to 130 solar devices on rural homes, including greenhouses, thermosyphon air systems, south glazing with storage, and hotwater preheat.
City of New York Department of Employment, utilizing the Energy Task Force, a nonprofit community group, to operate the project	$449,100	Targeted to New York City's Lower East Side, some 40 to 65 dwelling units will be retrofitted with solar water heaters, providing training for approximately 15 participants recruited from the area's community housing rehabilitation groups.
The Memphis-Shelby County (Tenn.) Consortium in cooperation with the South Memphis Development Corp., a nonprofit community development group, and its subsidiary, the Sunbelt Solar Corporation	$247,400	Closely tied to the TVA's solar commericalization campaign, 25 participants will be trained to install up to 50 solar water heaters of the type TVA will sell to its customers with an attractive $500 power credit.
The Lehigh Valley Manpower Consortium in cooperation with the Pennsylvania state Energy Office and the Reynolds Metal Company.	$297,700	Reynolds Metals Co. will train 20 to 25 participants to install solar water heaters and/or "window box" space heating units on 75 homes previously weatherized by the sponsor.
Tarrant County (Texas) in cooperation with Lennox Industries and the Fort Worth Skills Center.	$107,200	Fifteen participants will receive combined classroom and on-the-job training to install 30 solar water heaters.
Indian Development District of Arizona, Inc., based in Phoenix, Ariz.	$498,700	Twenty-five Native Americans will be trained to install solar water heaters on 80 homes of elderly persons on 11 reservations in Ariz.

The objectives of the Richmond proposal were twofold. First, the project was intended to train twenty-four unemployed and underemployed persons for the installation of solar water heaters. After training, these twenty-four persons were to be placed in unsubsidized employment in the private sector. Second, the project aimed at promoting solar technology in the Richmond area and stimulating citizen interest in its advantages. To this end, highly visable solar collectors were to be placed on the houses of fifty-four low-income families as part of the employment training program.

In addition to combining the employment training and energy conservation objectives, as proposed in Richmond, the program would have involved four local government agencies. The SUEDE program was to be administered by the city's Department of Developmental Programs on behalf of the Richmond Area Manpower Planning System (RAMPS). In addition, the Richmond Community Action Agency was to recruit, screen, and select program applicants as well as coordinate the project with trainers (to be provided by the Reynolds Metals Company) and the installation sites (fifty-four single-family dwellings selected by the Richmond Redevelopment and Housing Authority).

The project was designed to train six CETA clients "by means of hands-on work experience in the actual retrofitting of solar units."[7] These six trainees would in turn become trainers for two later groups of nine trainees each. For a total of twenty-four trained solar installation technicians, the total cost of the program was estimated at $150,000 ($92,000 from DOE/CSA and $58,000 from DOL, of which 80 percent was to come from RAMPS's Title I CETA allocation).

Conclusions

As a member of the administration of Richmond, Virginia, a medium-sized American city, I am aware of the potential costs to cities of some programs for energy conservation; but I am also acutely aware of the need for local communities to take some action in order to contribute to meeting national energy goals and to prepare for a future of accelerating energy prices.

In the process of this investigation, five major federal and two state agencies were contacted,[8] eight different communities were directly contacted,[9] and information was received from about twelve more. Equally helpful information was secured from eight nonprofit groups.[10] These contacts made it abundantly clear to me that the action is on the local level. Indeed, federal officials were the first to admit this. While I had assumed that the various federal agencies would have at their fingertips long lists of community energy conservation projects, I soon dismissed that notion. While there is some such listing going on in federal agencies and an evident desire to do more, the main thing I received from the federal government was encouragement to continue what I was already doing. This is simply not adequate.

There are three federal roles which, although they already appear in existing legislation and implementation programs, need to be more strongly emphasized. They are:

1. *The clearinghouse role.* While the federal agencies admit that this is their responsibility, they also admit to moving too slowly in performing it.

2. *The incentive-offering role.* While current federal legislation does offer a variety of energy related tax incentives and subsidies, these do not seem to be providing a sufficiently strong push behind the small scale efforts needed by both the public and private sectors at the local level.

3. *The risk-taking role.* It is my experience as both an appointed and an elected official that it is considerably more difficult to take innovative risks at the local level than at the national level. While it should be clear that some of the energy conservation programs which our ingenuity devises will fail, the need for such conservation is so great that we must risk some failures. The federal government can play a key role here by undertaking some projects where both the risks and potential rewards are high.

While those of us on the local level need more help from Washington, it is important to emphasize that there is no point in waiting for Uncle Sam. Every local community needs to be doing what New York City, Danville, Virginia, and Laramie County, Wyoming, are doing—developing and trying out new and innovative ideas. Whether it means selecting a town energy coordinator as in Vermont,[11] setting up city energy offices as in Florida, or giving city public works departments strong encouragement as in Richmond, the local public sector—especially during the present fiscal squeeze—needs to be using its ingenuity to the fullest.

Indeed, it is important to caution against too strong a federal role in the development of community-based energy programs. This can be demonstrated by an example from the Virginia Tidewater region, which was not reviewed earlier because it did not quite meet the criteria mentioned in the introduction.

Over the past several years, the public works departments of three Virginia Tidewater cities have been working as a consortium to solve some of their solid waste disposal problems. On the brink of negotiating an agreement with the navy to furnish it with steam produced from burning their solid waste material, their hopes for an innovative project were dashed, at least temporarily, when the navy withdrew from the project during the last week of April 1979. Claiming that the cost of steam produced from solid waste was too much higher than that produced from a coal gasification system, the navy effectively delayed, perhaps indefinitely, the Tidewater solid waste-steam project.

The problem here is that the navy is only responsible to the federal taxpayer and does not therefore take a sufficiently broad economic approach when assessing the feasibility of proposals which combine development and conservation objectives at the local level. From the federal perspective, the coal gasification system might well save taxpayers' money, but local taxpayers would also save money from burning solid waste. Some way must be devised to consider the whole picture in cases like this.

Another important lesson to be derived from the above review is that combining energy conservation with community and/or human resource development involves not only a number of funding sources but also a variety of government agencies at all levels of government, nonprofit community groups, and private sector industries. Clearly the administration of these programs will involve skills in coordinating and scheduling the activities of the various organizations involved, and well-honed interpersonal skills will be a needed asset to any administrator trying to cope with the numerous organizational and individual personalities involved in any such multi-organizational projects.

Finally, the above review suggests to me that, when considering the various energy resources, we have too often forgotten the most important resource of all—human energy, both mental and physical. The various government-sponsored programs for human resource development, especially CETA, need to be considered not as stopgap programs to solve unemployment problems, but as vehicles for making progress in applying human energy to solving our total energy problems.

The use of CETA personnel with CSA or DOE funds in weatherization or residential solar water heater installation is fine, but too limited and small scale. Why not encourage communities like Springfield, Vermont, which hopes to develop its own low-head hydroelectric facilities, to make use of CETA workers? Perhaps new and different legislation is needed, but ways should be found to make use of the human energy which is going to waste. In this way we may be able to provide effective alternatives to the chemical energy which is in such short supply.

Notes

1. Quoted from "Building and System Summary by Consulting Engineers," Barton Heights Branch Library, Proposal submitted in response to Program Opportunity Notice EG-78-N-01-4200, January 31, 1978 (rev. March 10, 1978), submitted by the city of Richmond, Virginia (the name of the library was subsequently changed to the "North Avenue Branch Library").

2. *Solar Energy: A Demonstration of Energy Conservation*, Department of Housing and Redevelopment, the city of Saint Petersburg, Florida, 1978.

3. *Development of the Utilization of Combustible Gas Produced in Existing Landfills*, PRDA EM-78-D-01-5153. Proposal by Department of Public Works, city of Richmond, Virginia, 1978.

4. For a detailed account of the types of activities undertaken as part of this project, see "Region VIII C.A.A. Association Energy Advocacy Project, Second Quarterly Report," Denver, Colorado, April, 1979.

5. "A Greening in Wyoming," Opportunity II, Summer 1978, 18-21.

6. *Ettrick Home Improvement Program*, Proposal Summary, Richmond Community Action Program, Richmond, Virginia, March 19, 1979.

7. *Grant Application for a Solar Utilization/Economic Development and Employment (SUEDE) Project for Low Income Housing*, submitted by the Richmond Area Manpower Planning System with the cooperation of the Reynolds Metal Company and the Richmond Community Action Program, Richmond, Virginia, August 18, 1978.

8. Federal agencies contacted were the Departments of Energy (DOE), Housing and Urban Development (HUD), the Community Services Administration (CSA), and the Environmental Protection Administration (EPA). In addition, the Virginia Office of Emergency and Energy Services as well as the Governor's Employment and Training Services Council were contacted in Richmond.

9. Baltimore, Md.; Chesterfield County, Va.; Claremont, Calif.; Clearwater, Fla.; Hartford, Conn.; Norfolk, Va.; St. Petersburg, Fla.; and Santa Fe, N.Mex.

10. The Center for Renewable Resources, the Citizen's Energy Project, the National Council for Citizen Participation, the National League of Cities, and Public Technology, Inc., in Washington, D.C.; Richmond Community Action Agency (R-CAP), the Virginia Association of Community Action Agencies (VACAA), and the Virginia Municipal League in Richmond, Virginia.

11. Pursuant to Vermont's Act 226 of 1976.

8

Geothermal Energy and Intergovernmental Cooperation in California: The GRIPS Approach

Elaine T. Hussey and
George K. Lagassa

Geothermal energy is by no means a new discovery. The ancient Greeks, Romans, Babylonians, and Japanese used hot springs, where hot water or steam flows naturally from underground to the surface, for hot mineral baths, thus establishing a pastime which continues to be popular throughout the modern world. In the late 1800s it became a common practice to drill hotwater wells in order to expand the potential of natural hot springs, and the seed of modern geothermal energy technology was planted. Use of the earth's heat specifically as an energy source is not particularly new, either, as electricity was first generated in 1904, at Lardarello, Italy, by using dry steam hydrothermal resources. Since then, geothermal has been used rather extensively, in those areas where access is easy, for four purposes: local or district space heating, industrial process heating, greenhouse heating and other agricultural purposes, and generating electric power. Table 8-1 outlines worldwide usages of geothermal energy as of 1978.

If we examine the information presented in table 8-1 with respect to the United States, two facts become quite apparent. First, the United States is the nation with the single largest geothermal electric generating capacity, owing to the harnessing of the dry steam geothermal resource in northern California, which began in 1960. Second, the use of geothermal energy for local space heating or commercial purposes is relatively small in this country. The use of geothermal resources for space heating or industrial process heat is highly localized and requires a specific "match" between resource presence and user.

While the internal heat of the earth is a theoretically inexhaustible energy resource, only heat which is concentrated near the surface of the earth is currently recoverable on an economically viable basis. Typically, these concentrations of thermal energy provide more energy than can be

The authors accept full responsibility for opinions expressed in this chapter. Nothing herein is to be interpreted as the position of the California Energy Commission or the state of California.

used locally and thus logically suggest on-site conversion to electricity for purposes of wider distribution. Table 8-2 qualifies the last statement somewhat by explaining the several different categories of geothermal energy theoretically exploitable and the appropriate uses for each type.

Note in table 8-2 that only the first two categories have been successfully accomplished, although the oil companies have been extracting oil and gas from geopressured resources for years. Only the third point under category two (hot water below 90 degrees centigrade) is restricted to local space heating. This means that, using currently feasible technology, the bulk of U.S. geothermal resources are optimally exploitable on a translocal basis.

The optimum size for electric power plants using current technology for harnessing dry steam geothermal resources is 110-155 Mw, considerably smaller and more manageable than the huge 800-1,000 Mw facilities re-

Table 8-1
Utilization of Geothermal Resources as of 1978

Nation	Space Heating, Industrial Process Heat, Agricultural Description	Electricity (Mw of Installed Capacity)
El Salvador		60
Hungary	1,200 housing units and municipal/commercial buildings in Szeged; also used for heating greenhouses and farm buildings and crop drying	
Iceland	100 hydrothermal wells provide 90 percent of residential needs in Reykjavik	63
Italy		408
Japan	Heating greenhouses since 1920 and for some industrial applications: sulfur recovery, commercial baking, salt recovery from salt water, experimental fish farming	169
Mexico		78.5
New Zealand	City of Roturua gets heat from 1,000-plus hot water wells (30,000 pop.) for agricultural purposes, industrial mill processes, drying timber, powering log-handling equipment	202.6
Philipines		169.2
Soviet Union	Municipal heating system for several cities of 15,000 to 18,000 population and for green houses, seedbeds, and an oil refinery	5.7
Turkey		0.5
United States	Used for commercial/residential heating in Boise, Idaho, since 1890s and in Klamath Falls, Oregon. Also used in southern Idaho and Oregon for greenhouses, farm buildings, schools, and resorts; in northern California for greenhouses; and in Nevada for onion drying	663

Table 8-2
Categories of Exploitable U.S. Geothermal Energy Resources and Their Uses

Category	Description	Uses
Hydrothermal convection resources	Characterized by hot water and/or steam in permeable rocks	
	Dry steam (primarily in northern California)	On-site electric power generation on a currently competitive basis
	Hot water (about 20 times as extensive as dry steam)	
	150-plus degrees C.	Possible generation of electricity
	90-150 degrees C.	Space and process heating and generation of electricity
	Less than 90 degrees C.	Space and process heating only on a local basis
Geopressurized hydrothermal resources	Trapped by impermeable clay beds, they are much hotter than normally pressured reserves (up to 273 degrees C.); sometimes saturated with methane gas; requires drilling	Heat, methane, and pressure may be extractable in the mid to long term. DOE predicts 1-2 billion cubic feet of methane may be recoverable by 1985
Hot dry rock	Dry, impermeable, subsurface rocks with temperatures between 300 degrees and 500 degrees C.; requires drilling and fluid injection	A major DOE-funded project is underway at Los Alamos Scientific Lab to develop related technology
Molten rock	Buried magma or volcanoes, with temperatures between 600 degrees and 1,500 degrees C.; could require very deep drilling	Technology not currently available

quired to capture the economies of scale of fossil fuel and nuclear power generation. Given the smaller increments of additional power provided by generating facilities of this scale and the shorter lead time involved in their construction, use of geothermal for electric power generation offers the additional advantage of permitting a much closer matching of electricity supply and demand, thereby contributing to more effective utility planning.

Yet, with every advantage comes a disadvantage, and geothermal energy is no exception to this common-sense statement. The major disadvantage of geothermal resources is that the whole gamut of their use-impacts is localized. Since the geothermal resource is not itself transport-able, it must be used on site. Coal, oil, or uranium, on the other hand, can be mined (or drilled), refined, and used at different locations, thus spreading their impacts across a wider population than is possible with geothermal. Thus, while geothermal power plants are optimally installed on a considerably more manageable scale than, say, power plants fueled by fossil fuel or nuclear resources, the inability to spread and diffuse its im-pacts means that it shares a significant characteristic with large scale energy projects in general; its advantages are widespread, while its disadvantages are localized.

Putting this characteristic in the context of our current perception of a national energy crisis and the federal government's apparent willingness to provide encouragement for whatever energy resources will contribute to total energy supply, it should be obvious that the potential for involvement in geothermal energy development is very high at all three levels of U.S. government. Each level is beset with its own peculiar problems and poten-tials, not the least of which is the possibility for conflict or cooperation with the other two levels of government. In examining the involvement of the federal, state, and local levels of government in the geothermal energy field, we will portray a highly dynamic and interactive system of in-tergovernmental relations. By focusing the last section of this chapter on the implementation of geothermal policy in the four-county region which con-stitutes the Geysers-Calistoga Known Geothermal Resource Area (KGRA), about ninety miles north of San Francisco, we shall see the potential, where the will exists, for constructive cooperation among governmental jurisdic-tions. Moreover, by focusing on the nexus of policy statements and real government action, we shall see the major role to be played by local govern-ment in the completion of energy projects with translocal significance.

Geothermal Energy in the United States

The broadest context in which to understand geothermal policy in the United States is that of the perception of a national energy crisis, defined largely as a deficiency of domestic energy supply relative to demand. To the end of ameliorating this domestic supply shortfall, a number of congres-sional acts have been designed both to encourage energy conservation and thereby lessen demand, as well as to increase the use of previously unused (or underused) domestic energy resources.

After the disbandment of the Atomic Energy Commission and its replacement by the Energy Research and Development Administration, Congress took two actions with particular relevance to the geothermal research field. First, it passed the Geothermal Research, Development, and

Demonstration Act[1] (September 3, 1974), which authorized the expenditure of $50 million to guarantee loans for the acquisition and development of geothermal resources in fiscal year 1976. Pursuant to this legislation, a Geothermal Resources Development fund was established which, by fiscal year 1980, provided a total loan guarantee authority of $350 million.[2] Second, in an apparent effort to counterbalance the built-in bias in favor of nuclear power resulting from the large proportion of ERDA's budget and personnel devoted to programs previously administered by the Atomic Energy Commission, Congress passed the Federal Nonnuclear Energy Research and Development Act on December 31, 1974.[3] This act declared congressional policy to develop a broad range of technologies for using domestically available energy resources in environmentally and socially acceptable ways. To this end, $20 billion was authorized for expenditure during the coming decade for nonnuclear research and development. In fiscal year 1980, $111 million was authorized to stimulate the development of hydrothermal and hot dry rock resources and to reduce the cost of geothermal wells by 25 percent in 1982 and 50 percent in 1986.[4] Together with the Geothermal Steam Act of 1970,[5] which authorized the Interior Department to lease federal lands for geothermal exploration and development, these acts constitute the legal foundation of federal geothermal policy.

Unfortunately, implemention has created a policy environment of considerable uncertainty and thus prevented the federal government from effectively expediting geothermal development.[6] One problem is the coordination of the several federal agencies involved in geothermal energy. Although their roles are somewhat more circumscribed, the Departments of the Treasury and of Agriculture, the EPA, and the National Science Foundation are also involved in geothermal policy implementation. Together with the Department of Energy and the Department of the Interior (DOI), these agencies/departments comprise the Interagency Geothermal Coordinating Council. Although DOE chairs the council and is explicitly granted lead agency status in geothermal development, this has apparently not permitted adequate coordination of the federal geothermal effort.

Probably the most significant indicator of this lack of coordination is to be found in the varying but extremely long time spent by key participating agencies to develop necessary implementing regulations. DOI took four years to develop its regulations with respect to obtaining leases for geothermal development on federal lands. ERDA took almost two years to issue regulations for its geothermal loan program. EPA spent nearly three years to issue guidelines for monitoring the environmental impact of geothermal development. The U.S. Geological Survey (which is primarily responsible for providing data on the availability of geothermal resources) took over two years to provide a promised modification of its regulations, aimed at reducing paperwork required prior to leaseholders conducting resource surveys on leased lands. The Bureau of Land Management (BLM) has been involved since June 1976 in developing new regulations and modifying old ones in order to accelerate geothermal development. Progress in this effort has been slow in coming, primarily because BLM has been preoccupied, as of late, with preparing its nationwide wilderness plan. In California, this problem has been compounded by the fact that BLM has been ordered to speed up the California desert plan component (to be completed by January 1980) of its broader wilderness plan. Moreover, the 1978 National Energy Act will require the development of additional implementing regulations before the full potential of that act can be realized, including the geothermal tax incentive provisions.

Within DOE itself, serious management problems exist with respect to the criteria for selection of particular geothermal projects and programs deserving of federal aid. The criteria are largely informal and not apparently based on any comprehensive set of rationally determined priorities[7] and are not aided by a developed management information system for keeping tabs on projects being reviewed. These particular problems are no doubt compounded by the more general difficulties which DOE is facing due to the significant and multiple internal reorganizations it has undergone in its short lifespan. The massive shuffling of personnel has prevented the continuity necessary for effective program management.

With respect to federal geothermal policy in general, suffice it to say that its explicit intention is to encourage geothermal development (about this there is great certainty!) but that its implementing actions have tended to create and sustain a policy environment of considerable uncertainty.

Geothermal Energy in California

According to the U.S. Geological Survey, approximately 60 percent of known and proven geothermal resources in the United States are in California. Thus the energy policy of that state is of major interest to anyone concerned about the development of that resource.

The most important statement of energy policy in California may be found in the Warren-Alquist State Energy Resources Conservation and Development Act of 1974.[8] While the act is most impressive for its comprehensiveness, in this context we need only point out a few of its major provisions. First, it found that past trends of rapidly increasing consumption of electricity were "wasteful, uneconomic, inefficient, and unnecessary" and a threat "to the state's environmental quality."[9] Second, it declared that it is the responsibility of the state to reverse this trend by engaging in comprehensive planning for the energy future of California.[10] Third, it declared that "there is a pressing need to accelerate research and development into alternative sources of energy and into improved technology of design and siting of power facilities."[11] Fourth, it established a consolidated procedure at the state level for power plant and site certification.[12] Fifth, it established a five-member State Energy Resources Conservation and Development Commission, complete with supporting technical and administrative staff and substantial state funding (hereinafter referred to as the CEC, for California Energy Commission).[13]

The first two provisions referred to set the tone for energy policymaking in California by defining the problem largely in terms of profligate energy use and by proposing that this problem be solved by extensive state government planning. The last three provisions are more germane to our specific discussion of geothermal resource development. As a result of the legislature's stated commitment to the development of alternative energy technologies, the new energy commission was organized with a division explicitly focused on the development and implementation of alternative technologies. Although the agency has gone through a number of metamorphoses since its establishment in January 1975, at the present time there are nine staff members within the alternatives "shop" who comprise a Geothermal Office with the express purpose of promoting geothermal development and applications.

A better indicator of the extent to which the state of California encourages geothermal development can be found by examining the Warren-Alquist Act as originally passed and recent amendments which deal with geothermal power plant facilities. The application procedure for power plants typically involves a two-stage process, consisting of an eighteen-month "notice of intention" (NOI) and an eighteen month "application for certification" (AFC) process, and must include the evaluation of three alternative project sites. However, from the beginning, geothermal power plant proposals were treated differently. The NOI/AFC process time was halved, to two nine-month processes, and the requirement for three alternative site evaluations was eliminated, due to the site-specific characteristic of the geothermal resource. During 1978-1979 the process for geothermal power plants was further shortened with the passage of an option allowing a single-phase, twelve-month, combined NOI/AFC process when the applicant has a proven resource base. For our purposes, the major significance of these amendments to the Warren-Alquist Act is the fact that they were explicitly designed to expedite the certification process for geothermal power plants, specifically, those "capable of providing geothermal resources in commercial quantities."[14]

The origins of this particular legislative action are found in yet another indicator of the state's commitment to geothermal development. Assembly Bill 3590 of the 1976 legislative session created the State Geothermal Resources Task Force to study geothermal development in California and to answer a series of questions related to four issues (resource assessment and conversion technology, environmental considerations, regulatory issues, and economics). The task force consisted of two members of the state assembly, two members of the state senate, three public members, and one member each from the major state bureaus having an interest in or jurisdiction over any phase of geothermal energy development. The director of the Department of Conservation served as chairperson.

The task force held eight days of public hearings throughout the state, at which eighty-five witnesses presented 1,700 pages of testimony. In addition, some twenty-six meetings were attended by many persons from the geothermal professional community. Their report, completed in June 1978, was a comprehensive statement of statewide and major site-specific concerns over geothermal development and contained a series of recommendations dealing with future state actions needed to expedite geothermal development. One of the major regulatory recommendations was for the CEC to establish a single nine-month review process for geothermal power plant siting.[15] This task force suggestion was one of the first to result in legislative action.

In sum, California's energy policy statements and actions are similar to the federal government's, as they aim clearly to encourage and expedite the harnessing of geothermal energy resources. In the words of then CEC chairmen Richard L. Maullin,

. . . our policy will be reflected in decisions intended to maximize the use of geothermal resources and to support the rapid expansion of geothermal power production. In short, geothermal energy will be a *preferred* source.[16]

The two areas of California with the greatest potential for geothermal development are the the Imperial Valley region (bordering Mexico and Arizona in southern California), where the existing hotwater resources are slated to produce 960 Mw of electric power by 1990, and the Geysers-Calistoga KGRA, about ninety miles north of San Francisco. The Geysers field has been producing electricity since 1960, when the Pacific Gas and Electric Company completed its first eleven Mw geothermal powerplants in northern Sonoma County. Because a significant portion of the geothermal resource in that area is in the form of dry steam, ease of access has already resulted in considerable subsequent development. At the present time, 663 Mw of geothermal electrical generating capacity is already on line, and 770 Mw of additional capacity are either under construction or in various stages of the regulatory process.

The organization of the CEC's Geothermal Office into two sections for promoting geothermal development in the Imperial Valley and the Geysers region, respectively, one section for encouraging direct heat utilization and one for local government assistance, not only reflects the distribution of geothermal resources within the state, but also indicates the state's recognition of the important role to be played by local jurisdictions in the development of these resources.

Given the extensive geothermal development that has already taken place in the Geysers field, and given the rather high potential generating capacity of that field if or when it is fully developed (estimates range from 3,000 Mw using solely dry steam, to 5,000 Mw, if we include hotwater resources), it provides an excellent case study of the role of local (in this case county) governments in geothermal development and in other energy projects with translocal significance.

Geothermal Development in the Four-County Geysers Region: The GRIPS Plan

The local role in geothermal development in the Geysers region was substantially complicated by the fact that the Geysers field is distributed across four rather diverse counties. As table 8-3 illustrates, the four subject counties (Lake, Mendocino, Napa, and Sonoma) range in population from 33,000 to almost 275,000, have county budgets ranging from $13 million to $95 million, employ professional planning staffs ranging from six to twenty-five strong, and lead life-styles varying from urban to extremely rural. Even more important, attitudes and institutional processes for dealing with geothermal development are also quite different. Thus, Sonoma County, where there are thirteen operating geothermal power plants, willingly accepts geothermal development as an integral part of its industrial base and has well-established processes for dealing with it, after almost twenty years of experience. By contrast, Napa County at one time totally banned geothermal development out of concern for its possible impact on the wine industry there. Likewise, Lake County, whose major geothermal resources are much closer to its population centers, began to raise questions about geothermal development in the early 1970s, and a number of lawsuits were filed to prevent the completion of specific proposed developments.

Actually, Lake County residents had been exposed to the negative attributes of geothermal power for quite some time, as a result of having suffered the rotten-egg odor of hydrogen sulfide emissions from geothermal powerplants in neighboring Sonoma County (sited in an area of Sonoma County with a population of about fifty). Thus, when geothermal exploratory activities began in Lake County, residents formed the Lake County Energy Council in early 1976, in an effort to control geothermal development by promoting the "intelligent development of energy resources in our county."[17] Membership quickly reached 1,400, and the organization remains quite active.

In general, the Geysers KGRA is a quiet, rural area occupied largely by

Table 8-3
Data on Four Counties in Geysers KGRA

	Lake County	Mendocino County	Napa County	Sonoma County
Population	33,000	64,400	93,900	274,300
County budget (FY 1977 total expenditures)	$13,294,754	$27,550,087	$27,285,803	$95,050,264
Per capita income	$5,435	$6,721	$7,610	$6,817
Planning staff	6 professional 4 clerical	10 professional 5 clerical	9 professional 2 clerical	25 professional 10 clerical
Development activity Power Plants (#/MW)				13 plants (663 Mw)
In regulatory process or under construction	3 plants (330 Mw)			4 plants (440 Mw)
Potential (Mw)				

those drawn to the incredibly beautiful environment and slow-paced life. Major industries are agriculture (orchards, vineyards, stock raising, dairy farming, and grain production), recreation, tourism, and forestry products. Excluding existing geothermal development in Sonoma County, there is minimal commercial and industrial activity, and it is thus not surprising that the residents displayed some reservation about more extensive unplanned geothermal development. For geothermal does have impacts. It has social impact in the form of possible incentives for industrialization and urbanization of a largely agricultural and rural area. Its environmental impact takes the form of hydrogen sulfide emissions and other air pollution, higher noise levels, and the possible contamination of water supplies as a result of the discharge of geothermal fluids, substantially jeopardizing fish and wildlife habitats as well as human health. In addition, like all electrical processes, transmission lines form a visual backdrop for development.

The depth of concern for the potential impact of geothermal development in Lake County was made abundantly clear when the County Board of Supervisors, representing what was then the poorest county in the state, appropriated $10,000 in October 1976 to fund a study which would evaluate more carefully the planning needs for appropriate and balanced development of the geothermal resource. Thus was born GRIPS, the Lake County Geothermal Resources Impact and Planning Study, an attempt to come to grips with the tremendous change being foisted upon the county by geothermal development. GRIPS was not intended to obstruct geothermal development in the county, but to balance it with other community values. In the words of the original GRIPS plan itself,

> the immediate objective of the project will be to develop a comprehensive evaluation of the various environmental, economic and social consequences, both positive and negative, which could result from geothermal development in Lake County. The fundamental purpose of this evaluation is to provide to those who must make decisions about the future of geothermal development, the best information available as to the consequences of their decisions.[18]

When overtures were made to the U.S. Energy Research and Development Administration (later DOE) for financial support for the project, it was suggested that ERDA would be more receptive to this kind of planning organization if it were to reflect the entire four-county resource area. Negotiations among the four counties began almost immediately; and, during the winter of 1977, it was agreed that the four counties would, under contract with the CEC, jointly prepare a plan for data acquisition to assist in determining the impact of geothermal development in the region. The contract with the state was funded by $30,000 from the CEC, $20,000 from ERDA, and in-kind contributions from the counties themselves. Signed on May 23, 1977, it specifically required (1) the preparation of a bibliography and a library of existing information; (2) a categorization, evaluation, and assessment of the adequacy of the existing data base to determine whether it would meet the needs of the agencies involved; (3) identification of needs for additional data; and (4) preparation of a report and management plan for implementing studies and constructing a more comprehensive data base. At this time, the plan was retitled the Geothermal Resource Impact and Projection Study.

As the four counties began to work together more extensively, they decided to take advantage of a provision of California state law which permits local governments to form a joint powers agency (JPA) which has, subject to the provisions of the enacting charter, the legal authority to do collectively whatever the constituent local governments were previously allowed to do only on an individual basis. Thus, on February 8, 1978, after a unanimous vote in all four counties, Lake, Mendocino, Napa, and Sonoma counties formally incorporated as a Joint Powers Agency—the GRIPS Commission. Prior to the GRIPS incorporation, it was decided that the CEC and ERDA should be represented on the commission only as ex-officio, nonvoting members. This action was taken in anticipation of possible conflict-of-interest charges with respect to the CEC and ERDA representatives, as they would be both providing and accepting contracts and funds.

Shortly after formation of the JPA, a new $78,000 contract (with $45,000 passed through from DOE) was signed with the CEC to assist in achieving the fourfold objectives of the GRIPS Commission, as follows: (1) to document and integrate the interests of federal, state, and local agencies in planning the development of a common information base for integrated assessment of geothermal resource impact projections; (2) to develop a specific management structure and technical plan for creating, assembling, and utilizing a common information base; (3) to implement the common information base and integrated assessment system for geothermal resource impact projections; and (4) to create a system to make data available for coordinated policy determination and decision-making among governmental jurisdictions.

Incorporation of GRIPS into a joint powers agency should not be allowed to mislead us into thinking that GRIPS is another layer of government. GRIPS is not, nor was it intended to be, another layer of government. It is not a regional government, nor is it a permitting agency, and it has no powers to accept or deny a particular project. In essence, GRIPS is a focal point for the data collection needed prior to timely permit decisions and for the sharing of information on all levels of government. Changing GRIPS's name a second time, in early 1979, to the Geothermal Research Information and Planning Service reflects this understanding of its function.

The Accomplishments of GRIPS

The mere existence of GRIPS is something of an accomplishment in and of itself, since it provides a structure within which four diverse local jurisdictions can hammer out rational plans and policies for dealing with their common concern for geothermal development. But the potential and actual accomplishments of GRIPS are far more tangible than this.

After a series of six workshops with the Lawrence Livermore Laboratory (under contract with DOE to provide environmental studies at the Geysers), dealing with issues of air quality, noise, geology, water quality, socioeconomic impact, and biology, and after several workshops with local government officials, the GRIPS plan was released in July 1978. The plan contains a status report on the availability of the environmental data needed by state, local, and federal agencies for planning and managing the geothermal resources of the Geysers, and a series of suggested projects for filling related information gaps. It also identifies the major priorities for action: hydrogen sulfide emission control, noise and land-use conflict management, landslide and erosion problem resolution, and the protection of rare and endangered species. Although similar to other energy development concerns, the unique apect of this plan was that it was developed by four counties saying, "These are our priorities, and we need answers."

Clearly GRIPS is not just an arm of higher levels of government. While it does not ignore or reject the needs of state and federal agencies, it does act with some independence. Thus, when the Lawrence Livermore Laboratory (LLL) delivered a work plan for a DOE-funded social/cultural research project at the Geysers, GRIPS noted the implications of its unilateral preparation. A series of meetings with LLL followed, with the result that LLL came back with a work program more appropriate to the needs of the local governments involved.

GRIPS offers a unique mechanism for assuring that federal and state research is valuable and useful to local decision-makers. Contracting with GRIPS for such research needs guarantees that the research results will be useful and used in the local decision-making process. Several such research contracts have already been signed and carried out by GRIPS, including a contract to plan for the monitoring of air quality at the Geysers, a joint GRIPS-BLM effort (through the state Office of Historic Preservation) to prepare a cultural resources inventory, and a DOE contract to do additional studies of the peregrine falcon (categorized as a rare and endangered species), which has nested in the Geysers region.

GRIPS has, of course, had its failures. As of this writing, it is still looking for a funding source for achieving one of its major objectives—the preparation of a master environmental assessment plan and accompanying data base. Only by providing a comprehensive environmental data base can GRIPS fulfill its mandate to member counties, the U.S. Department of Energy and the California Energy Commission.

But the GRIPS future is still bright, owing largely to a $90,000 contract recently signed with DOE. The contract is for the explicit establishment of geothermal development policies within the four GRIPS counties. Successful completion of this project will insure that the four counties will have established well-thought-out procedures for dealing with geothermal developers, thus providing the certainty that developers need to plan new projects effectively.

Conclusions

We have examined the role of federal, state, and local governments in geothermal resource development. We have also emphasized that the federal and state efforts have been aimed primarily at encouraging geothermal development as a means of serving broad national, regional, or statewide interests in a supply of reliable energy adequate to meet the demand. Although geothermal power plants are optimally constructed on a relatively manageable scale, the basic characteristics of the geothermal energy resource result in a highly localized concentration of its social, economic, and environmental impacts. Thus, operationalizing the general policy presumption in favor of geothermal development requires that state and federal agencies take specific actions that impact on real people in specific locations. At this point, at the nexus between policy principle and real government activity, it is imperative that more localized jurisdictions be brought into the decision-making process. GRIPS provides an excellent model for doing so.

It has been said that once the "feds" get involved, the locals are out; but this has not been the case for geothermal development in California's Lake, Mendocino, Napa, and Sonoma counties. In this case the federal government has been quite willing to work with local governments, soliciting input and participating but not overpowering. Likewise, for their part, the local governments have recognized the need to work together and to cooperate in their common interests. GRIPS facilitates this state of affairs by providing for necessary local government cooperation with each other and with state and federal agencies, without preempting jurisdictional prerogatives.

Notes

1. P.L. 93-410.
2. U.S. Department of Energy Budget to Congress, Budget Highlights, January 22, 1979 (DOE/CR-0004), p. 8.

3. P.L. 93-577.

4. Budget Highlights, p. 8.

5. P.L. 91-581.

6. U.S. General Accounting Office, Staff Report, "Federal Efforts Have Not Accelerated Geothermal Energy's Use Nor Expanded Its Potential," Draft of a Proposed Report (EMD 79-79).

7. See U.S. General Accounting Office Staff Report, "The Multi-Program Laboratories: A National Resource for Non-Nuclear Energy Research, Development, and Demonstration" (EMD 78-62, May 22, 1978).

8. California Statutes, 1974, c. 276, p. 501, section 2.

9. California Public Resources Code, sec. 25002.

10. Ibid., sections 25001, 25003.

11. Ibid., sec. 25004.

12. Ibid., chapter 6.

13. Ibid., sections 25200-25224.

14. Ibid., sec. 25540.2.

15. State of California, "Report of the State Geothermal Resources Task Force," June 1978.

16. Testimony of Richard L. Maullin, Chairman, California Energy Resources Conservation and Development Commission, before the Joint Committee on the State's Economy, "Electrical Supply Planning: Strategies for the Future," Los Angeles, Calif., October 25, 1977, p. 15.

17. Membership Statement, the Lake County Energy Council, 1976.

18. Lake County Geothermal Resources Impact and Planning Study GRIPS, Socio-technical Systems, Encino, Calif., October 1976.

Myths and Practices of Solar Commercialization

Jerry Yudelson

The federal government and the four Regional Solar Energy Centers are all preparing "commercialization plans" for passive solar uses and solar water heating. These plans are flawed in conception and likely to be insufficient in implementation, largely because of unexamined assumptions and unarticulated myths about solar commercialization.

These myths involve a false definition of the energy crisis, improper methods of energy accounting, excessive faith in the efficacy of government programs, poor understanding of the complex nature of the economic performance of solar energy systems, and inadequate attention to social issues central to achieving a rapid transition to dependence on renewable resources.

This chapter examines these myths critically and suggests a variety of means for reformulating them into more useful guides for solar commercialization.

Myth 1: The United States is faced with an energy crisis which can be resolved only by increasing the supply of available energy resources.

We must note at the outset that the notion of an energy crisis is the kind of false rhetoric that we should dispense with in these discussions. In its meaning, a crisis implies resolution: the patient either gets well or dies. We are not in that situation. We have a long-term agreement to live sensibly on the American continent; we have no place else to go; and we are going to have to live with increasing constraints on energy supply by reducing demand and switching to renewable supply sources. The energy "crisis" is endemic, is not going away, and is more like a chronic illness than a one-time crisis. What we should consider instead is that we have an energetic opportunity, an opportunity to make major social advances and to bring society back into ecologically responsible bounds.

People who are involved in the solar field see this larger picture and view the energy "crisis" as symptomatic of an ongoing, long-term breakdown of urban industrial societies. They recognize that growth in our already high levels of energy use represents a fundamental force for imbalance in our society and must soon be lowered. Thus they perceive the basic problem not as energy use per se, but as the attendant social and environmental disruption caused by it. Pollution is the basic near-term constraint on energy use, not supply shortages.

123

Actually, solar advocates are not alone in their understanding of the energy problem. Rather, they are a part of an emerging cultural paradigm which focuses on individual development and self-discovery, institutional experimentation, and community service. Although this new paradigm is much broader and more comprehensive than solar energy per se, it is to this worldview that solar energy programs are more properly directed. The major principles of this new paradigm are:

> Our economy needs to be one of permanence, sustainable into the distant future, living mainly on renewable flow rather than capital resources.

> Economics has to be viewed as a dynamic science of creating long-term value rather than a static analysis of resource allocation.

> Direct experiences coupled with understanding, not theory and models, are the roots of knowledge.

> Scale is a crucial determinant of quality of life; and because virtually all of our large institutions are too big, we need to decentralize our government, corporate control of our economy, and our oversized social institutions. Smaller scale operations are beneficial for our economy and for our survival on this planet.

> Access to resources is a key issue for communities. We need more public use of the private sector.

> Government's ability to manage society and to keep transaction costs low is very limited.

> We need a more socially appropriate technology, more clearly responsive to community needs.

> People are beginning to feel a great need for "living-in-place," for being responsible for their own bioregion. Movements are beginning aimed at reinhabiting bioregions on a sustainable, self-reliant basis.

> Little physical energy is really needed for social health or personal happiness.

This emerging paradigm is very energizing. However, the myths of a fading era are powerful drugs, sedatives to hinder creative action. The first one to be overturned is that the energy "crisis" is a temporary problem that can be overcome by large scale efforts to increase aggregate energy supply.

Given this changing perception of the energy problem, a different set of policy priorities emerges. These include zero growth in primary energy use within five to ten years (through economic incentives and mandatory conservation), long-term *decrease* in energy use, higher levels of personal and social well-being (through programs to reduce energy use and improve environmental quality), and economic sufficiency for all.

Energy policy must give full consideration to problems of social equity in using higher energy prices and mandatory conservation to meet energy supply and environmental quality goals. An aid to achieving this goal is to foster the recognition that we must become a conserver rather than a consumer society.

Energy policy must be built around "net energy yield" considerations; a social-ecological maturity; respect for the integrity of natural ecosystems; maintenance of social flexibility; development of a more appropriate energy, resource, and settlement technology; and basic reliance on renewable resources.

Energy policy should promote regional self-sufficiency, emphasizing smaller scale, more decentralized production, redirection of urban growth patterns, and use of local initiatives in resource conservation. Comprehensive (but not compulsive) regional planning will be necessary to integrate energy production and use with environmental quality goals, land-use patterns, and redirected economic development for serving social development policies.

Energy policy must respect the need to maintain the healthy integrity and diversity of human arrangements and natural ecosystems, to promote human growth in a fundamentally stable and aesthetically pleasing natural order. Such policy should give more incentives for developing cooperative economic relationships based on small scale, soft technology, mutal aid, moderation of demands, and meaningful, convivial working situations. Disincentives should be created to discourage the harsh system of large scale technocratic industry/government structures and the continuing emphasis on material affluence.

Energy policy should encourage regional, decentralized, small scale approaches rather than unworkable national policies which require police-state measures to enforce. National policies should promote the development of regional bioeconomic approaches (based on the carrying capacity concept), which integrate economic development, energy use, environmental protection, life-giving technology, sustainable cities, and decentralized urban development. This approach would go far beyond any single-purpose land use, energy supply, social welfare and economic growth approach, since it will be guided by an emerging ecological ethic and a biocentric rather than an anthropocentric approach.

Myth 2. The currently accepted method for energy accounting is the best and the only method for measuring energy use.

How much energy was supplied in 1978 by solar energy? According to the federal government's energy clock, it was too small to count. According to my calculations, solar energy supplies at least 30 percent of the energy used in the American economy. It is the energy input to all of our crops and to crop drying in the fields. It is the energy input to forests and forest products and to grazing lands. It is the energy input to the pollution control and to services provided by natural ecosystems. It is an input to raisin drying. If we dry the raisin in the sun, solar does not get any credit, but if we dry it in a big room with a gas oven, then the federal government accounting system says that we are now using energy and writes so many Btus in the column for natural gas. How much passive solar are we already using? No one can tell us, since energy is only counted when it is sold as a commodity.

Indeed, the whole concept of accounting is fundamentally incompatible with the use of solar energy. If we really achieve a substantial increase in solar energy use, we may not even know it. Especially if passive solar design becomes popular, many experts may not be able to determine its contribution to supply, since it does not count much as Btus gained. Not only is it the case that solar energy is not sold as a commodity, but there are very few devices which will be sold, since passive solar is a system, a well-designed house, not a fuel or even a product. All of these factors are going to make it both very difficult and very complicated to know where we are in solar energy and nearly impossible to evaluate the effectiveness of related government programs.

Moreover, it seems rather foolhardy to suggest that we can actually predict what level of solar energy we will be using in the year 2000. This is the game of the "Quad Squad" in Washington, D.C. Any sensible observer knows that our economic system is undergoing such profound change that any projects based on the current structure of the economy and on current tax and price policies for energy will turn out to be very wrong. If the solar hot-water level predicted by the federal government takes place (14 percent penetration by the year 2000 for solar hot water, including only about 60 percent of new housing in the year 2000) we will be in great trouble, really in hot water.[1] In fact, if every new house in the year 2000 does not have major passive solar use and orientation and solar water heating wherever it is available, we are going to be in very bad shape. So these predictions are smart this year, done by honorable and fully certified consultants, but they are very stupid if we look twenty years ahead at what our energy needs will be.

In any event, most estimates of how much solar we can get in the year 2000 are based on so-called market-penetration models. These models confuse policy goals with projections based on the use of questionable measurement techniques which use consumer perceptions of the economics of solar systems to estimate sales. In fact, the amount of solar energy that we will have in the year 2000, or conversely the amount of fossil fuel energy which we will be able to conserve, is heavily dependent upon government policies—federal, state, and local—to restructure energy economics and to rearrange the economic incentives that people see. We did not just arrive at a system of cheap electricity and fossil fuels in this country. Conventional energy sources were, according to a 1978 report to the U.S. Department of Energy,[2] heavily subsidized by tax breaks and direct federal outlays, to the tune of well over $150 billion over the last quarter-century. If these policies are changed, even a little bit, predictions for the use of solar energy in the year 2000 may be invalidated even before we reach that date.

Myth 3: Federal policy alone can constitute a national energy program.

The view that the federal government is primarily responsible for solar energy and that spending federal dollars can by itself make solar happen is simply false. Much of the federal solar effort has been directed at studying the problem and establishing new institutions, such as the Solar Energy Research Institute and the four Regional Solar Energy Centers. Yet a clear direction for those institutions has never been established, and none of the direct grant programs can be termed a clear success. We have nearly 1,000 people working directly in the federal solar program (excluding DOE support contractors and the national laboratories) with confusion and frustration the most frequent report, particularly from the newer institutions.

While the federal government spins its solar wheels, solar energy seems to be happening in the states. Such states as California, New Mexico, Arizona, and Colorado, where there has been consistent political and economic support for solar initiatives, can all boast real success in solar commercialization. Nevertheless, an analysis of nationwide trends in solar development by the states tends to the conclusion that the market for solar energy is determined largely by the support which is given by government and solar industry organizations at the state and local levels. The state of Florida, for example, which has an ideal climate for solar applications, suffers from a lack of political zeal which is reflected in the limited success of its solar energy program. By contrast, the success of California's SolarCal programs is largely attributable to the political support it has received from Governor Jerry Brown and organized advocacy by the solar industry itself.

Created in 1978 by order of Governor Brown, the SolarCal Office was astutely located in the state's Business and Transportation Office and is therefore particularly well situated to interact with the business community. By working together with such business constituencies as homebuilders, lenders, realtors, agricultural industries, and the solar industry and industrial plant owners, the SolarCal Office acts as a "broker" in encouraging commercial applications of solar technologies. Program elements include educational seminars, publications, assistance with regulatory processes, direct encouragement, financial assistance programs, and extensive publicity for commercial applications of solar energy systems. Partly as a result of these efforts, there will be over 40,000 solar applications in California in 1979.

Given the substantial success of such state-based solar energy programs as California's, it is not unreasonable to conclude that the federal government should curtail and simplify rather than expand its involvement in solar energy. Many federal efforts in the solar field have proven counterproductive and suggest that a too active federal role may actually hinder solar development.[3] A healthier solar energy policy would be one that is an aggregation of more local actions, a policy derived from the bottom up rather than imposed from the top.

Unfortunately this notion is likely to be resisted, largely because acceptance of the federal government as the key actor in energy policy is sustained by a member of other mythlike assumptions, all of which require debunking.

> The presumption of higher wisdom in government institutions, the belief that government knows what to do, is simply not well founded. For all the respect I have for the work of some individuals, it is clear that the federal government, and, in some respects, many state programs, have had to follow the lead of individual innovators to get anywhere.

> The assumption that spending more federal dollars increases government effectiveness. In fact, we may very quickly reach the point of diminishing returns for direct federal outlays in the solar development field. To avoid this we need to switch to more indirect financial incentives, such as tax credits, utility rebates, and low-cost loans.

> The blithe assumption that more government programs will help. In fact what we find is a lot of confusion of programs and annual reorganizations of every one of them. If we took half of the 1,000 employees employed by federal solar programs and spread them out equally among the fifty states, there would be ten people working in every state. Most states at this point have only one or two persons working in solar, so this distribution would increase solar programs five- or tenfold at the state level, closer to the action. In this context, I would like to introduce a principle that some philosophy students may recognize. It is called Yudelson's Razor and simply states that large organizations and new programs should not be multiplied beyond necessity. This principle is really something to think about as one looks at the proposals for more and more federal programs.

> The belief that many renewable resource developments are prevented by legal and institutional barriers which must be removed by government.

That there are some barriers is true, but that they immediately need removal is false. In fact, many of the federal programs and to some degree the state programs of barrier removal will only have the result of removing all the barriers for a solar industry that does not exist. The so-called legal/institutional barriers ought to be pushed hard until we can see which are the most important, but we must remember that the real barriers are public attitudes and the level of public interest in exploring energy alternatives. Most of the barrier removal programs that now exist are just making a lot of money for energy consultants who conduct studies.

Myth 4: Solar energy use is a good idea in principle, but it is too costly to be a viable alternative to conventional energy resources or to make a significant contribution to energy supply.

When people say that solar energy is not cost-effective, they do so because they fail to consider the cost of what solar will replace—synthetic fuels from coal and shale. These are the long-term energy resources currently being touted, and it now costs $30 to $40 a barrel.[4] Solar is very competitive with these sources, as well as with new sources of gas (Alaskan gas or Eastern Hemisphere LNG) and nuclear-generated electricity.[5]

Likewise, in assessing the broader economic impact of solar systems, the detractors of solar fail to recognize the secondary benefits of solar development for local economies. Obviously solar retrofits, unlike passive solar design of new homes, will produce new primary jobs. But beyond this, the most important economic benefits will result from local reinvestment of the substantial sums of money saved on utility bills. Although many people still think that the economy will suffer without large new inputs of energy and that solar energy cannot possibly supply all of the incremental demands, that notion is proving to be false. Conservation improves local economies due to cumulative respending of utility bill savings on more labor-intensive and wealth-producing activities. Moreover, energy not used in homes becomes available to business and industry, at a reasonable cost, for directly productive enterprises. The aggregate economic benefits, nationwide, of a massive push for energy conservation and renewable energy alternatives could be quite substantial.

Certainly we can be wealthier than we are now, but only if we abandon our excessive preoccupation with increasing the overall level of energy supply. This will not, however, be accomplished on a business-as-usual basis. Continued reliance on large businesses and large utiltiies to take the lead will only lead us to heavier concentrations of economic and political power. Clearly, we have to start looking for new institutions at the same time that we try to redirect utility and business invesments to renewable resources.

Community organizations and local governments may need to get more involved in the commercial sector; and, because small enterprises supply most of our jobs, innovations, and community services, they will need additional financial, technical, and marketing assistance.

Comparable in effect to the myth that solar is not cost-effective or otherwise economically viable is the related belief that a change to solar can only occur gradually. In fact, in the economic history of this country, there have been massive shifts in paradigms and massive shifts in economic structure which have happened within the span of one generation. From 1940 to 1962, oil and gas (petroleum products) added 30 percent to their market share of energy, from 40 percent to 70 percent. People who think it's very difficult to get 25 percent solar by the year 2000 should study previous energy transitions. In fact, with an aggressive program of incentives for solar development we can easily achieve more than that. But to do so we must show the absurdity of the argument that there is a threshold for commercialization and that until that point is reached in the economics of a system, it is not ready. In fact, we know that people were buying solar energy when it cost ten times as much as it does today. These are the types of people we ought to support in the future. Before we can assess the commercial viability of solar energy in mature markets, we must first focus our attention on initiating solar markets.

Myth 5: We can leave it to the professionals to design an effective energy policy which will apply to and equally benefit us all.

Perhaps the greatest and potentially most damaging myth is that we can leave it to the professionals to rescue us from the "energy crisis." This illusion quickly dissolves when we remember that it was the professionals who earlier forgot how to design an energy-conserving building or city. In fact, most of the innovations that we are now working on in the solar field come from people who were not formally design professionals—bright people not bound to the conventional wisdom (and mythology) of the professions. In this context, I can cite one of the best pieces of good science that I have seen, from a young man in Denver who used incense to track the air flows in passive homes to discover why some designs work better than others. Some of the best writing I have seen comes from people who stayed up all night with their passive homes to observe things. These people, like Kepler and Copernicus, who relied on their own insights and not on the canons of their colleagues, are the people we need to look to and to support.

To this end, I recommend a major federal program which I am sure would work. I would like to see $10 million go to 200 innovators with track records in energy. Give them $50,000 each and tell them to go away for two years. Tell them, "We do not want your progress reports; do what you think is best." If only two of those people produced something valuable, it would be money well spent, certainly better spent than much federal money. Let's support people rather than institutions or professions.

We must also remember that most professionals are employed by bureaucracies which, by their very nature, tend to impose uniform solutions and uniform standards, even when problems are quite diverse. It goes without saying that uniform nationwide standards for solar installations and design are not appropriate to the cultural and climatic variation of the continental United States. But even at the regional level, uniform standards can be less than optimum. If we consider microclimate, cost and regional culture as design determinants, we discover that there is infinite variation in economically and ecologically appropriate design. Designs can and should vary greatly in going from one small valley to the next, as people will want passive solar designs that closely match the climatic, social, and cultural characteristics of the particular bioregion in which they live. Such diversity is difficult for the bureaucracy to tolerate, but it is life-enhancing. Uniformity is easy and efficient, but slow death.

Finally, by leaving energy solutions to the professionals and the bureaucrats, we run the great risk that the costs and benefits of energy programs will not be equitably distributed. In the field of solar energy, it is often assumed by federal officials that all we need is a commercialization program. In fact, if we only focus on commercial solar, many people will be left out. The poor, renters, elderly people, and large cities will not have access to and will therefore not share the benefits of solar development. It is very important that all solar programs and incentives reflect detailed considerations of social equity, even if such concerns run counter to the more typical bureaucratic ethic of efficiency.

Recommendations and Conclusions

Clearly we need solar energy. It is an appropriate technology. It has a long-term value of reducing thermal pollution and carbon dioxide pollution of the planet. It is sustainable. It is locally available and cheap. There are many more jobs associated with it, at more appropriate skill levels; and it is understandable at the community level. It involves good science and good design, but can be used by anyone. It requires relatively little capital, and it is decentralized in terms of source, use, and control. It helps to lower the overall energy flux of society, gives a lot of flexibility in future planning, is closely matched in quality to its end-uses, and is amenable to use by emerging institutions and can also be used by adapting to existing institutions. But the highest value of solar energy is that it may help to change many values and attitudes popularly held today. Opening the door to the "conserver society" may be its greatest contribution to energy supply, far more than just the quads of energy produced.

But how can we get from here to there? What positive action programs need to be adopted and implemented by government and industry in order to achieve more effective and extensive solar applications? A clear sense of priorities leads me to propose the following actions at the federal level for 1980:

A national 50 percent refundable tax credit, with full credit and funding for passive solar technologies.

A 30 to 40 percent investment tax credit for use of renewable resources, especially in industrial process heat systems.

Getting the federal house in order with full funding for the Federal Photovoltaic Utilization Program and with full implementation of previously enacted congressional actions.

A well-funded Solar Development Bank to assist consumers and small businesses with low-cost, long-term loans.

Use of solar energy in all new federal buildings, accompanied by a fully funded program to retrofit all federal buildings with cost-effective solar and conservation measures by 1990.

Assuring that all federal housing programs and policies are consistent in promoting solar utilization, including activities at the Department of Housing and Urban Development, Federal Housing Administration, Veterans Administration, Farmers Home Administration, Government National Mortgage Association and the federally chartered secondary market ("Fannie Mae" and "Freddie Mac").

Full use of the media to promote solar purchases by consumers.

In general, policy at the federal level should be guided by the following principals: (1) state and local solar action programs should receive more extensive support; (2) more federal money should go into direct and indirect incentives (such as loans and tax credits) than into increased program budgets ($5 to $10 billion per year in incentives can easily be justified and can be financed from utility revenues and a severance tax on nonrenewable resources); (3) the states should be provided more assistance as they encourage private financial institutions to perform better in the solar energy field; and (4) more support should be provided for innovative individuals than for institutions.

At the state level there is need for variation in policies and programs, but there are lessons of nationwide significance to be learned from the experience of the SolarCal Office. SolarCal is trying to carve out a new niche, to pioneer new roles for state commercialization efforts. We are functioning as a broker between the solar user and the solar business or passive system designer, as a catalyst for solar use by industry, as a coordinator of government and industry promotional efforts, and as a mediator in disputes between builders and local code officials. These programs are low-cost and effective, a combination which we will all need in this post-Proposition 13 era of reduced government spending.

The aim of the SolarCal Office commercialization program is to stay rational in concept and practical in emphasis and execution. We work closely with the solar industry and commercial user groups, to stay responsive to their needs for information, technical assistance, financing, and cutting governent red tape. To achieve many of its commercialization goals, the SolarCal Office and Council have produced a SolarCal Action Program with forty-six specific actions for state, federal, and local government, the solar industry, lenders, business groups, community organizations and individuals.[6] The Statewide Action Program aims at securing 1.5 million residential and commercial solar applications by 1985. It focuses on a partnership among government, the private sector, academia, and communities and emphasizes such issues as financing, consumer protection, marketing and public information, job training and development, public facilities, and community-scale initiatives.[7] This SolarCal Action Program can be used as a model by other state and local governments for developing similar programs to assist widespread solar commercialization.

Many myths of solar commercialization have become articles of faith in designing solar utilization programs. Many of these myths are counterproductive and will only hinder the development of action programs that will give us a significant use of solar energy over the next five, ten, or twenty years. The programs, priorities, and perspectives of the SolarCal Office and SolarCal Council in California provide an approach which, based on state and local government actions in concert with private-sector initiatives, can serve as an effective countervailing force to the power of these myths.

Notes

1. U.S. Department of Energy, "Draft Plan for Commercialization of Solar Water Heating," Division of Solar Energy (Washington, D.C., January 1979).

2. Battelle Pacific Northwest Laboratories, "An Analysis of Federal Incentives Used to Stimulate Energy Production," PNL-2410, Revised, December 1978.

3. For a fuller discussion of the counterproductive results of many federal efforts see W.A. Shurcliff, *New Incentives in Low-Cost Solar Heating* (Andover, Mass., 1979), pp. 239-259.

4. The Solar Lobby, *Sun Times*, Washington, D.C., January 1979. Also see R. Stobaugh and D. Yergin, *Energy Future* (New York: Random House, 1979), p. 53, which places the incremental cost of imported oil at $35 to $85 per barrel.

5. D. Chapman, "Taxation and Solar Energy," a report prepared for the California Energy Commission (Sacramento, April 15, 1978).

6. SolarCal Council, "Towards A Solar California: The SolarCal Action Program" (Sacramento, January 1979).

7. See also J. Yudelson, "Potential for State Assistance to Community Solar Energy Enterprises," in *Proceedings of the National Conference on Local Public-Private Ventures*, Philadelphia, December 1978.

10 Innovation by Negotiation

Sumner Myers

Public concern about energy and productivity has led to increasing government sponsorship of technologies for private and mixed markets where the federal government is no longer the primary consumer. This new situation is beyond the experience of most government officials and raises several basic issues in public policy and administration.

Two such fundamental issues are addressed in this chapter. First, what should be the government's investment policy in support of the development and commercialization of technologies, energy or other, for private and mixed markets? And, second, what role should government play in order to maximize the likelihood of its investment success while minimizing its intrusion into traditional domains of the private sector?

By definition, the commercialization of technology must be accomplished through the private sector. Commercialization of publicly funded technologies, therefore, requires that the government jointly invest with one or more private industry partners in order to develop and market those technologies. This, in turn, requires that the government and its partners negotiate with each other about the inputs and outputs of each stage of the innovation process, a situation which differs markedly from the days when government, as primary consumer, could specify the product outcomes of its development projects.

With some exceptions (for example, housing) the government has had little experience in investing with private industry to bring to the marketplace new products that users will choose to purchase. The government's approach to commercialization derives largely from its successful experience in military and space programs where it could specify the innovations it wanted. But "innovation by specification" is inappropriate where the end product is targeted for customers who can exercise choice about whether to purchase the product or not. And that element of choice is the basis of market uncertainties which can be ameliorated to the satisfaction of both parties only through the process of negotiation.

Negotiation itself is a principal characteristic of our political system. For example, budgets and schedules are everyday products of negotiation which require political skills. But negotiating joint business ventures to

---

Author's note: all government/industry cases described in this document represent firsthand experiences except "Composite Materials."

promote technological innovation requires a kind of business skill which has heretofore not been needed by most public officials.

Negotiation concerns future expectations of satisfaction which no two men are likely to estimate in the same way. Thus, the process of innovation will be negotiated by parties whose goals are both convergent and conflicting. If both parties enter the process in a cooperative spirit, they will strive for goals that can be shared equitably. This does not mean that every goal will have the same value to each party. But it does mean there is a greater possibility for the parties to reach their respective goals than would otherwise be the case.

Negotiation is competitive as well as cooperative. It involves competition which is not bounded by a set of clearly defined rules. Negotiators are not clearly limited in the actions they can take or the agreements they can or cannot make. As Nierenberg explains it, the process of negotiation is not bounded by a priori rules, and associated risks are understood by participants only on the basis of long experience, not cookbook formulas.[1]

Because there is an overwhelming tendency for bureaucrats, public or private, to work by rulebooks, there is a continuing search for a set of guidelines that will completely eliminate the need for personal judgment. The cases cited in this chapter, however, indicate that there is little chance of finding such guidelines. Bureaucrats must, instead, strive to narrow the range of negotiable issues to those which do require personal judgment. As Karass points out, negotiations involve difficulties of risk assessment and blurred reality and thus always involve a "zone of not knowing."[2] Narrowing issues to this zone helps the negotiating process by indicating where talent and insight must be brought to bear on behalf of the public interest.

As we shall see, current guidelines are too broad to be operationally useful for moving government-sponsored technologies from development through commercialization. Indeed, to the extent that the guidelines encourage government officials to abandon judgment, they may be counterproductive. The cases discussed below indicate that commerical success depends on business marketing insight brought to bear at the right time and place. Some of this insight might be provided by the government's partner. But, in the final analysis, the government dare not depend on its partner alone. Rather, it must get its own business talent on board to help negotiate its technologies to commerical success.[3]

Commercialization: Purpose and Method

Commercialization is the process through which technology passes in becoming a new product which, hopefully, people want to buy. The process is long and uncertain. The purpose of negotiation is to reduce that uncertainty, especially uncertainty due to project duration and marketing.

In general, uncertainty results from imperfect information and the inability to predict what will happen in the future. The degree of uncertainty increases as the project's duration extends further into the future. While uncertainty is also a function of the degree of technological advance being sought, all things considered, technological uncertainties are relatively small. For example, Myers and Sweezy found that of 200 innovations which failed, only 11 percent were failures of technology. In contrast, almost half of the 200 innovations failed for market-related reasons.[4]

The long process of commercialization comprises a number of stages, generally beginning with invention or research initiation and ending with full production and diffusion of the new technology. Money is required at each of these stages, and because there is usually no immediate return on such expenditures they must be regarded as joint investments in the future of a successful product. As discussed later, successful negotiation at each stage opens the way to the next stage.

At each stage of the joint investment, each party to the negotiation determines the present value of a flow of future satisfactions (and dissatisfactions) and compares it to making no deal at all or holding out for a better deal. The negotiator's role is to raise his partner's assessment of the present value of the future's satisfactions. To do this he must have a clear understanding of what his partner's goals and motivations are.

Government's Role

The government is motivated to maintain a competitive marketplace, not as an end in itself, but because the marketplace can ordinarily achieve a more efficient and equitable allocation of national resources than can any other mechanism. The market mechanism, however, is not perfect, nor does it, by its very nature, ensure that political and social demands will always be met through the interaction of supply and demand factors. If the market could easily perform public policy services, there would be little, if any, role for government in the commercialization process beyond, perhaps, the sponsorship of basic research, which is nonappropriable. However, there are public welfare objectives that will not be achieved if left to market activity. In such cases, government intervention to improve the general welfare is justifiable.

For instance, *timeliness* of technological development may be worth more to the public in general than to any private firm in particular; the timely development of energy technologies is considered to be critically important in our effort to break OPEC's hold over our economy. Indeed, DOE is charged with speeding the development and commercialization of energy-related technologies.[5]

Money can be used to hasten technological development where there is a trade-off between time and money. According to Twiss time and money are not independent variables, but are to an extent interchangeable. Thus important programs which are moving too slowly can often be accelerated by judiciously pumping money into them.[6]

When it is appropriate for government to fund the acceleration of particular technologies, the question is, how much acceleration can be achieved and how much is it worth? The government negotiator cannot expect to know a particular company's time schedule for the development, much less commercialization, of a particular technology. And, of course, he would be naive to accept without reservation what his prospective industry partner tells him about that schedule. This means that, for bargaining purposes, someone who knows the technology, the market, *and* something about the particular company must help the government estimate what the company's priorities are.

Many "free market" economists, on the other hand, see virtually no role for government beyond funding nonappropriable technologies. Their somewhat tautological reasoning is as follows: Private industry will invest in technologies that are economically viable, that is, "good technologies." That leaves the uneconomic, that is, "not good" technologies, to be funded by government. Why should the government fund technologies which are "not good"?

The question is faulty. The fact is that many technologies may be profitable, but may not be considered good enough investments if the particular firm has other, *more* profitable, opportunities at hand. However, the firm's lower priority, or "bridesmaid," technology may be of greater public benefit than the technology which attracts the firm's investment.

Here the role of government is to encourage the technology of higher public benefit to be developed despite what may appear to be its lower profitability to the firm. In order to do so, government has to offer a "dowry." If the government provides enough money, the effect will be to increase the firm's return on investment of the bridesmaid technology and thereby make it a more attractive project for the firm to select. As in the case of time value technologies, the government negotiator does not know precisely where the bridesmaid project stands on the company's list of priorities except that it is below the investment cutoff point. The purpose of negotiation is to find out and bargain from there.

The negotiator needs some sense of how much money he might offer to get the bridesmaid and time value technologies developed and commercialized. This sense derives from his estimate of the marginal contribution to the public welfare. For example, the Harvard Business School study, *Energy Future*, estimated in one marginal cost case that the value of reducing oil imports from OPEC is approximately $40 per barrel.[7]

In another case, using an avoidable measure of energy value, researchers found that the most recent disruption to the U.S. oil consumption system was caused by a shortfall of 12 million barrels per month, about 2.5 percent of our monthly consumption of oil, both imported and domestic. On that basis DOE has estimated that, if gas lines that resulted became an everyday part of life, 200 million hours per month would be wasted on them.[8] At $3 per hour to cover both the cost of the car and its driver this represents $600 million of waste.[9] The $600 million of wasted time might have been avoided by a technology which produced or conserved 12 million barrels of oil per month. Thus, on an avoidable cost basis the government could have spent up to the equivalent of $50 per barrel of oil on the alternative energy technology.

The Project Selection Phase

Although government laboratories may develop technologies, private industries, not public agencies, commercialize the new products in which the technologies are embodied. The involvement of private firms in joint ventures with government begins, of course, with project selection. How, then, can the government negotiator induce private industry to select projects that are of particular benefit to the nation as a whole?

In brief, the government must hold forth the promise of profit opportunities high enough to justify the risks involved. Moreover, given the risk, the potential of government-supported technology must look better than any other opportunities the target firm might have at hand.

If the government is to induce private industry to select a particular project for development, the government must understand that firms are not just trying to make a "reasonable" profit. Rather, they are trying to make the biggest profit they can, while avoiding risk. This objective is the focus of industry's project selection strategy which is to pick investments which are both low risk and high payout.[10]

Using these criteria, companies will rank each idea according to its return on investment (ROI), thereby generating a priority list of investment opportunities. Projects will be funded from that list down to a cutoff point determined by the company's limited resources. If the government negotiator is to induce a particular company to develop a particular technology, it must compete with the company's other opportunities for a place above the firm's investment cutoff point.[11]

Theoretically, if the risk is low enough and the profit opportunity great enough, the firm will snap up the technology in question—provided no better investment opportunity presents itself. But while the comparative advantage of government-supported technology should speak for itself, as a practical matter the government often has to negotiate industry into selecting the particular technology for development and, ultimately, commercialization. In doing so, government must understand some other factors that determine a company's investment priorities.

As a practical matter, companies do not rigidly follow principles that maximize profits, if only because the art of forecasting R&D costs and benefits is less than perfect. As Twiss pointed out, forecasts of R&D project costs and benefits are almost invariably inaccurate and are not, therefore, reliable guides for project selection.[12] Thus decision-making about innovation in the industrial firm is fundamentally based on confusion and uncertainty.[13] The government negotiator can and should take advantage of these confusions and uncertainties by offering the firm an opportunity to "satisfice" its way out of its information dilemma—that is, by encouraging the firm to accept technological investments which are just satisfactory or "good enough"[14] and not necessarily optimum.

In short, given the limited value of forecasting, instead of searching for the best alternative, firms will often settle for a technology that meets certain threshold criteria and is easily at hand. It may therefore pay for the government negotiator to be as generous as necessary to get the company to start a development project of public interest. Once started, the tendency of the company is to keep going—to continue to "satisfice" rather than later substituting more promising projects for the government-sponsored one.

The government's potential partner might well prefer to invest in these more promising alternatives, but he may be without the resources to do so. A fair number of innovations (15.5 percent) simply run out of money.[15] And so while the firm may abhor the idea of government sponsorship, its reluctance might be overcome by making enough money available. It is a negotiating principle that "it is better to have 10 percent of a good thing than 100 percent of nothing."

Even the government, however, is subject to the problem of scarce resources. It might therefore wish to offer its prospective partner certain "off-budget" inducements, such as tax incentives, which the company can transform into higher profits or lower risks. As table 10-1 shows, there are other ways of providing incentives without laying out federal dollars. Because many of them require legislation, however, such inducements are probably limited. In any event, surely the most direct way to align private interest with public purposes is to use money as an incentive—discretely and creatively. Thus, the most practical route to commercialization probably involves a mix of incentives, some requiring outlays of federal money and some not (see table 10-1).

The Negotiating Process in Commercialization

The longer the time horizon for a development/commercialization project the greater the uncertainty. This situation is difficult enough for one party

Table 10-1
Illustrative Incentive Approaches

Incentive Approach	Requires Outlay of Federal Money	No Outlay of Money Required
1. Assure a commercial market for technology suppliers	Provide financial assistance to end-users of technology, for example, low-cost loans to buy heat pumps	Government regulations, for example, Clean Air Act assured market for SO_2 scrubbers
		Permit temporary monopolies, for example, permit energy producer to load his plant with customers before licensing competing plant
		Sell government plants to private industry complete with customers (for example, uranium enrichment)
2. Assure price for energy produced by new technology	Government acts as buyer of last resort at attractive price or otherwise makes up difference between market price and new production price	Mandate minimum support price for energy, for example, Kissinger plan
3. Reduce technological risk for adopter		Warrant technology
4. Reduce costs of technology to adopter	Underwrite certain first of kind costs, for example, light water reactor	Waive or postpone royalty payments
		Underwrite operating costs through tax reduction or credits
5. Help provide investment capital to adopter	Government loans, contributions to equity capital	Government guarantee of senior debt

Source: derived from a paper by Donald G. Allen prepared for presentation to the 1976 Annual Meeting of the American Society for Public Administration, Washington, D.C., April 21, 1976.

to the process. When both government and industry must negotiate issues affecting future progress it is essential that they *reduce the uncertainty* by dividing the commercialization process into definable and agreed-upon stages, each with a decision point which brings them together to negotiate about what to do next.

Sequential Decisions and the Sweezy Model

According to Mogee, empirical studies suggest that although the same criteria tend to be used in all phases of project evaluation, the weight attached to the criteria may change as the project proceeds and progresses.[16] Thus judgment is required at points in the sequence of related decisions.

In the Sweezy model currently used by DOE there are five such points at which decision criteria are applied. Negotiation takes place at the initiation of each stage of the commercialization process with regard to what is to be accomplished in succeeding segments. Both the government and industry negotiators must agree jointly that if the criteria set forth for that stage are met each has a commitment to carry the project all the way to commercialization.[17] This must be done so that one party to the joint venture does not unexpectedly terminate his participation and with it the whole project. Industry needs that kind of protection; uncertainty of continued funding and political support make the government notorious for canceling projects at its own convenience.

Similarly, the government needs protection from industry's response to better investment opportunities that might arise. If the conditions negotiated at the initiation of a segment of work are in fact met, industry must promise to keep going on the project even if some better investment opportunity should present itself.

There are five decision points specified in the Sweezy model: (1) research initiation, (2) development initiation, (3) field test, (4) production initiation, and (5) full production.

If the criteria specified for each stage of the work have not been met, a decision may be made jointly either to terminate the project as a whole or to go back and do some additional work in order to meet those conditions. A series of benchmarks exist within each stage of the work against which to assess progress made within that stage. For each benchmark a clearly recognized action, event, or test has been established to signal whether or not the project has passed that benchmark. These benchmarks cover six types of decision factors: technology, market, capital, management action, public interest, and public incentives. By observing and reporting on these benchmarks to each other, the public and private sector managers can work independently of each other on a "management by exception basis" until progress through all of the indicated benchmarks brings them to the decision point for renegotiation.

The Need for Marketing Insight

Negotiation is about matters whose outcome is highly uncertain; in the context of commercialization those matters have primarily to do with marketing. Mansfield showed that, of every 100 projects, fifty-seven were completed technically, only thirty-one of the fifty-seven were commercialized, and a mere twelve of the thirty-one were market successes.[18] It is important to note that these ratios were achieved by institutions that specialize in bringing new technology to the market, private industry. We should therefore expect an even worse showing by government, which has virtually no expertise in this most difficult of all areas. No wonder, then, that when faced with a mandate to commercialize the innovations it sponsors, government leans so heavily on its private industry partners.

There are, however, several situations in which private industry leadership is inappropriate but marketing insight is needed—for example, where (1) the government's marketing approach must be spelled out in the first place in order to attract industry participation (solar heating and cooling); (2) the government's market is much larger and different from the market perceived by its contractors (electric vehicles); (3) the industry partner may have an interest in the technology other than marketing it as a product (furnace tester); (4) the industry is reluctant to develop a product for the market, but is unwilling to say so (composite materials and transbus).

Guidelines have been developed by government from previous experiences in order to help public officials exercise the sound business judgment which is required throughout the commercialization process. The trouble with such guidelines[19] is that they are either too general to be operational or, when they seem specific, they tend to be mechanically applied, often with counterproductive results. Unfortunately the seeming safety of guidelines encourages government people to avoid intuition and judgment, whether their own or others. Guidelines are simply no substitute for business judgment, as the case studies in the following section will illustrate.

Guidelines which call for "involvement" of potential adopters become meaningless unless the government negotiators learn to talk with, rather than at, their partners. Superficial "involvement" might actually have lulled government into a false sense of security when, in the cases of transbus and composite materials, the government negotiators had been overly confident of success because they *had* involved potential adopters along the way. Similarly, guidelines which require that the industry partner assume a greater cost burden than government can be counterproductive. With the Furnace Tester Program, government officials had mistakenly felt that all was going well simply because the industry partner was sharing so much cost. Once again, there can be no substitute for good business sense throughout the commercialization process and particularly during periods of negotiation.

Examples from Federal Government Experience

In each of the first three cases presented below, note the role played by the creative marketing experts and canny businessmen brought in to help the government negotiator. Their insights determined how each unbounded process went.

Solar heating and cooling (attracting industry through a government market approach). In order to attract industry to develop and commercialize solar heating and cooling technologies, DOE had to indicate what the market potential was for such systems. DOE sought to address this issue by referring to some excellent market research studies done for solar heating systems. One such study resulted in a finding that 90 percent of the people interviewed would refuse to buy a solar system if it cost $8,000 more than the conventional system.

All was doom and gloom in the halls of DOE beause the solar and heating and cooling systems they were developing were projected to cost $16,000 to $24,000 more than conventional systems. The problem was referred to an outside marketing expert who had succeeded in commercializing the electric heat pump. He saw the matter differently.

Far from viewing this as bad news, he was delighted that 10 percent of the people interviewed might buy a solar system even if it cost $8,000 more than a conventional heating system. He pointed out that, based on his previous experience, DOE needed only 4 percent of the market—77,000 units per year—to gain a foothold on it.

The marketing expert also emphasized to DOE that in this country "nothing is bought, everything is sold." He further recommended that, rather than try to convince industry that solar heating and cooling was a salable technology because its life-cycle costs to the user worked out favorably, DOE take the approach that the "early adopter" market was large enough to be profitable. At a meeting where this approach was presented, industry completely understood the DOE strategy and joined forces with the government.

Electric vehicles (government and industry markets differ). DOE, sensitive to its lack of marketing expertise, often relies on cooperating companies to "do it their way since private industry knows best." A team of marketing experts brought in to review the Electric Vehicle (EV) program saw it differently.

After reviewing the EV program the experts unanimously agreed that, future battery technology notwithstanding, there was "no way in the world that electric vehicles could compete head-on with conventional automobiles." They recommended, therefore, that EVs be "positioned in the market" to be totally different from conventional automobiles. And, to be consistent with this marketing approach, it was most important that DOE's electric vehicles *look* totally different from conventional automobiles. This meant that DOE would have to take a direct hand in the aesthetic design of the vehicles to be sure that they would, indeed, look different.

The team's recommended policy was a complete reversal of current policy, which was to let producers incorporate electric systems into conventional automobile bodies such as the Volkswagen Rabbit. The resultant product—a conventional automobile with an electric motor—did have a certain amount of sales potential. For example, one producer estimated that he would sell 4,000 to 5,000 vehicles per year and make a handsome profit. But while he might succeed, the government would fail; that number is much too small to have any measurable effect on the nation's energy system.

Digital furnace tester (industry has interest in the technology but not in the market). One of the largest instrument manufacturers in the country put up $600,000 to develop a digital furnace tester. The government matched that amount with $200,000 to speed the innovation to the marketplace. The government, confident that it had made a good deal, asked the private company to present its market plan for commercializing the digital furnace tester.

The company's plan indicated that potential sales volume was on the order of $1 or $1 million per year. A businessman who was on DOE's negotiating team asked what percentage this was of the company's total annual sales. The answer turned out to be .2 percent—so small that it could be nothing more than a nuisance. Further discussion revealed that the company really had no intention of marketing the product itself; it was only interested in the technology that would be embodied in the product.

Composite materials and transbus (industry is reluctant to develop or use the product but will not say so). The government negotiator must at all times listen carefully to the feedback he is getting from those he is trying to involve in his projects. Bad news is often not communicated sharply enough in situations where manufacturers and users are in some kind of continuing relationship with the particular government agency. In addition, there is strong tendency for government technocrats to hear only what they want to hear.

NASA worked for years with the aircraft manufacturers to develop and incorporate NASA-sponsored composite materials in the flight surfaces of their aircraft. NASA's expectations were high. But in the event, these materials were used in such small quantities that NASA was extremely disappointed.

The cooperating companies, anxious to maintain a good relationship with NASA failed to voice their misgivings loudly enough to overcome NASA's wishful thinking. In the final analysis, however, the companies had to act in their own interests even at the risk of damaging their continuing relations with NASA.

Similarly, DOT had worked closely for years with several manufacturers to develop the specifications for a transbus—a radical low floor design which depended on an unproven twin rear axle. A number of transbus prototypes were built and demonstrated. When the bus was finally put out for bid, however, none of the manufacturers responded, claiming that the bus was "unbuildable." DOT was both surprised and shocked. But one might ask why they should have been.

Why, over the years of negotiating the transbus specifications, had DOT not sensed that industry was reluctantly "going along," perhaps to maintain good relations with the federal agency that provides 80 percent of the money used for bus purchases? In any event, when the chips were really down, each manufacturer decided that no bid price was high enough to justify the damage to its reputation that would result from mass producing what it felt would be an overly expensive and unreliable bus.[20]

In each of the foregoing cases, business and marketing perceptions were diametrically opposite government perceptions. Indeed, from the government official's point of view they were counterintuitive. Government officials despaired when they learned that 90 percent of market wouldn't buy their solar systems; businessmen were delighted that 10 percent might. Government felt that producers should be responsible for how their vehicles should look; the marketing team unanimously agreed that it was DOE's responsibility. Government felt that a $2 million market was big enough to interest any company; asking the right question showed this was wrong. And, finally, government thought it was making progress because it was talking with bus and aircraft manufacturers; the manufacturers felt that government was doing too much talking and not enough listening.

Negotiation for Success

The same lack of perception and misunderstanding arises time and time again even in cases where public officials think they are acting on good advice or with good judgment. Demonstration projects, for example, have caused acute government embarrassment when they should not have, usually because public officials misunderstand the purpose of demonstrations. In the public sector, the demonstration project has become a major instrument for diffusing government-sponsored technological innovations, but it has also become a particular peril for both the sponsoring agency and its industry partners. Without effective negotiation government officials will continue to misdirect their efforts and suffer public embarrassment and failure.

An innovation will diffuse when potential users can "see" that the relative advantage of the innovation is both great enough and certain enough to be worth the dollar and human costs required to adopt it. A physical demonstration of the innovation both reduces uncertainty and aids perception. If the relative advantage is shown to be great enough, the demonstration will generate a "demand pull" for the innovation.

In effect, the demonstration helps potential users decide what they want by showing them what they can have. Basically, adopters choose among two general categories of products: (1) qualitatively new products (or systems) which are supposed to enhance performance or provide a new capability and are often evaluated qualitatively; and (2) productivity products, which are supposed to save resources, capital, material, labor, or energy and are usually evaluated quantitatively in economic terms. Whatever the adopters' objective, however, they must be convinced that the product they are offered is of significant advantage.

In general, though, the government experience with demonstration projects over the past several years has been crowned with less than success. The Morgantown, West Virginia, Personal Rapid Transit (PRT) demonstration is a notorious case in point. The system, which was still essentially in the experimental stage of development, was presented to the public far too soon. Officials had hoped to develop PRT in situ at Morgantown, rather than at a test track, and to complete the development of this complex technology within three to five years. Much of the trouble resulted from a confusion about the meaning of the term "demonstration," which had become ambiguous.

In the private sector, demonstration means showing off the relative advantages of a new product in order to help potential customers decide whether or not to buy the product. In that meaning, a demonstration project would be mounted only after the technology is, as RAND puts it, "well in hand." When the outcome of a demonstration is relatively certain, the demonstration serves as an example.

In the public sector, however, the word "demonstration" has taken on another meaning; it is widely used to describe projects whose outcomes are so uncertain that they are better described as experiments. Demonstrations that are primarily experiments must be managed differently from demonstrations that are primarily examples (see table 10-2). Ideally, experiments should have low visibility. While sponsors hope for success, they must anticipate failure. It goes without saying that embarrassment is minimized and credibility protected when failures are not too obvious. Unfortunately, political pressure impels experiments to be managed as examples, virtually forcing demonstrations to do too much, too soon, and in public.

In spite of this political pressure, however, the government can learn much from the way in which private industry uses demonstrations to market its new products. But in the context of public sponsorship, the government official must be aware of the peculiar dangers inherent in publicly sponsored demonstration projects. Here, he is largely on his own. In negotiating a project with his private industry partner he can expect little help because, despite the record, his partner seems to think that the government knows what it is doing when it is spending large sums of money. From experience, of course, we know that this is not always the case. To be successful in

Table 10-2
Demonstrations as Experiments and as Examples

	Experiment (Tests Feasibility)	Example (Shows Utility)
Audience	Sponsors	Customers
Project design objectives	Low visibility	High visibility
	Quantitative control and evaluation	Sufficient control for credibility
	Simulated pertinent environment	Full operational environment
	Smallest scale to get information	Fullest scale to approximate reality
Management posture	Healthy skepticism	Optimistic assurance

Source: based on work supported by the Office of Transit Management and Demonstration, Urban Mass Transportation Administration, Department of Transportation.

demonstration projects, as with other phases of the commercialization process, the government negotiator must have business insight. But he must also understand that his business will be conducted in a highly charged political environment.

Negotiating Success: The Business Strategy Team

Having learned the techno-political skills necessary to prevent innovations from failing, the government must be prepared to learn the negotiating skills that are necessary to innovation success. In order to do this, government must begin by (1) recognizing commercialization to be the negotiating process it is; (2) reaching out to get on its team, people who have the necessary business insights and marketing intuition; and (3) learning to absorb the wisdom made available by such "outside" people. This chapter has concerned itself primarily with (1) above. Our recommendation focuses on (2) and (3), getting the right people and absorbing their wisdom.

Our recommendation to involve outside industry people is hardly a new one. In fact, a major recommendation of the Charpie task force to DOE was to ". . . develop a procedure for drawing on the know-how of the outside [industry] in developing program strategies. . . ."[21] The task force was well aware that the necessary business talents are rarely found in government service. Indeed, a task force analysis of several hundred executive résumés found only eleven people in DOE with the necessary qualifications to deal with commercialization issues—and these were top-level bureaucrats too far from the level at which commercialization decisions were actually made.

Several programs at DOE have adopted the Charpie approach by using industry teams at the program and project decision levels. They now engage on an "as needed when needed" basis a few top industry executives with proven business acumen and marketing intuition, but with no conflicts of interest. These people are integrated into Business Strategy Teams which, once assembled, provide program managers and project directors with the insights necessary to "read" the industry people with whom they are dealing. The team closely follows each project's development and comes together to help DOE negotiate with its private industry partners at critical decision points. The results to date are extremely encouraging, as indicated by the cases described earlier.

The use of Business Strategy Teams has had an additional benefit; it has generated mutual respect between the public sector negotiators and their industry partners. This improved working environment of cooperation and mutual respect has emerged out of the fact that DOE managers now understand what they are hearing from their private industry counterparts. Previously, the two parties had been talking past each other. And, to make matters worse, many industrialists had held DOE managers in disdain because the latter pretended to business and market expertise which they clearly do not have.[22]

Some Options for Policy and Administration

The foregoing discussion has addressed two critical issues regarding joint government/industry investment in the development and commercialization of technologies for private and mixed markets.

1. What should government's investment policy be regarding technology for development and commercialization?
2. What role should government play in order to maximize the likelihood of its investment success?

We have found that government failure to address these questions coherently at the operational level has resulted in countless project failures and is likely to lead to more of the same. Given the twin problems of an energy crisis and productivity slippage, continued failure to answer these questions will jeopardize our economy and might, ultimately, jeopardize our very system of government.

According to Bean and Roessner, three basic criteria should guide the federal government in the selection of projects for development and commercialization: (1) the social benefits of a federal investment should be greater than its social costs; (2) the net benefits of the investment should at least equal or exceed the net benefits from alternate government benefits, the opportunity cost; and (3) market incentives are not adequate to induce private industry to undertake the investment in the absence of government intervention.[23] These general criteria can be made specific enough to be operational by integrating them into a decision calculus related to the kinds of technologies described in this chapter.

Government investments in productivity technologies should be keyed to their value to the nation as a whole. The approach to estimating such values can be based on a government policy that emphasizes demand-pull. Under such a policy, the government would help commercialize technologies for productivity improvement by stimulating their purchase. It can do so by using federal subsidies to raise to acceptable levels, 20 percent, the ROI that the customer would enjoy from adopting and using the new product in question. The government is justified in doing so provided that its subsidy generates public benefits large enough to meet or exceed OMB's mandated rate of return for government investments, 10 percent. Note that if the public value is difficult to quantify in dollar terms, chances are that the product deserves no public support.

Qualitatively new products are more difficult to evaluate for government investment than either energy technologies or productivity products. As we have seen, benefit/cost data forecasts for new products have proven so inaccurate that both government and industry are forced to operate largely on hunches and intuition. Private industry, by its nature, usually has the in-house talent to do so. The government, however, is much less well equipped. This means it must protect its investment by reaching out for people who can bring the necessary business talent to bear at each investment decision point.

In some cases, government might avoid up front investments entirely in favor of ex-post reward payments. We urge that the government explore techniques for encouraging private industry to accept all of the risks of developing and commercializing qualitatively new product technologies that are in the public interest by increasing the size of the reward that comes with success.

In order to carry its innovations to success the government must begin by learning how to avoid failure. As we have seen, an important cause of failure is the political pressure that forces government to demonstrate its technology in public too soon—the tendency to treat experiments as examples. These pressures often come directly from the Congress itself, and hopefully, in time, the Congress will learn that it is responsible for many technological failures. But in the meanwhile government technocrats must learn, first, not to overreact, and then to absorb or deflect these pressures.

Finally and most importantly, the outcome of bringing business and marketing talent into the government's negotiation process depends almost entirely on the willingness of government executives to absorb the wisdom brought to them by outsiders such as the Business Strategy Teams. A certain amount of receptivity, if not humility, is needed here. Alas, both qualities are in short supply in the federal government. Public executives generally have just enough business "booklearning" and more than enough money to reinforce the natural tendency to ignore advice that differs from their own preconceptions. This chapter therefore must strongly recommend to government executives involved in the process of negotiating innovations that if you don't agree, listen harder.

Notes

1. Gerard I. Nierenberg, *The Art of Negotiating: Psychological Strategies for Gaining Advantageous Bargains* (New York: Hawthorne Books, 1978), p. 23.

2. Chester L. Karrass, *The Negotiating Game* (New York: Thomas Y. Crowell, 1970), p. 231.

3. The difference in talent and orientation between government and business executives is described by David Tornquist, *The Characteristics and Roles of the Actors in the Joint Public/Private Commercialization Model; March 21, 1979.* IPA Technical Memorandum 78-2.

4. Sumner Myers and Eldon Sweezy, *Federal Incentives for Innovation—Report R 75-04, Why Innovations Falter and Fail: A Study of 200 Cases Prepared for Experimental and Development Incentives Program (NSF)* for the Denver Research Institute, January 1976, p. 26.

5. Public Law 93-409, Solar Heating and Cooling Demonstration Act of 1974; Public Law 93-473, Solar Energy Research, Development and Demonstration Act of 1974, sec. 2 (6); Public Law 93-577, Federal Nonnuclear Energy Research and Development Act of 1974, sec. 3 (a); Public Law 94-413, Electric and Hybrid Vehicle Research, Development and Demonstration Act of 1976, sec. 2 (6) (b) (1).

6. Brian Twiss, *Managing Technological Innovation* (New York: Longman, 1974), p. 151.

7. Anthony J. Parisi, "Harvard Study Urges Conservation and Solar Use Over Synthetic Fuel," *New York Times*, July 12, 1979, p. A-1. The $40 figure reported in the *Times* is based on a telephone interview with Dr. Stobaugh, an editor of the Harvard study. The study itself sets the figure between $35 and $85 per barrel. See also Robert Stobaugh and Daniel Yergin, eds., *Energy Future* (New York: Random House, 1979).

8. T.R. Reid, "DOE Figures Gas Lines Could Waste Millions," *Washington Post*, July 5, 1979.

9. American Association of State Highway and Transportation Officials, *A Manual on User Benefit Analysis of Highway and Bus Transit Improvement, 1978* (Washington, D.C., 1978).

10. Booz-Allen and Hamilton, *Management of New Products*, 1968, p. 10.

11. The Conference Board found that over three-quarters of 203 firms surveyed used ROI as a principal measure for judging new product concepts. See *Evaluating New Product Proposals* (New York: The Conference Board, 1973), p. 19.

12. Twiss, *Managing Technological Innovation*, p. 144.

13. Mary Ellen Mogee, *The Process of Technological Innovation in Industry: A State-of-Knowledge Review for Congress* (Washington, D.C.: Library of Congress, Congressional Research Service, 1978), p. 41.

14. A. Herbert Simon, *Administrative Behavior* (New York: The Free Press, 1975).

15. Myers and Sweezy, *Federal Incentives*, p. 26.

16. Mogee, *The Process of Technological Innovation*, p. 38.

17. Eldon E. Sweezy, *The Commercialization Decision Framework*. IPA Technical Memorandum 78-1, August 1978.

18. Edwin Mansfield, *Research and Innovation in the Modern Corporation* (New York: Norton, 1971), p. 62.

19. See Walter S. Baer, L.L. Johnson, and E.W. Merrow, *Analysis of Federally Funded Demonstration Projects* (Santa Monica, Calif.: Rand Corporation, 1976); and N.B. McEachron, H.S. Javitz, D.S. Green, J.D. Logsdon, and E. Milbergs, *Management of Federal R&D for Commercialization* (Menlo Park, Calif.: SRI International, 1978), both prepared for the Experimental Technology Incentives Program, U.S. Department of Commerce.

20. For an assessment of the technical feasibility of building Transbus see Mitre Corporation, *An Analysis of the Transbus Procurement*, prepared for the Transportation Research Board of the National Academy of Science, July 1979.

21. *The Demonstration Project as a Procedure for Accelerating the Application of New Technology* (Charpie Task Force Report), Vol. I (Washington, D.C.: U.S. Department of Energy, 1978).

22. See Mary R. Hamilton, *Public-Private Sector Relations and Energy Policy*, presented at the Annual Meeting of the American Association for the Advancement of Science, Houston, January 6, 1979.

23. Alden S. Bean and J. David Roessner, *Assessing the Government Role in the Commercialization of Federally Funded R&D* (unpublished paper).

11 Public Policy and Efficient Use of Energy

Marc Ross

Energy resources are extensive, but energy which is both cheap to extract and cheap to use is very limited. The cost of providing and using a unit of energy will continue to increase. Furthermore, the provision of energy is becoming increasingly problematical, as illustrated by the recent Iranian revolution and the accident at Three Mile Island.

The long-term policy response of the United States to the energy problem is to initiate projects to create new universal sources of energy such as fluid fuels from coal and oil shale, and electricity from nuclear fission and from "clean" coal processes. Evidence of difficulties which have buffeted most of these schemes has littered the news media: a coal industry in the doldrums, postponed "synfuel" plants, and canceled nuclear power plants and nuclear development programs in the years since the oil embargo, a time when one would have thought that alternatives to oil would thrive. These failures typically involve a combination of technical and political developments leading to a very high cost and a perception of high, if uncertain, hazards.

These are two principal directions for energy policy in the next few decades: (1) continuing efforts to increase the supply of energy and (2) improving the effectiveness with which energy is used. I will call these the supply strategy and efficiency strategy, respectively. Note that the concept of efficiency is distinct from sacrifice, for example, driving less and lowering indoor temperatures in winter.

The supply strategy involves a truly massive private investment to develop oil and gas fields in unconventional places, coal mines, coal transportation facilities and fluid-fuel extraction facilities, nuclear fuel facilities and electric power plants. It also involves massive government assistance to subsidize these capital expenditures, to provide research and development, and to moderate environmental restraints on the energy industry.

Likewise, the efficiency strategy involves a massive private investment to improve the performance of buildings, transportation systems, and industrial equipment. It also involves government research and development

This article is adapted very loosely from part of a book by the author and Robert H. Williams, *Energy: Regaining Control through Innovation* (McGraw-Hill Book Company, Summer 1980).

153

in energy-saving instrumentation and techniques. Government might also create incentives and regulations, or energy price and financing conditions, to encourage more efficient equipment and processes.

In this chapter I will briefly discuss the efficiency strategy, its economics, its relationship to public administration, and its relationship to the supply strategy.

Energy Carriers

We talk of energy. A variety of forms of energy is meant. There are the *primary* sources that man initially interacts with: fossil fuels, sunlight, wind, water at an elevation, uranium, and so on. These forms of energy are often converted, perhaps more than once, before use. It is convenient to classify the forms in which energy is transported and/or stored before final use as energy *carriers*. There are four main types of carriers: fluid fuels (gaseous and liquid fuels), solid fuels, electricity, and thermal energy such as steam. The properties of an energy carrier, especially the storability, transportability, ease of handling, and environmental acceptability, establish its relative usefulness for a particular end-use.

The labor and skills required for distribution and for handling at the site of end-use are important determinants of the appropriateness of a carrier. In small scale applications—buildings, transportation, and small industry—problems of distribution and handling inhibit the use of solid fuels. Environmental problems of coal and uranium also inhibit their use by smaller scale users.

As a general rule, the storability of energy forms is closely related to tranportability. Fuels with high energy density—coal, oil, uranium—can be economically shipped in batch mode (barge, railroad, truck, and so on). Those that are expensive to store, such as electricity, are most efficiently transported by line, or continuous, mode. The storage and transport properties of the liquid fuels give these carriers an enormous advantage in applications, such as transportation.

A key fact is that it costs about a thousand times as much to store energy by a means which provides electricity as it does to store energy as a liquid hydrocarbon in a tank! As a result it is impractical to substitute electricity for liquid fuel in many time-varying uses as well as in most vehicular uses. Thus, although many buildings are heated and cooled by electricity, much of that "peaking" power is generated by using oil.

The nation has, in fact, two principal energy systems. One is dependent on fluid fuel carriers, with substitution among petroleum derivatives and methane and its derivatives (or other fluid hydrocarbons) being relatively easy. The other is dependent on electricity. Further electrification (the pattern of growth in electricity's share of total energy use) has just about run its course in the United States, because, for most remaining uses of fluid fuel, substitution of electricity is extremely disadvantageous. For the present kinds of uses of fluid fuel, enhanced supplies of fluid fuel and/or more efficient equipment and processes, not substitution of electricity, must be looked to for solutions of the energy problem.

Conserving Energy and Reducing Costs

There is some confusion about the goals of an efficiency strategy because cost minimization can be based on different criteria which imply very different projected levels of fuel consumption. The criterion based on the *price* of energy is minimization of the cost of an energy-using activity to the individual consumer or firm. The cost of energy to the consumer is simply the price of energy. (Proper evaluation requires that price increases during the time period under consideration be taken into account). The cost to be minimized is the cost of energy plus the capital and operating costs of the activity. One can, for example, express the capital cost in terms of a fixed annual charge (assuming an interest rate) and add that to fixed annual operating and energy costs to obtain the total cost which is to be minimized. Full application of this cost minimization principle typically would lead to substantial fuel savings because of recent energy price increases.

A different economic criterion based on the *replacement cost* of energy is minimization of all incremental costs to the nation involved in an energy-using activity. The incremental or replacement cost of energy to the nation is much higher than the price of energy for two reasons: the replacement cost of energy is based on new sources of supply; these are much more costly than existing facilities because fields of cheap oil and gas are no longer waiting to be discovered. In addition, any use of energy imposes "external" or "social costs" such as pollution, damage to worker health, and threats to national security, economic stability, and climate. (The point is, of course, that energy imposes much higher external costs than most other products). While evaluation of social costs is highly problematical, costs of new supply can be estimated. At present, the replacement cost of energy carriers delivered to final customers is about twice the price.

It is characteristic of efforts to improve energy efficiency that the cost versus fuel savings curve has a very broad minimum. This relationship is shown schematically in figure 11-1, where costs are plotted vertically, including the annual cost of energy (based on price) and the annual finance charge (to pay for the capital investment), and fuel saved is plotted horizontally.

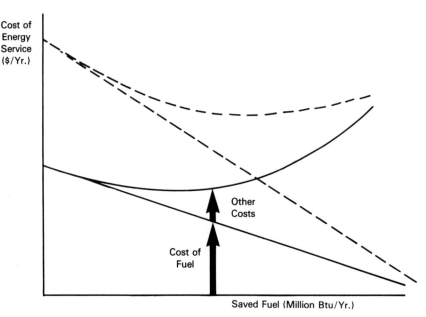

Source: adapted from Marc Ross, "Efficient Use of Energy Revisited," *Physics Today* (February 1980).

Figure 11-1. The Cost versus Fuel Savings Curve

Let us explore the meaning of this curve in detail using the example of improvement (retrofit) of existing housing with respect to winter-season-heating (see figure 11-2). The various retrofits are ordered from left to right, according to the associated *cost of saved energy*. This is the annual finance charge (which will pay off the capital cost in a given period of time, plus interest charges, including tax corrections) divided by the annual fuel savings. Typically, a night-setback thermostat, plugging of important air flows into and out of the building shell, ceiling insulation in an uninsulated house, window improvements such as special shutters or draperies, and furnace improvements such as electric ignition and fuel and flue restriction, have very low costs of saved energy. More ambitious insulation jobs and storm windows and doors typically have a higher cost of saved energy.

The optimal program of retrofits involves carrying out retrofits to the point where the cost of saved energy of the last retrofit equals the cost of energy that characterizes the economic criterion that one has selected. (Of course, such optimization requires knowing the consequences as well as the cost of each retrofit; unfortunately this is a more diffiuclt problem than might be thought.)

At the present time, it is very advantageous to extensively retrofit almost all housing—assuming that good work is done. I have estimated,[1]

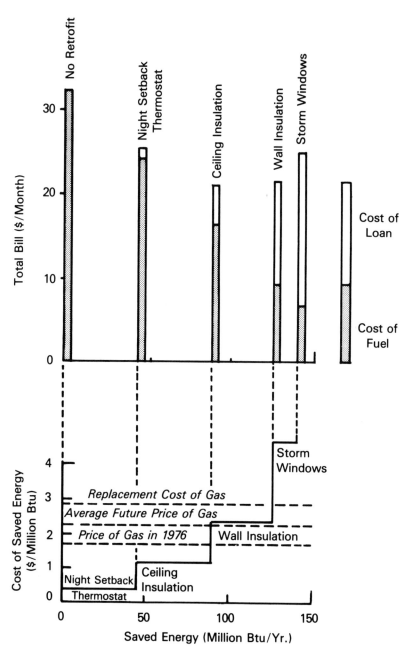

Source: adapted from Marc Ross and Robert Williams, *Energy: Regaining Control through Innovation* (McGraw Hill Book Co., Summer 1980).

Figure 11-2. Housing Retrofit and Cost of Saved Energy

very roughly, that under the first, or energy price, criterion an average investment of $500 per dwelling unit would be justified, leading to about 30 percent fuel savings. Under the second, or replacement cost, criterion the optimal investment would average about $1,500 per dwelling unit, with fuel savings of 60 percent. Of course there is an enormous variation from house to house and region to region.

Let us look more deeply into the distinction between the two economic criteria. If retrofits are carried out according to the energy price criterion, substantial direct economic benefits accrue to the nation because new energy supply facilities can be deferred. As a result of these retrofits all energy customers would experience a slower pace of energy price increases. Since these benefits are spread over all energy customers, the individual householder is motivated to carry out only a few retrofits. If these benefits could be focused on the decision-maker, the householder, the motivation would be stronger (the household investment rising in my estimate from about $500 to about $1,500). There are several ways this could be done, that is, that something like the replacement cost criterion could be brought into play. Three possibilities are

1. Incentives, such as tax credits, could be offered to householders for certain retrofits.
2. Energy utilities could be allowed to finance retrofits and incorporate the capital cost into their rate base. Thus, the energy industry's replacement cost economics could be applied to housing retrofits.
3. The price of energy could be raised to the replacement cost level (even to a level which covers some social costs). This could be accomplished by taxing fuels and returning tax receipts to the people on a per capita basis.

Each of these schemes would focus benefits on the householder and thus bring investment decisions on conservation technology more in line with competing investment decisions on new energy supply. Each scheme would require extensive legislation and has a number of interesting features, so adequate discussion is beyond the scope of this chapter. I will, however, point out some key features.

The first, or incentive, scheme is fairly popular with the Congress. It has the critical flaw that incentives have limited applicability because the manifold opportunities of technical change cannot be exploited, as discussed below.

The second, or utility financing, scheme has been introduced for electric heating in Oregon. It has the advantage of tapping the services of organizations which are in close contact with every building. In addition, and quite surprisingly, a utility could offer "free" retrofits to customers. A program of such retrofits would lead to energy price increases to cover the "interest" costs of the retrofits. These price increases would be about the same as the price increases resulting from adding the corresponding amount of new energy supply capacity.[2] The fundamental concept of this approach is that it is much less costly for energy companies to sell energy services such as heat and light than to sell energy as such. This is the meaning of bringing the energy industry's economics to bear on improvements in the efficiency of energy use.

The third scheme is represented, but only very crudely, by the proposal to let oil prices rise and tax the windfall profits. Ideally energy prices should be increased through a tax mechanism so they reach a desired level, and the receipts should substitute for existing taxes or be rebated.[3] The concept is of course that consumers of energy should buy energy at prices covering its full costs. In general, the excess receipts should be returned to people on a basis unrelated to their energy purchases, to be used for whatever purposes they like. Furthermore it would be counterproductive to an efficiency strategy to use these funds to subsidize energy supply facilities.

Regulation and Incentives Have Limited Applicability

In the present political climate regulations to require improved energy performance and, more especially, subsidies to motivate investments in improved performance seem very attractive. The most important regulation affecting energy use is the fuel economy standard for automobiles. The performance of 1985 model cars (the fuel economy of a manufacturer's models averaged over production, as measured by EPA) is required to reach at least 27.5 mpg, or twice the fuel economy of the early 1970s. This remarkable improvement is being met by auto manufacturers with surprisingly little reduction in the performance and interior dimensions of cars.

The efficacy of regulation in this case is of course due to the very small number of manufacturers and models and the uniformity of the mass-produced product. Even here there are problems: the test standard is likely to deviate substantially from actual average performance.[4] The variance in actual performance in the individual car due to variation in use may well be very large. There may be loopholes which enable some people and firms to evade the intent of the standard. In the case of autos the most important of these problems is probably the use of light trucks for passenger travel. Trucks over three tons have not been regulated until recently. Even now the fuel economy regulations for three- to 4.5-ton trucks are very mild for the sound reason that there is a legitimate need for such vehicles, and at their weight really high fuel economy cannot be achieved. The use of these light trucks as passenger vehicles has been booming.[5]

In my view it is important not to rely solely on regulation of performance, even in the case of standardized mass-produced products like cars. Rising fuel prices (as well as the possibility of fuel shortages) is a very important complement to regulations.

Cars and certain standardized appliances are relatively well suited to performance regulation. Housing is much less so. A critical problem is that actual performance is very difficult to regulate; it is much easier to calculate performance on the basis of design and even easier to specify items of construction. Thus minimum insulation R values are often specified and, in some cases, maximum window area has been specified. The trouble is that such specifications are unlikely to be optimal and may well, depending on the building, be counterproductive. Improved measurement and analysis will, however, make it possible to move toward regulation based more closely on performance. While such a program might be relatively effective for new houses, I believe it would be quite unsatisfactory for existing housing.

As with regulations, incentives related to house heating improvements are often seriously flawed. For example, incentives may specify adding ceiling insulation where plugging air flows is what is needed. Incentives generally exclude multipurpose measures such as skylights, south-facing windows, and massive walls (for passive solar heating) which also bear a load. There are excellent administrative reasons why incentives must be specified in this way.

Regulations and incentives are still less valid in the industrial area. The best-known example is the fuel switching policies whose flip-flops have been damaging to industrial planning. Consider two other examples. It has been suggested that more efficient electric motors be mandated, but this might inhibit putting extra money into control equipment which would often be a much more effective measure.

Another example is a potentially counterproductive incentive: investment credits for in-plant cogeneration of electricity and steam. The problem is that, while the less capital-intensive cogeneration technologies may be preferred, the incentive might lead to a different choice.[6] Even worse, this same incentive applied to the very capital-intensive central power stations works against any form of in-plant cogeneration.

These examples do not, however, fully illustrate the difficulty. Even a very well thought out regulation or incentive must fail to capture the advantages offered by the manifold nature of technology. Manufacturers can and do alter the design of products, processes, particular items of equipment, and day-to-day operations depending on the particular qualities of their plants. In addition, any final product results from bringing together many intermediate products, with choices to be made about the role of each. In the complex interplay of these choices any particular incentive or regulation, aside, perhaps, from one that encourages information and control equipment, would be likely to be counterproductive.

The reader may believe that a strong administrative effort could be made to successfully overcome these problems. I believe this would not be wise. Programs should be designed to minimize the administrative strain. Many energy programs established by Congress in the 1970s foundered because the administrative difficulties were too great.

The Potential for Improved Efficiency

Important elements for an effective efficiency strategy have been suggested in the above discussion. In essence a market approach based on higher energy prices is proposed. This, combined with a short term reequipping program to assist disadvantaged people and firms, appears to be far more promising than a nonprice approach combined with regulatory, incentive, and assistance programs. Presentation of a coherent program is, however, beyond the scope of this chapter. It remains to address the broad effects of such a strategy on the national situation.

Although physical and economic information on existing energy use and, especially, on new technologies is seriously limited, and methods for projecting technical change are controversial, to say the least, certain fairly reliable conclusions emerge from attempts to project the effect of technical change on fuel consumption in the United States.[7]

1. Since 1973 some major efficiency improvements have occurred. They will continue to occur.
2. The extent of fuel savings will be very sensitive to public policies.
3. If effective public policies would be adopted to encourage improved efficiency, then dramatic reductions in projected energy use would occur in the next two decades.
4. Such reductions would turn the nation's energy-supply goals upside down.
5. Effective supply and efficiency strategies are in direct conflict with each other. Choices need to be made.

I will discuss each of these points briefly. Industrial energy use has fallen about 3 percent per year per unit of production since 1973.[8] No end is in sight for such improvements. An important factor in this favorable response is that many industries have technical staffs able to respond to the new energy situation. Another key factor is that the price of energy to industry has risen faster than for other customers. Household heating fuel prices have also increased relatively rapidly. Those customers who were, perhaps, best able to respond, owners in existing dwellings, have reduced fuel consumption about 15 percent.[9] Much of this was not achieved by technical change, however; most of the techncial opportunities for improvement remain to be exploited. Progress is also being made in automobiles because of fuel economy standards, although actual performance of the fleet is disappointing in comparison with expectations.

The sensitivity of projected fuel savings upon policy is revealed in a number of the studies. This issue was discussed in some detail earlier in the chapter.

The efficiency improvements projected by various studies, in the event the United States pursues an efficiency strategy, would more than double the energy efficiency of the U.S. economy in the next several decades. Meanwhile saturation effects are occurring with respect to energy-intensive activities, as a result of such factors as the change in birthrates, saturation of specific transportation and space conditioning products, refined design of manufactured products, and the shift to services. (For example, the use of information-related products is growing explosively while the bulk use of steel, concrete, and wood products is falling behind the growth of total production.) The combined effect of these two developments and the gradual increase of solar-related energy supply would be to *decrease the demand for fossil and nuclear fuels in absolute terms.*

Under these circumstances it would be advantageous to promote the use of benign fuels—natural gas, for example—rather than problematic and dangerous fuels such as coal and uranium. The virtue of coal and uranium has been that their provision could (seemingly) be vastly increased to meet growing demand. With demand declining, the nation could drop its attempts to promote these fuels.

With reference to energy supply I conclude that, in the longer term, tax subsidies, economic regulation, and government-industry partnerships to promote creation of supplies and to keep a lid on the price of energy are inappropriate. This supply strategy is not only unpromising, but it conflicts with the successful pursuit of efficiency improvements because the latter would render many of the supply efforts completely unnecessary. The process of government planning and support for massive supply programs could not tolerate these inconsistent goals.

An effective efficiency strategy will not be adopted as long as industry and the nation are committed to multi-billion-dollar tax subsidies for energy supply (and the associated management by government). An effective efficiency strategy will not be adopted as long as consumers and the nation are committed to trying to contain the price of energy rather than containing the overall cost of energy services such as heat, light, and transportation.

Notes

1. See "The Technical Approach to Energy Conservation—Prospects in Three Major End Uses," part II, chapter 5 of Sam H. Schurr, Joel Darmstadter, Harry Perry, William Ramsey, and Milton Russell, *Energy in America's Future, The Choices Before Us*, Resources for the Future (Baltimore: Johns Hopkins Univ. Press, 1979).

2. Marc H. Ross and Robert H. Williams, "Drilling for Oil and Gas in our Buildings," a Center for Energy and Environmental Studies report, Princeton Univ., July 1979.

3. This issue is addressed at some length in my book with Williams. For a general discussion see Talbot Page, *Conservation and Economic Efficiency, An Approach to Materials Policy*, Resources for the Future (Baltimore: Johns Hopkins Univ. Press, 1977). A proposal for using an energy tax along with a rebate as a tool to raise the price of electricity to the replacement cost has been presented by A.H. Rosenfeld and A.C. Fisher, "Marginal Cost Pricing with Refunds per Capita," submitted to the 1978 Hearings of the California Energy Commission on Load Management, July 1978.

4. Bary McNutt and Robert Dulla, "On-Road Fuel Economy Trends and Impacts," U.S. Dept. of Energy, Office of Conservation and Advanced Systems, 1979; see also *Transportation Energy Conservation Data Book*, Edition 3, ed. D.B. Shonka, Oak Ridge National Lab. ORNL-5493, February 1979.

5. "The Technical Approach to Energy Conservation."

6. Robert H. Williams, "Industrial Cogeneration," *Annual Review of Energy* 3 (1978).

7. It is beyond the scope of this chapter to summarize these attempts. Among some of the more prominent studies which seriously examine efficiency improvement are M.H. Ross and R.H. Williams, "The Potential for Fuel Conservation," *Technology Review* 79 (February 1977); Eric Hirst and Bruce Hannon, "Effects of Energy Conservation in Residential and Commercial Buildings," *Science 205* 656 (August 17, 1979); Demand and Conservation Panel of CONAES (Committee on Nuclear and Alternative Energy Systems), "U.S. Energy Demand: Some Low Energy Futures," *Science 200* 142 (April 14, 1978); Roger Sant, "The Least Cost Energy Strategy," published September 1979 by the Energy Productivity Center of the Mellon Institute; and Ref. 1.

8. *Energy Users News*, April 2, 1979, p. 6.

9. American Gas Association, *Energy Analysis*, February 3, 1978, p. 4.

**Part III
The Problem of Electricity**

Because existing electric power grids represent the fulfillment of economies of scale, they are inherently more centralized and large scale than many other energy systems. As such, they are the personification of hard-path energy strategies, and their existence poses a serious challenge to the advocates of small-scale technology. The selections in this part examine this challenge and discuss policies for dealing with the existing systems for bulk power generation and transmission. Chapter 12, by George K. Lagassa, explains the logic of regional power grids and existing means for government regulation of electric utilities and specifies strategies for overcoming the centralizing bias of this logic. Chapter 13, by Peter W. Brown, Lawrence W. Plitch, and Martin Ringo, pursues this logic in greater depth by outlining the legal and institutional obstacles to small-scale hydropower development.

Chapter 14, by Janet B. Johnson and Richard T. Sylves, and chapter 15, by Kai N. Lee, both discuss bulk power electric systems from the perspective of their broader sociopolitical impacts. Johnson and Sylves portray the preemption of local prerogatives as a result of new state laws for power plant siting in the middle Atlantic region. They conclude that this phenomenon signals a radical diminution in the ability of citizens to influence important decisions which affect their daily lives. Kai Lee uses the example of the Pacific Northwest to illustrate the advantage of taking a regional approach to electric utility regulation. He recommends that the power available from the Bonneville Power Administration be used as a lever to encourage regional energy and natural resource conservation, energy subsidies to the poor, and energy-efficient economic development.

Finally, the chapter by Douglas N. Jones examines the new demands placed on state utility commissions by various provisions of the 1978 National Energy Act and explores the administrative questions associated with state implementation of federal policy.

12

Implementing the Soft Path in a Hard World: Decentralization and the Problem of Electric Power Grids

George K. Lagassa

Those who espouse diverse, small scale, renewable resources as a means to solve the energy crisis frequently point out that their proposed policy stratagems involve considerably more than converting to the use of unconventional energy resources and technologies. Rather, following the "soft path" implies a fundamental change in the sociopolitical and economic framework of the Western industrialized world. As such, it brings into question the very structure of the contemporary administrative state, the current distribution of wealth and power, and the political economy of transnational corporations and centralized high technology. Laced with tinges of antiindustrialism,[1] antiurbanism, and a heavy dose of antitechnology, it emerges as a global critique of modern Western society and a doctrine which is quite revolutionary in both content and implication.

The soft path doctrine may also be seen as a somewhat more focused coming-of-age of the protest movements of the 1960s. The "power to the people" rhetoric has changed, but the sentiment is the same. It is founded on the same sense of alienation and powerlessness as the movement of the 1960s, and its expected end results are very similar—decentralized government and administration, community control, and popular influence over the political and economic decisions that affect our daily lives.[2]

To any good democratic citizen, these are quite admirable goals. However, merely stating these goals or even developing the outlines of an alternative "soft path" runs the very real danger of being ignored. Indeed, the electric utility industry has gone to some effort to develop a comprehensive critique of Amory Lovins's soft path and has thoroughly convinced itself that, because the soft path is an overly romantic vision of an impossible energy future, it is justly deserving of disregard and oblivion.[3] This does not bode well for the successful implementation of soft path strategy, since the electric utility industry is the energy industry which would be most radically changed in any soft path scenario.

To overcome this resistance to unconventional energy alternatives and,

---

Portions of this chapter originally appeared in "State Utility Commissions as Vestigial Organs: The Need for Regional Governance of Electric Utilities," *Kansas Law Review* 28 (Winter 1980).

more importantly, to avoid the real possibility of being routinely ignored as utopian romantics, it is imperative that the soft path advocates develop a reasonable and realistic program of implementation. Such a program for achieving soft path goals will necessarily be constrained by what already exists and will, therefore, be something of a compromise. As such it will have to abandon the notion that the hard and soft paths are mutually exclusive and incompatible.[4] Given the political and economic power and the force of habit which sustains existing hard path energy strategies, such an either-or argument is destined to failure. A realistic program for the successful adoption of unconventional, small scale energy technologies cannot be revolutionary. Rather, it must be built on evolutionary change which gradually incorporates elements of the soft path into current systems for dispensing energy resources. Immediate scaling down of existing energy systems and decentralization of government regulation thereof is neither possible nor desirable.

To illustrate this point, the remainder of this chapter will examine the logic and historical rationale behind existing systems for the generation, transmission, and distribution of electric power in the United States. While electric power by no means exhausts the various types of centralized energy systems which exist in the Western industrialized world, choosing it for analysis in this context is justified by two factors. First, electric power is not itself a primary energy source. Rather, it is a major consumer of primary energy and is, as such, a major component of the conventional hard path energy strategy of the industrialized world. Present systems for fossil and nuclear fuel recovery, refinement, transportation, and storage all contribute to and support the rationale of existing systems for dispensing electric power. Second, electric power systems have been the subject of considerable criticism by soft path advocates. Regional power grids supported by huge base-load generating stations have, according to soft path critics, the following negative attributes: they do not match energy quality and scale to end-use needs and are therefore inefficient and inappropriate in their use of energy; they are fraught with infrastructure costs and associated diseconomies of scale which would be avoided by smaller scale energy systems; and they are administered by distant authorities which justify their decisions on the basis of their possession and control of specialized, technical information. In short, existing electric power systems are both the cornerstone and the epitome of hard path strategy.

A History of Scale Expansion in the Electric Utility Industry

When Thomas Edison's first power plant was built in New York City in 1882, the need for government involvement was minimal. Local government permission was required prior to the installation of power lines on or under city streets, but rate regulation was not yet seen as a necessity. Electric power users were primarily the well-to-do and were relatively small in number and, inasmuch as the industry was new, its prices were limited by its obligation to establish prices which were at least somewhat competitive with those for alternate energy sources. Thus, at its inception the electric utility industry was appropriately subject to local community control. However, as electric power began to be viewed as a necessity and not a luxury, the electric companies and their operations began to grow. In order to expand their markets, the companies had to make sizable capital investments, not only in generating capacity but also in transmission and distribution facilities. To prevent the unnecessary and potentially wasteful duplication of such facilities which would result from sales competition, the electric utilities were granted the status of natural monopolies—industries which operate more efficiently in a noncompetitive market. Thus, electric companies were granted the exclusive right to market power within particular geographic areas or franchise territories, and their prices were subject to government regulation in an effort to prevent monopoly status from leading to artificially high monopoly prices. As the industry became intercity in scope, it became apparent that such regulation should take place at the state level, and rate regulation by state commissions gradually became the accepted practice. The starting date for state regulation of electric utilities was 1907, when the New York State Public Service Commission was established and the Wisconsin Railroad Commission was granted authority over electric utilities. By 1922 such regulatory authority existed in all but one of the forty-eight states (Texas), and today it exists in all fifty states.

The important point to note here is that changing government regulatory authority was a response to and an attempt to keep up with changes in the technology and scale of the electric utility industry. As the industry became intercity in character, local control became inappropriate and state regulation became imperative, both to protect the consumer from being exploited by a natural monopoly and to assure investors of a fair return on their investments. Auxiliary to their prime function of rate regulation, state commissions were also typically granted two other controls over electric utilties. The authority to approve local franchises for the right to distribute power was intended to maintain efficient, contiguous "franchise territories"; and the authority to certify the need for proposed electric power generation and transmission facilities aimed to protect both the consumer and the investor by preventing industry overcapitalization.

Also noteworthy is the very limited extent of federal government involvement at this time. Under the 1920 Federal Water Power Act, the Federal Power Commission was established and granted licensing authority with respect to the construction of dams and reservoirs on navigable waters.

While the FPC clearly had some early influence over electric power development—coincidentally, over the largest power plants then technologically feasible—the principal purpose of the Federal Water Power Act was the promotion of navigation. More extensive federal government jurisdiction over electric utilities was simply not required by the existing scale of the industry. Thus the lion's share of electric utility regulation was accomplished at the state level.

Such regulation was adequate until the electric utilities began to sell power in interstate commerce. In 1927, in *Public Utilities Commission* v. *Attleboro Steam and Electric Company*,[5] the U.S. Supreme Court refused to allow the Rhode Island PUC to raise the rates on wholesale power charged by a Rhode Island company to a Massachusetts company on the grounds that "the regulation places a direct burden upon . . . interstate business [and] . . . is . . . beyond the power of the state . . . but if such regulation is required it can only be attained by the exercise of the power vested in Congress."

In resonse to this ruling, which created what came to be called the "Attleboro gap" (the absence of rate regulation for interstate power sales), Congress passed the Federal Power Act of 1935 (Title II of the Public Utility Act), which substantially expanded the authority of the Federal Power Commission by allowing them to regulate rates charged for wholesale power sold in interstate commerce. Again, government responded, this time a bit belatedly, to inadequacies in electric utility industry regulation caused by changes in the scale of operations of the industry.

Subsequent expansions in the scale of the electric utility industry were a fulfillment of the wishes of both the industry and the federal government. At least since the early 1920s, the electric utility industry has been enamored with the "superpower" concept—the notion of a large scale, strongly interconnected and coordinated electric power grid. The period 1920-1925 witnessed a variety of industry studies,[6] all of which predicted technological developments which would foster a gradually expanding scale of electric utility operations. Such technological breakthroughs as the development of high-strength, heat-resistant steel alloy, the development of boilers capable of containing supercritical steam pressures over 3,000 pounds per square inch, and the gradual advances in transmission technology fulfilled industry prophecy and encouraged the use of bigger and bigger generation and transmission facilities. Moreover, scale expansion was in no small way supported by the apparently insatiable American appetite for electric power, as U.S. electric power sales grew approximately twenty fold from 1935 to the present.[7]

This expansion in the size and scale of the industry has also been encouraged, though only halfheartedly until the 1960s, by federal government policy. In addition to granting rate regulatory authority sufficient to fill the

Attleboro gap, the 1935 Federal Power Act authorized the FPC to promote (though explicitly not to require) cooperation and coordination of services among fragmented electric utility systems, "for the purpose of assuring an abundant supply of electric energy throughout the United States with the greatest possible economy and with regard to the proper utilization and conservation of natural resources."[8]

Moreover, the Public Utility Holding Company Act of 1935 (Title I of the Public Utility Act of that year) did more than respond to the expanding economic scale of the electric utility industry. The act allowed the federal government to break up the concentration of economic power within the industry and to eliminate abuses resulting from pyramiding of equity investment and single corporate ownership of electric utilities and their equipment suppliers. Standards for holding company ownership of utility companies were established and the Securities and Exchange Commission (SEC) was given related enforcement powers. Most important for our purposes, the SEC was given the authority to prevent holding company acquisition of existing electric companies unless "such acquisition will serve the public interest by tending towards the economical and efficient development of an integrated public utility system." The act defined "integrated public utility system" as follows:

> . . . a system consisting of one or more units of generating plants and/or transmission lines and/or distribution facilities, whose utility assets . . . are physically interconnected or capable of physical interconnection and which under normal conditions may be economically operated as a single interconnected and coordinated system confined in its operations to a single area or region, *in one or more states*, not so large as to impair (considering the state of the art and the area or region affected) the advantages of localized management, efficient operation, and the effectiveness of regulation . . . [emphasis mine].[9]

In short, while the federal government wished to break up the concentration of economic power in the utility holding companies, which developed in the 1920s and the 1930s, the law made an explicit exception for holding companies which operated integrated regional electric systems.

Clearly, a combination of factors contributed to the gradual development of the huge multi-stage electric systems which characterize the electric utility industry today. Technological breakthroughs allowing considerable expansion in scale of operations, rapid growth in demand for and consumption of electricity, FPC authority to encourage voluntary interconnection and system coordination, and SEC authority to prevent utility mergers which did not tend toward the development of integrated public utility systems—all have contributed to the growth of multi-state regional electric systems in the United States. To these factors should be added TVA encouragement of scale expansion by example, the declining cost of electric power generation made possible by achieving new economies of scale from 1947-1967, and government subsidies for the development of nuclear power.

The Benefits of Integrated Electric Utility Systems

Certainly, the most important reasons for the development of integrated electric systems are to be found in the inherent technical and economic advantages of such scale expansion. The most obvious benefit of electric utility planning and operation on an integrated system basis is that it allows the achievement of economies of scale well beyond those which can be achieved by independent, isolated, substate franchise systems. Optimum power plant size, understood as that size which permits the generation of power at the lowest marginal cost, is considerably larger than that which is needed by most utility franchise systems. Therefore, the only way to capture these economies of scale is for two or more franchise systems to share the power generated at such huge plants. Simply put, it is cheaper to produce electricity in one large plant than in several small ones.

In addition to the basic savings in generation cost, several other specific advantages to the industry result from integrated power systems.

Decreased Operating Cost by Means of Economic Dispatch

In power pools which coordinate operations as well as planning, centralized dispatch allows the pool to respond to incremental load increases by generating additional power at those power plants where generation can be done at the lowest marginal cost. As demand continues to increase (or as peak load is approached), additional power is provided to the system by power plants with gradually increasing marginal operating costs. This assures that the most expensive power will not be used until it is absolutely necessary and results in a basic cost saving to the consumer.

Decreased Cost of Necessary Reserve Margin

Rational planning of power systems requires that every utility system, no matter how small or how large, must have more generating capacity than peak load. This is required to offset the uncertainty of peak load under certain conditions, the possibiity of unexpected equipment failures, and the need for scheduled equipment outages for routine maintenance purposes.[10]

The objective of having a margin of reserve capacity is to maintain optimum system reliability. More simply put, when we flick the switch, we expect the lights to go on primarily because the electric system is basically reliable. Where power systems are regionally planned and interconnected, the cost of reserve capacity can be shared and the aggregate system reserve requirement will be substantially lower than if reserve were planned on an individual company basis.

Decreased Cost of Serving Peak Load

Where two franchise systems experience peak load during different seasons or at different times of the day (load diversity), they can benefit by coordinating system planning and operation. Such coordination allows the effects of load diversity to be somewhat muted by mutual reciprocal assistance during peak load periods. In short, the burdens of peak load can be distributed among several electric companies, and peak load capacity within individual franchise areas does not have to be as high as it would be in the absence of such a sharing of burden. Furthermore, installed peak load capacity can be operational more frequently and can thus generate revenues rather than sit idle. In a manner of speaking, a portion of peak load within individual franchises can be treated as base load (constant demand) when looked upon from a broader regional perspective. This phenomenon in turn encourages the construction of much larger base load generating facilities, jointly financed by several companies, to provide service to several franchise areas or an entire region.

Given the obvious advantages of integrated power systems the Federal Power Commission's authority to encourage coordination and interconnection (pursuant to the 1935 Federal Power Act) seems largely unnecessary. We would expect that electric utilities would voluntarily form power pools or coordinated groups in rational response to very real economic incentives. To a certain extent, this is true. During the 1950s and early 1960s system interconnection was proceeding, though, in retrospect, at a relatively slow pace. The Tennessee Valley Authority and the American Electric Power Company, blessed by the advantage of single ownership and management, did strengthen their own internal interconnections across a wide geographic area. The Pennsylvania-New Jersey-Maryland power pool (PJM) was formed, and during the late 1950s informal coordination among New York State's electric companies did result in a decision to strengthen the transmission grid of the late 1940s by overlaying it with 345 Kv bulk power transmission lines to be operational by the early 1960s.[11]

Apparently the FPC believed that progress toward full system integration was adequate, since it did not very avidly pursue its authority to encourage coordination and interconnection until the 1960s, with the preparation of the 1964 *National Power Survey*.[12] Although the form and content of the survey clearly encouraged the strengthening of regional power networks to assure service rehability, it came too late to prevent the 1965 Northeast power failure. This cascading power failure, which covered the greater part of six northeastern states for up to seven and a half hours, was caused by inadequate regional interconnections within the Canada-United States Eastern Interconnection (CANUSE).[13] Probably its most important consequence was that it prompted the FPC to make use of its authority under the Federal Power Act to encourage electric system integration. This they did by calling for the development of explicit utility company agreements and coordinating organizations on a regional basis. The FPC report on the blackout encouraged the strengthening of transmission interconnections within and among regions[14] and resulted in the establishment of the National Electric Reliability Council and nine constituent regional reliability councils in 1968 (see figure 12-1). These regional reliability councils, which exist primarily for planning and not operating purposes, are supplemented by other somewhat smaller but tighter coordinating organizations. These organizations engage in varying degrees of operating cooperation and range from holding companies with central dispatch (the American Electric Power System, the Tennessee Valley Authority, the Southern Company, and Commonwealth Edison, and Central Illinois), to power pools with central dispatch in which participating companies are independently owned (New England Power Pool, New York Power Pool, Pennsylvania-New Jersey-Maryland Interconnection, the Michigan Pool, Cincinnati-Columbus-Dayton Pool, Illinois-Missouri Pool, and Interconnected Utilities of Eastern Wisconsin), to loosely coordinated systems without central dispatch (such as the Rocky Mountain Power Pool, the Eastern Missouri Basin Power System, the Central Area Power Coordination Group, and others).

In the context of our discussion of the viability of soft path strategies for electric power, it is important to note what the FPC chose not to recommend after the 1965 blackout. A little-known fact about the blackout is that the two areas that were most weakly interconnected to the CANUSE system were able to avoid the power failure. Because southeastern New Hampshire and Maine and the state of Michigan were each connected to the regional system by only one high-voltage line each, they were able to disconnect before the power surge reached them and therefore prevent a cascading failure of their respective systems.

This fact, which was by no means emphasized in the FPC report, suggests that a rational response to the blackout would have been to encourage other power systems within CANUSE to weaken their interconnections, and thus lessen the vulnerability associated with interdependence. Such a recommendation would have pointed away from the development of regional

WSCC	Western Systems Coordinating Council	NPCC	Northeast Power Coordinating Council
MARCA	Mid-Continent Area Reliability Coordination Agreement	MAAC	Mid-Atlantic Area Coordination Group
SPP	Southwest Power Pool	ECAR	East Central Area Reliability Coordination Agreement
ERCOT	Electric Reliability Council of Texas		
MAIN	Mid-America Interpool Network	SERC	Southeastern Electric Reliability Council

Source: Federal Power Commission, *National Power Survey: A Report* (Washington, D.C.: U.S. Government Printing Office, 1970), p. I-17-16.

Figure 12-1. National Electric Reliability Council Regions, Canadian portions not included

transmission grids and toward decentralized franchise and/or community self-sufficiency. Regardless, the FPC report called for a strengthening of regional system integration. The reason for this recommendation should be obvious from what was said above. That is, to have counseled a policy of franchise self-sufficiency would have meant foregoing the economies of scale which result from regional interconnection and would certainly have undermined the trend, popular with consumers, of decreasing real prices for electric power from 1947-1967. Moreover, while there are dangers in broad regional interdependence, there are also advantages of increased system reliability in an adequately interconnected system. The FPC reasoned that the actual advantages of system integration outweighed its possible disadvantages and that the possibility of future cascading power failures could, in any event, be guarded against by improved coordination of utility operations and proper facilities planning and construction.

As a lesson in bureaucratic policymaking, it is equally important that the FPC's recommendation was dictated by the prior industry commitment (in the form of extensive capital investments) to regional interconnection. A policy of franchise self-sufficiency would have meant the abandonment of these investments and would have been contrary to prevailing attitudes in the industry, as well as at least twenty years of prior electric company behavior. Significantly, this all transpired at a time when system integration was relatively weak and underdeveloped. That a policy of immediate decentralization would be deemed feasible today, after a decade and a half of subsequent scale expansion and system integration, is quite unlikely; and those who advocate this policy are deluding themselves by believing otherwise. In fact, as we shall see in the next section, the trend has been toward increasing centralization of governmental regulatory authority as a response and an accommodation to the needs of regional power networks.

Facilities Siting and Environmental Protection

After the 1965 blackout, the electric utility industry embarked on its biggest capital development program effort to date. To this end, numerous power companies scheduled the construction of huge power plants (many of them nuclear) and associated extra-high-voltage transmission facilities, most of which were planned on a regional basis. Given the large size of these proposed facilities, it became quite obvious that they were not primarily designed to serve the needs of the localities in which they were being sited. County and municipal governments, pushed by grass-roots citizens' organizations and further encouraged by the growing environmental awareness of the American public, mobilized to prevent the construction of many of these facilites. At the disposal of the opponents were numerous weapons for delaying and obstructing the installation of electric power facilities—local zoning requirements, local building permits, and increasing numbers of environmental protection regulations at all levels of govern-

The electric companies were simply unable effectively to plan new facilities in this environment of legal and political uncertainty and pushed for one-stop siting procedures at the state level as a means to preempt the numerous and diverse state and local requirements. For their part, the environmentalists saw one-stop siting as an opportunity for the creation of a single forum for early-public participation in siting decisions and for presenting a united front to the utility companies. As a result, the early 1970s witnessed the enactment of a number of state laws formalizing and partially consolidating previously fragmented procedures *at the state level*. In most states, political compromise dictated the creation of a new state agency for energy facility certification, in addition to the state public utility regulatory commission.

Because state siting laws are preemptive of local regulations, they were not passed without substantial controversy. This is not surprising, since the need for such laws is derived from a classic problem of democratic theory—the conflict between individual or minority rights and the welfare of the majority. State siting laws come down decidedly in favor of the latter. That is, the environmental and aesthetic costs of huge power plants and transmission lines are borne by the localities in which they are sited and are thus suffered by a minority, while the benefits go elsewhere—to the region as a whole or to urban areas where spatial limits prevent local siting. State siting laws create a new forum for debating facility siting, which forum allows the statewide or urban interest in reliable electric power service to be stated with greater force and legitimacy. Pastoral rural environments are thus less able to resist the demand that they accept a power plant or transmission line which provides no obvious or direct countervailing benefits. I, for one, regret that this state of affairs has to exist, but I am not convinced that it could be any other way. The fact is that we live in a highly urbanized and interdependent world, and no amount of antiurban sentiment is going to change that. Unless we choose to follow the Cambodian strategy of coercively depopulating the cities, it is predictable that rural communities will continue to be obliged to compromise their life-styles for the benefit of larger urban populations. Barring revolution, adoption of the Cambodian model in this country is highly unlikely. In any event, its coercive and authoritarian aspects are clearly undesirable.

The Need for More Centralized Regulatory Authority

Once we accept the reality of our urban industrial economy, we are driven to accept (or at least tolerate) more centralized power plant siting procedures. In fact, given that the electric utility industry is planned, and in some places operated, on a regional basis, we are led to question whether state-based siting procedures are centralized enough. When viewed from the regional perspective which the industry itself is increasingly adopting, state siting procedures, far from being too centralized, are insufficiently centralized. Thus, a 1976 report of the New England Regional Commission was critical of the fact that although the state organizations for power facility evaluation in New England have attempted to address the full spectrum of issues related to facility siting, they have done so only on a state by state basis. The structures that have evolved are not conducive to the establishment of a standardized power facility planning and evaluation process.[15]

Several potential and actual problems result from this suboptimum administrative arrangement.

First, the existence of a multiplicity of state-by-state power facility licensing procedures disallows the authoritative selection of the best possible site in the region. One advantage of power pooling, reduction of the environmental costs of power production by the selection of the site which offers the least environmental impact, is foregone. To capture this advantage requires regional coordination.

Second, state governments may authorize power plants and transmission facilities which are wasteful and duplicative when viewed from a regional perspective. More likely, in the era of the "anywhere but here" attitude, states may fail to authorize facilities which are needed as part of a regional network.

Third, the establishment of state-based energy facility siting agencies, in addition to existing regulatory commissions, has created a new form of fragmentation. Rate setting and facility siting are administratively separated, thus discouraging effective assessment of new rate designs which encourage conservation as an alternative to additional capacity. Moreover, once the new facilities are erected, the discretion of the rate setting authorities is substantially limited, as such facilities automatically figure in to rate base.

A similar concern was voiced with respect to the more general electric utility regulatory activities of state utility commissions in the FPC's report on the 1965 Northeast power failure.

> When the Federal Power Act was passed . . . no special provision was made for jurisdiction over reliability of service for bulk power supply from interstate grids, the focus of the act being rather on accounting and rate regulation. Presumably the reason was that service reliability was regarded as a problem for the states. Insofar as service by distribution systems is concerned, this is still valid, but the enormous development of interstate power networks in the last thirty years requires a reevaluation of the governmental responsibility for continuity of the service supplied by them, since it is impossible for a single state effectively to regulate the service from an interstate pool or grid.[16]

In line with this recommendation, the FPC requested in 1969 that Congress grant it authority to compel coordination and interconnection on its own motion, when it would improve service reliability.[17] Despite the obvious benefits to the utilities of voluntary interconnection, the FPC argued that the electric utility industry needed to be pushed toward system integration. Only with the authority to require interconnection and joint planning and operations, the FPC argued, could government overcome occasional industry reticence which may result from divergent managerial philosophies in different companies, different fuels policies in different states, conflicting management personalities, and possible incentives for overcapitalization by electric companies. The industry itself was opposed to any such expansion of government regulatory authority and Congress therefore failed to grant this authority for over a decade. However, congressional attitudes about the proper role of the federal government began to change as crude oil prices climbed and gas lines lengthened. Finally, in 1978, the Public Utility Regulatory Policies Act (PURPA),[18] one of the five acts which comprise the National Energy Act, substantially increased the authority of the Federal Energy Regulatory Commission (which replaced the FPC as a result of the 1977 Energy Reorganization Act) to order interconnections on its own motion and to otherwise encourage pooling and industry rationalization.

Implications for the Soft Path

At least on the surface, this provision of PURPA is the epitome of hard path strategy. It serves to further centralize authority over electric utilities at the federal level; puts this authority in the hands of distant technical experts who are insulated from popular control; and, by encouraging power pooling, sustains the need for huge fossil fuel and nuclear bulk power plants and associated transmission facilities. While this is all quite true, as the above argument should have made clear, it is also inevitable. The constraints of prevailing industry and public bureaucratic attitudes, prior financial commitments, and the political influence of the industry converged to prevent any substantially different result. Given this fait accompli, soft path activists have two responsibilities: first, to build on the advantages of more centralized government authority by using it to serve soft path goals; and, second, to guard against the presumption in favor of large scale generation facilities (built into regional power networks) even when demand for electric power could be more appropriately served by smaller scale (domestic and commercial) and cogeneration facilities.

With respect to the first responsibility, the reasoning is very simple. The electric utility industry has been very resistant to the soft path strategy. Therefore, implementation of such a strategy will have to be forced on the industry by government. Because the lion's share of electric utility regulatory duties (most rate setting, power plant siting, and related need for power determinations) are the responsibility of the states, regulators are not in a very strong position to foist soft path strategies on the industry, which is largely organized on a multi-state, regional basis. Conversely, since the geographic scope of state jurisdiction is smaller than that of actual utility planning and operations, the industry is in quite a strong position to resist particular soft path strategies.

For example, according to Lovins, electric utility rate structures should be redesigned in such a way as to encourage greater conservation of electric power. Declining block rates, which provide cheaper rates to large users, should be replaced by flat or inverted rates.[19] Peak load rates should be instituted in order to flatten the demand curve for electric power and thereby eliminate the need for additional standby capacity. While implementing these innovative rate designs on a state-by-state basis cannot hurt, such an approach not only limits the aggregate effectiveness of these innovations but also creates certain inequities, the potential for which serves to undermine the support for such rate changes. The abolition of declining block rates will not be supported by industry in state A if they perceive that they will be at a competitive disadvantage relative to industry in a neighboring state which continues to be allowed to consume substantially the same power at a lower rate. Indeed some industries may threaten to pack up and leave for a different state where the utilities commission is more friendly. Likewise, peak load pricing by one state in a multi-state power grid may have only a limited impact on aggregate peak demand if other states do not follow suit, especially if demand is relatively equal in the several states in the region.[20] Why should state A accept the burden and inconvenience of such a rate design when state B, which uses substantially the same power, does not? Establishing such rate innovations on a regional basis would overcome these disadvantages.

The Carter administration's 1977 proposals for a nationwide rate structure[21] based on conservation-inducing designs would have overcome these problems, though without accounting for regional variations. While this proposal was somewhat compromised in PURPA, the notion of uniformity of rate designs across state lines was not totally abandoned.

Specifically, under PURPA state PUCs are required, within three years, to consider and publicly justify their respective rejection or acceptance of six federal rate making standards, as follows: (1) rates charged each class of electric consumer must reflect the actual cost of providing electric service to that class, (2) declining block rates should be abolished, (3) rates should reflect the cost of providing service at different times of the day, (4) rates should reflect the cost of service during different seasons, (5) industrial and commercial customers should be offered the opportunity to pay lower, interruptible service rates, and (6) utilities should utilize load management techniques which are practicable and cost effective and which are likely to reduce peak load requirements. In addition, PURPA established five mandatory standards, including a prohibition against master metering in new buildings, specific limits on automatic adjustment clauses, and a prohibition against rate-supported political and promotional advertising. The Secretary of Energy is also authorized to intervene in state rate making proceedings in order to advocate any of the above standards or any other conservation-inducing rate designs or techniques.

While it is too early to predict the impact of these provisions, it is probably safe to say that the advantages of rate uniformity as a means of soft path ends are relatively small. However, this is not to say that they are insignificant. The soft path advocates should make extensive use of the public participation provisions of PURPA[22] to urge the adoption of conservation-inducing rate designs on as wide a basis as possible.

One other way to make positive use of the further centralization of government authority which is required to assure adequate public control over regional power grids is to seek legislation or regulations which guarantee broad public and private access to these grids. One of the major obstacles to small scale electric generation facilities is the unreliability of supply which characterizes such approaches. The availability of power from a small scale hydropower facility will vary seasonally. Surplus power will be generated during spring runoff but will probably be inadequate for local needs during the winter months, when many rivers and streams are frozen, or during summer months, when hot, dry weather may lower the power potential of many streams. Likewise, generation of power by small scale solar or windpower installations or by means of cogeneration, either commercially or domestically, is subject to the same instability. If such facilities are connected to the regional transmission network, the users which they supply can be guaranteed a reliable supply of electricity. During periods of surplus, excess power can be sold to the grid or wheeled (transmitted by a third party) to another consumer. During periods of power deficiency, power can be purchased, via the grid, from a commercial utility. Guaranteeing access to the grid by small scale generators merely provides the same reliability advantages to all power producers that has previously been enjoyed only by the large utility companies. Increased reliability is, after all, a major justification for the existence of regional grids. The above suggestion merely asks the question, "Reliability for whom?" and suggests that the answer should be "Everyone."

Actually, the above recommendation is far more profound than it might appear on the surface. By suggesting that small scale power generating facilities can make an economically justifiable contribution to total power supply, it runs quite counter to the notion that electric power can be provided economically only when it benefits from economies of scale. In fact, what my argument suggests is that the chief benefits from large scale obtain primarily with respect to transmission and not generation.

If we carry this argument one step further, we can see that certain aspects of the earlier natural monopoly argument are quite questionable. We have already seen that one of the major benefits of regional system integration is the ability to capture economies of scale in generation which are foregone by isolated, local franchise systems. We have also seen that the potential for such economies of scale was a major justification, in addition to that of avoiding wasteful duplication of transmission and distribution facilities, for treating electric utilities as natural monopolies.[23] Curiously, this argument has never been convincingly made with respect to oil refineries or the automobile industry, both of which also involve huge capital investment and benefit from similar economies of scale. Nor is it made with respect to natural gas producers by those who advocate deregulation of natural gas prices. These examples suggest that the generation of electric power may not in fact be a naturally monopolistic industry and that only the transmission and distribution systems of the electric utility industry logically require natural monopoly status. Especially today, with the distribution and transmission infrastructure of the industry largely in place, access to markets is almost unlimited; and there is no theoretical reason why a condition of competition, or at least monopolistic competition, could not be established with respect to generation of power. To achieve this condition would, of course, require the vertical divestiture of the electric utility industry so that generation, transmission, and distribution of electric power would be done by separate companies. The price of power at the generating station could conceivably be deregulated while transmission systems would be subject to federal or regional regulatory jurisdiction and distribution to state, substate district, or local jurisdiction. Under this arrangement, the transmission grid would be the electric power counterpart to the natural gas pipeline system. Major generating companies as well as smaller independent companies would have complete access to the transmission system and would be free to sell electricity to anyone on the regional system who finds it economically feasible to sign a contract.

Obviously the likelihood that such vertical divestiture will take place in the near future is infinitesimally small. Aside from the technical and administrative difficulties of maintaining system reliability under conditions which would militate against coordination of generation facilities planning, the industry would be quite unwilling to give up its monopolistic position. Nevertheless, the suggestion is a useful one because it serves to clarify the advantage which existing electric utilities have over other small scale electrical generating companies. Monopolistic control of transmission and distribution by the same companies engaged in generating power can be an effective tool for preventing competition from small scale producers, municipal utility systems, or rural cooperatives who are denied access to the transmission grid. Moreover, if pooling really does capture otherwise foregone economies of scale, then smaller companies which are not parties to pooling agreements must charge higher rates than pool members and may subsequently find themselves at a disadvantage in the competition for investment funds.

That the electric companies are willing to use their monopolistic position to prevent new competition is illustrated by the refusal of the Otter Tail Power Company "to sell or wheel wholesale power to municipalities formerly served at retail,"[24] despite the expiration of their franchise agreements with those communities. Although the U.S. Supreme Court upheld, on antitrust grounds, a lower court's order "for wheeling to correct Otter Tail's anticompetitive and monopolistic practices,"[25] one of the four towns involved in the litigation backed down and renewed its Otter Tail franchise before the lower court made its ruling.

Certain provisions of PURPA are implicitly based on the antitrust implications of transmission networks, and therefore aim to provide greater access to the grids by small scale power producers, particularly hydropower facilities. Specifically, FERC is authorized to order interconnections on its own motion or the request of specified applicants, including any electric utility (which would include smaller investor-owned companies, municipals, and rural cooperatives), small power producers (80 Mw or less), and cogenerators. Providing access to the grid will no doubt overcome a major obstacle to the generation of electricity with waste heat from industrial processes (cogeneration) or by small producers using solar, wind, biomass, waste, or other renewable resources. Presumably this provision of PURPA will be applied to surplus electricity generated at individual households by means of photovoltaic cells, fuel cells, or windmills, though this will be determined by the specific regulations established by FERC pursuant to PURPA.

Significantly, PURPA does not authorize FERC to order a utility to provide wheeling services (that is, third-party transmission services from producer to consumer) for small producers. Wheeling orders are to follow only upon the application of an electric utility or federal power marketing agency (such as TVA or the Bonneville Power Administration). Explicitly excluded from the qualified applicants are small scale producers and cogenerators. Moreover, no power, from whatever source, may be wheeled directly to its ultimate consumer. This means, in effect, that the utility which provides the wheeling service will purchase power from the producer requesting the wheeling service and itself sell power to the ultimate consumer or another utility company. This provision is explicitly designed to prevent price competition between utilities. In the words of the conference report on PURPA,

the conferees do not intend that the commission order wheeling which significantly alters the competitive relationships among utilities in competition with one another for the same customers.[26]

Clearly PURPA was not motivated by a desire to bring into question the natural monopoly status of the existing electric utility industry. As we shall see, Congress was equally unwilling to confer the advantages of this status on small scale producers.

Given the exclusion of small-scale producers and cogenerators from the wheeling provisions of PURPA, all power sold by small scale producers must be sold to the local utility company, which will in turn resell it to the ultimate consumer. Obviously, the price to the ultimate consumer will be somewhat higher, given the presence of the utility company as a middleman in any power transactions. This means that, to be competitive with power produced by utility companies, the cost of power generated at small scale facilities must be less than that generated at utility company facilities, making the economic feasibility test that much more difficult for small scale facilities to pass. To overcome this problem, soft path advocates should urge amendments to PURPA which would allow the provision of direct wheeling services to small scale producers. Although the cost to the ultimate consumer will still include a wheeling charge, it will not include middleman charges on the product itself and will therefore provide a more favorable climate for the economical harnessing of small scale energy resources.

Short of this amendment, soft path advocates should become actively involved in FERC regulation setting procedures to assure that the prices which are paid by utilities for power from independently owned small scale facilities are not disadvantageous for the small scale producer.

Given the monopsonistic position of the local utility purchasing power from small scale generators or cogenerators, PURPA subjects this power for resale to federal rate regulation. Unfortunately the PURPA standards for these rates are both vague and contradictory. The vague standards apply to the upper limit on the rates which may be paid for such power—they are not to exceed "the incremental cost to the electric utility of alternative electric energy."[27] The conference report clarifies this vague standard somewhat in favor of the small scale producer by suggesting that "alternative electric energy" should not be understood as being limited to "alternative sources which are instantaneously available to the utility,"[28] but should include alternative sources which may have to be made available in the future. The contradictory standards pertain to the far more important lower limit on rates to be paid small-scale producers. Specifically, PURPA requires that the rate paid "shall not discriminate against cogenerators" or "small power producers,"[29] and therefore should not be too low; but at the same time, it shouldn't be so high as not to be "just and reasonable to the electric consumers of the electric utility" or "in the public interest."[30] In explaining this point, the conference report made it quite clear that Congress did not want the consumer to be obliged to subsidize the small scale producer and that the small scale producer is not to be assured a guaranteed rate of return, as are the utilities.

Clearly, members of Congress are considerably more equivocal with respect to what should be the lower limit on these rates than they are with respect to the upper limit. Since it is precisely this lower limit which will determine the economic feasibility of particular small scale projects, it is absolutely imperative that soft path advocates monitor and participate in, to the maximum possible extent, related FERC rule making procedures and subsequent rate making cases.

The chief danger to be guarded against by soft path strategies for dealing with regional power grids is the presumption that interconnected networks require only huge generating facilities. Various provisions of PURPA—including additional provisions for financing the planning and construction of small-scale hydropower projects[31]—offer considerable ammunition for combating this "big is beautiful" (or even necessary) attitude on the part of the electric utility industry. To make sure that this ammunition is not wasted, the advocates of diverse, small scale, renewable resources should become actively involved in the implementation of PURPA at both the state and federal levels.

Beyond the strategies discussed above, some additional effort should be made to curtail the unquestioned growth of regional power grids beyond that which we already have or which is necessary to take full advantage of existing (or soon to be on line) generating capacity. The fact remains that, economic efficiency notwithstanding, electric power grids are not energy efficient. After conversion and transmission losses, less than half the potential energy of primary low entropy fuels is put to use via interconnected grids. I have already argued that to scrap these facilities would be equally if not more wasteful. They are realities which we must accept and adapt to. This does not mean, however, that we should not discourage their unnecessary growth.

The increasing scarcity and related high costs of the fuels which fire the largest power plants will no doubt change the economies of scale of these facilities and lessen their economic advantages relative to small scale facilities using renewable, and therefore less costly, resources. But the "big is beautiful" attitude is certain to have staying power, and the soft path advocates should make every effort to prevent this outdated idea from becoming operational. To this end, soft path advocates should seek to enact or otherwise support public policies which encourage careful energy accounting and more efficient alternatives to centralized power production. For example, total energy systems which not only generate electricity on a small scale basis but also use waste heat for neighborhood or building space heating are based on a broader view of what is economical and have proved quite feasible for apartment buildings in New York City as well as in numerous neighborhoods and districts in Scandinavian nations.[32]

Total energy systems are, of course, quite threatening to the monopoly position of the electric utility industry. Industry opposition was made obvious as early as 1968, when the Edison Electric Institute established a "Program to Combat Isolated Generation"[32] aimed at counteracting the growing popularity of total energy systems at that time. The program apparently had some effect as, after learning that the designers of the World Trade Center in New York were planning to heat and light the two WTC buildings with a total energy system, Consolidated Edison Company of New York offered special promotional rates too low to be passed up. Thus the World Trade Center gets all of its electricity from Con Ed. As a result, at least one new bulk power plant was required in upstate New York, and several new extra-high-voltage transmission lines had to be added to the transmission network. These new facilities would have been quite unnecessary if the World Trade Center had been supplied by means of a total energy system.

Soft path advocates should begin to take action now to prevent the recurrence of such needless waste in the future. Such an effort might have been futile in the 1960s, but now that the cost of new power plants is so extraordinarily high and the utility industry can no longer hold out the promise of lower electric rates, the time is ripe for a soft path counteroffensive. Beyond encouraging new state laws designed specifically to prohibit promotional rates such as those used by Con Ed to make the World Trade Center its customer, soft path advocates can also make use of the National Environmental Policy Act and comparable state laws which require environmental impact statements for virtually every large power plant being built in this country. Specifically, environmental impact should be interpreted so as to include impact on energy resource conservation, thereby allowing the inefficiencies of huge power plants and associated transmission grids to be brought into the discussions of the proposed facilities.

Conclusion

The core of the above argument has been that, their obviously hard path implications notwithstanding, regional electric power grids are an accomplished fact and should be accepted as such. Considerable resources have already been devoted to their construction, and to scrap them now would not only be politically unfeasible but also economically and thermodynamically wasteful. Thus, the soft path advocate must adapt to the reality of centralized power grids by supporting new structures designed to bring regional grids under adequate public control. Moreover, every effort should be made to assure that access to the grid system remains open to all electric power generators, including small scale producers (domestic and commercial alike), cogenerators, small utility companies, municipals, and rural cooperatives. More specific elements of these strategies are listed under "Adaptive Strategies" in table 12-1.

Table 12-1
Realistic Strategies for Implementing Diverse, Small-Scale, Renewable Resources for Generating Electric Power

Adaptive Strategies
Urge more centralized government control over regional power grids.

Encourage uniformity of rate design for inducing electric power conservation within regions.
   Use PURPA presumptions in favor of conservation inducing rate designs.
   Participate in related FERC rule making proceedings and subsequent state and federal rate cases

Counteract presumption in favor of big generating facilities built into regional system concept by working to guarantee access to grid by small scale producers
   Participate in FERC proceedings on interconnection and wheeling orders
   Participate in FERC rule making proceedings on rates to be paid for power from small scale generating facilities.

Assure full development of small scale generating facilities
   Lobby for complete appropriation of authorized funding for federal planning and construction loans for small scale hydroelectric facilities

Affirmative Strategies
Work toward discrediting natural monopoly argument with respect to electric power generation.
   Amend PURPA to allow direct wheeling of power from producer to ultimate consumer

Urge legislation or regulations to prohibit promotional rates which discourage total energy systems

Urge legislation which will provide financial incentives or a facilitating structure to help finance high initial capital costs of total energy systems.

Make use of environmental impact statement requirements to show availability of total energy systems as an alternative to additional bulk power generating facilities.

Beyond accepting what is and adapting to it as best as possible, soft path advocates should question the logic of regional power systems and show their inappropriateness for certain purposes, not the least of which is efficient use of primary energy supply. Coeval with this effort should be another one to prevent unnecessary additional scale expansions in the electric utility industry. To this end, total energy systems should, where appropriate, be encouraged as a means for servicing new demand for electric power, instead of additional bulk power generating facilities. Specific strategies for accomplishing these goals are listed under "Affirmative Strategies" in table 12-1.

Any realistic assessment of this country's energy future during the next twenty to fifty years must include elements of both the hard and the soft path approaches. In the long term, it is very likely that something like the soft path will become dominant. However, in the shorter term, a rational soft path strategy for a transition to the new era must adapt to, not destroy, existing hard path systems.

Notes

1. See Ian A. Forbes, "Energy Strategy: Not What but How," unpublished manuscript, Energy Research Group, Belmont, Mass., March 21, 1977.

2. For a statement of this position see Kenneth A. Megill, *The New Democratic Theory* (New York, 1970), and "The Port Huron Statement," reprinted in parts in Mitchell Cohen and Dennis Hale, eds., *The New Student Left: An Anthology* (Boston, 1967).

3. Edison Electric Institute, "A Series of Critical Essay On Amory Lovins' 'Energy Strategy: The Road Not Taken?'" *Electric Perspective* No. 7713 (New York: E.E.I., 1977).

4. As is explicitly stated in Amory B. Lovins, "Energy Strategy: The Road Not Taken?" *Foreign Affairs*, October 1976, pp. 65-66.

5. 273 U.S. 83.

6. These included a "Super-Power Survey of the Washington-Boston District" prepared jointly by the federal government and a number of major east coast electric companies, and similar studies done by the Transmission Committee of the Empire State Electric and Gas Association, the Super-Power Committee of the Pacific Northwest, the Power Survey Committee of the Great Lakes Division of the National Electric Light Association, and the Giant Power Survey of Pennsylvania.

7. See Edwin Berlin, Charles J. Cichetti, and William J. Gillen, *Perspectives on Power: A Study of the Regulation and Pricing of Electric Power* (Cambridge, Mass.: Ballinger, 1974), chapter 1.

8. 16 U.S.C. 824a(a).

9. 15 U.S.C. 79b(a)(29)(A).

10. This argument is reminiscent of that made with respect to administrative systems in general in Martin Landau, "Redundancy, Rationality, and the Problem of Duplication and Overlap," *Public Administration Review* 29 (July-August 1969).

11. Direct Testimony of Harry G. Saddock, Engineer, Niagara Mohawk Power Corporation, Public Hearings on the proposed 765 kV Transmission line from Pannell to Volney, New York, Pursuant to Article VII of the New York State Public Service Law, p. HGS-5.

12. Federal Power Commission, *National Power Survey: A Report* (Washington, D.C.: U.S. Government Printing Office, 1964).

13. Federal Power Commission, *Northeast Power Failure, November 9 and 10, 1965: A Report to the President*, December 6, 1965.

14. Ibid., p. 9.

15. New England Regional Commission, *Power Facility Siting Guide-Lines in New England*, Energy Program Technical Report 75-8 (Boston, 1976), p. II-40.

16. FPC, *Northeast Power Failure*, p. 6.

17. See Section 202 of the Federal Power Act (16 U.S.C. 824), which grants authority to compel such interconnection and coordination only in an emergency and only on a temporary basis.

18. P.L. 95-617.

19. Lovins, p. 75.

20. For a theoretical discussion of when an individual is motivated to provide collective goods, see Mancur Olson, *The Logic of Collective Action* (Cambridge, Mass.: Harvard Univ. Press, 1971).

21. See *Congressional Quarterly Almanac* 33 (1977):708-745. President Carter's entire energy package, as originally proposed, is outlined in his April 20, 1977, address to a joint session of Congress.

22. PURPA, P.L. 95-617, November 9, 1978, 92 Stat. 3117, sections 121-124, 212.

23. See David H. Davis, *Energy Politics*, 2nd ed. (New York, 1978), p. 143.

24. 410 U.S. 366, see also *Gainesville Utilities Department et al.* v. *Florida Power Corporation*, 402 U.S. 515.

25. Ibid.

26. Conference Report to Accompany H.R. 4018, House of Representatives Report No. 95-1750, October 10, 1978, p. 92.

27. PURPA, section 210(b).

28. Conference Report, p. 99.

29. PURPA, section 210(b).

30. Ibid.

31. Ibid., Title IV.

32. See Wilson Clark, *Energy for Survival: The Alternative to Extinction* (New York: Anchor Books, 1975), pp. 233-244.

33. Reported in "Do-It-Yourself Power Catches On," *Business Week*, November 30, 1968, pp. 62-64.

13

Obstacles and Incentives to Small-Scale Hydroelectric Power

Peter W. Brown,
Lawrence W. Plitch, and
Martin Ringo

There is perhaps no energy technology as well developed and unburdened by technical immaturity as that associated with small scale hydroelectric power. With the development of the water turbine in 1832 and the establishment of the first hydroelectric power station in Appleton, Wisconsin, in 1882, water power as a source of electricity became an early reality. The reaction-type turbine, as perfected by Francis, and which now bears his name, established itself as the leader in the field of low-head hydroelectric technology by 1875; and, by 1932, the use of hydroelectric power in the United States had reached a peak of 41.4 percent of the total installed electric generating capacity in the country.

Unlike the newer technologies, such as photovoltaics, nuclear fusion, and synthetic fuels, which await their crest on the learning curve, small-scale hydro (SSH) facilities have been producing electricity for over a century and have been producing mechanical power since as far back as the ancient Egyptians. As a result, there are thousands of existing SSH dams scattered among our hills and valleys which are substantially intact and which were abandoned only during the last thirty years as a result of the cumulative effect of the relatively cheap fossil fuels and increased steam generation efficiencies.

These abandoned sites offer a unique and valuable resource in our efforts to serve energy needs and demands, and the advantages which they offer over the alternatives are quite substantial. Moreover, existing sites offer obvious advantages over other, yet to be developed, SSH locations. First, because they are previously used resources, an initial determination of the sufficiency of the rate of water flow and head size (distance from impounded water level to level of water below the dam) has already been made. Second, the refurbishing of small existing dams has little or no harmful effect on the environment, especially when compared to the construction of a new impoundment. Finally, the existence of a substantial portion of the necessary power structures will eliminate an otherwise significant amount of construction and engineering expense.

Given these and other advantages, substantial effort has already been devoted to determining the power potential and availability of the numerous SSH sites still existing in the United States today. The first resource assessment study completed was the now famous "Ninety Day Study"[1] conducted by Richard McDonald of the Institute of Water Resources and formerly director of the Small-Scale Hydroelectric Program of the U.S. Department of Energy. This study, which comprised a first cut analysis of the resource in the United States, indicated that the maximum potential for small-scale hydroelectric development at existing dams in the United States was 54,600 megawatts of capacity with an expected energy production of 159.3 billion kilowatt hours of electric energy per year (assuming a 33 percent plant factor for the subject facilities). The energy product of the resource represented an oil consumption equivalent of 727,000 barrels of oil per day (assuming an average thermal efficiency of 40 percent in oil-fired plants and an equivalency factor of 600 KWh/barrel of oil), well in excess of the 300,000 to 400,000 barrels per day that was the shortfall during the oil and gasoline shortage of June-July 1979. Moreover, that same barrel equivalency figure represents 8 percent of U.S. oil imports from OPEC nations at its zenith in 1977. The report further pointed out that a large segment of the resource was located in the New England area and in the Pacific Northwest region.

At the present time, the institute (which is administered by the Army Corps of Engineers and is located in Belvoir, Virginia) is conducting a follow-up national hydropower survey, intended to refine the information provided by the original "Ninety Day Study." Having collected additional data and undertaken further analysis, the corps now projects capacity of 5,700 megawatts producing 17 billion kilowatt hours of energy annually at existing sites and 7,600 megawatts of capacity producing 27 billion kilowatt hours of energy annually at undeveloped sites. These totals, which are the subject of continuing refinement, translate to a daily savings of 200,907 barrels of oil per day.

The further refinements indicated above are being carried out within the regions of the nation. For example, the New England River Basins Commission is continuing to refine its resource data about the New England region with its Hydro Power Study.[2] This report indicates that there is probably a larger number of existing dams in regions than previously identified by the corps. However, the report indicates that the estimates of capacity and energy at these sites are probably overstated. The total installed capacity of some 9,605 existing dams in New England was estimated by the New England River Basins Commission to be 1,907 megawatts (a figure which is also subject to further refinement).

With the preliminary identification of thousands of existing SSH sites well under way, it has become apparent that a sizable proportion of these dams are presently cost competitive with other more conventional means for generating electric power. Largely due to the increased cost of fossil fuels, the cost of small-scale hydro power, relative to the cost of electricity from these other sources, has become comparable to what it was during the first two decades of this century, when hydro development experienced its most rapid expansion. As the cost of fuel continues to escalate, more and more of the identified SSH sites will become economically feasible to develop.

That the economics of SSH are sufficiently attractive is further borne out by the fact that large industrial manufacturers, in both the United States and in Europe, have devoted considerable resources to the task of developing and marketing packaged units of SSH turbine and generator equipment. It is obvious that by committing their own resources to this resurrected energy technology these large corporations confidently expect sufficient returns on their investments to forego alternative financial opportunities.

The questions raised by the above discussion are apparent. If SSH development is technologically mature, if the existing sites have been located and identified and the resource assessed, and if a great number of the economically feasible sites have been determined to be cost competitive with today's prices of energy, why are these plants not on line, generating electricity for our homes and our businesses? Why are there only a few plants presently producing power from refurbished small scale hydroelectric sites? What are the major stumbling blocks in the path of developing SSH power at existing sites to the point where they can reduce our nation's dependence on scarce, nonrenewable fossil fuels? There is good reason to believe that the answers to these questions lie in the legal and institutional obstacles which have been erected over the years. In fact, of all the components which make up the input cost of hydroelectric development, the relative cost of regulation may be the only one which has increased as fast as the cost of oil, the principle competition to hydroelectric power. The legal and institutional issues are infinitely more numerous and complex than the economics or the technology of small-scale hydro. The few successful developers of which the authors are aware have each made his or her mark by resolving significant legal or institutional issues that would otherwise have prevented completion of the project.

It is thus taken as a working hypothesis that there are significant costs of regulation imposed on the SSH developer. This information is insufficient, by itself, to aid policy formation. Where in the regulatory environment can these costs be reduced with a net benefit to society? Obviously, all regulation could be removed, thereby removing the cost, but this is neither feasible nor desirable. The relevant tasks here are to identify where regulation is inefficient at obtaining its stated goals and to discover what possible policies are available to remedy this institutional problem. Most existing regulations are based on reasonable assumptions and constraints. Viewed en masse one can see the magnitude of the impact. However, the mere berating of this mass of legal and institutional obstacles is inappropriate and futile. Successful development can only be accomplished by accurately identifying the individual laws and regulations, assessing their impacts on development, and changing the law to accommodate society's interests in renewable energy resource development, preservation of the environment, and the efficient allocation of scarce societal resources.

What can be done to reduce environmental harm? What can be gained from tax benefits? How are the utility companies induced to interconnect with and buy power from small scale hydroelectric developers? The primary emphasis at the Energy Law Institute has been on these legal and institutional questions, as opposed to the narrower economic and engineering questions that pertain to small-scale hydroelectric development. It is with these issues in mind that the following overview of legal and institutional obstacles to SSH development is presented.

Major Legal, Regulatory, and Institutional Issues

The major regulatory and legal issues surrounding SSH development may be separated into water law issues, licensing issues, environmental regulation issues, power marketing issues, and tax and subsidy issues.

Water Law

The first legal hurdle confronting an SSH developer is the necessity of acquiring the property rights in the waterway which is to be harnessed. There are two principal bodies of law on water rights in the United States. Neither body of law should pose significant obstacles to SSH development.

Under the water law of eastern states, that is, riparianism, owners of land abutting a waterway own to the thread, or center line, of a non-navigable stream. The bed of a navigable stream is held in public trust by the state. Before the state may lease or sell the bed to a dam developer, it must determine that the public's right of navigation will not be abused and that the sale or lease is in the public interest. The "public interest" test is an analysis involving the balancing of the multiple and competing uses of the waterway. Riparians, that is, owners of land abutting the stream, have the right to the reasonable use or natural flow of the water flowing past their land. The generation of hydroelectric power is considered a reasonable use of flowing water.

In the western states the doctrine of prior appropriation pertains in determining water rights. Under this doctrine the person who *first* seeks to use the water has right to the water so long as the water is put to its highest and most beneficial use. This difference evolved due to the relative scarcity of water in the Western Plains States. Holders of water rights may lose their rights if they are not perfected or used for the purposes intended within a certain time after their acquisition. Since SSH involves *in stream* use of the water, for the most part, the appropriation doctrine would permit SSH development.

Licenses

Almost every SSH project will be required to obtain a license from the Federal Energy Regulatory Commission (FERC) pursuant to the requirements of the Federal Power Act. Although this process is complex, FERC recently has taken important steps to expedite and simplify the process.

FERC issues three types of licenses: a minor project license (projects of less than 1.5 Mw of capacity), a major project license for projects at existing sites (projects in excess of 1.5 Mw) and a major project license for projects at new sites. The licensing system for minor projects or major projects at existing sites will be simplified by new, proposed FERC regulations.

Hydroelectric projects can come under FERC jurisdiction in any of four ways:

1. *Projects located on navigable waterways.* A license must be obtained from FERC if a hydroelectric project will be located on a waterway which has been, is, or may become navigable. Navigability is defined in terms of commerce (for example, was the waterway used for floating logs to mill?).

2. *Projects affecting interstate commerce.* Hydroelectric projects must also obtain a license from FERC if they affect interstate commerce, even if located on a nonnavigable waterway. Commerce may be affected in either of two ways: (1) operation of the project in such a way as to affect the flow of water in a navigable waterway of which the nonnavigable waterway is a tributary, or (2) connection of the project to an interstate transmission grid, even though the project has no interstate sales.

3. *Projects which utilize federal land.* Hydroelectric projects which will utilize "public lands and reservations" belonging to the federal government must obtain a license from the FERC. Not all federal lands are included in this requirement. "Public lands" are those which may be devoted to private use under the public land laws. Such lands are generally administered by the Department of Interior. "Reservations" include national forests, Indian reservations, and other federal lands withheld from private use. Neither term includes national parks or national monuments. The FERC has the power to reserve federal lands for hydroelectric development.

4. *Projects which utilize surplus water or water power from government dams.* The Property Clause of the U.S. Constitution has been construed to apply to electricity generated at a government dam and to water made available at a government dam. Consequently, the FERC licenses the use of federal tangible property, just as it licenses the use of federal real property, for the generation of hydroelectric power.

The Federal Power Act permits a developer to request FERC to exempt a particular project from the federal licensing process. A developer may file a "Declaration of Intent" with the FERC and seek a waiver of the federal license requirement, or, if the developer is installing a hydroelectric facility in a water conduit or water main which is not closely related to a dam, he or she may ask for exemption from licensing. In this latter regard the Public Utility Regulatory Policies Act of 1978 recently authorized the FERC to exempt "conduit" hydroelectric projects from the licensing requirements and, even more recently, the FERC promulgated regulations establishing a simple, quick procedure for obtaining the exemptions.

In issuing a license the FERC must consider the economic feasibility of the project, comprehensive development of the waterway, and the environmental impact of the project. Several federal agencies must be contacted by the FERC before it can issue a license. Although the FERC is the lead agency on any federal SSH license, the involvement of and necessity for comments from other federal agencies can often cause undue difficulties and delays.

Coextensive with the federal licensing process is the state process. Compliance with such requirements is necessary because FERC will insist in almost all instances that all requirements of state and local law be met prior to issuing a federal license. In many states more than one state agency will issue a permit. One of the principal difficulties in obtaining the state permits is that each of the various state agencies typically require separate permit applications requesting essentially identical information. Those state agencies that are most commonly involved in the resolution of SSH are departments of natural resources, fish and game commissions, offices of historic preservation, public utility commissions, and water pollution control agencies. Their mission is chiefly to seek to mitigate the impacts to the environment of the particular project. Figure 13-1 is a flow diagram of a typical state's licensing process.

Environmental Regulation

1. *NEPA.* The National Environmental Policy Act (NEPA) requires each federal agency, before it takes any action, to weigh the impacts of that action on the environment. If a federal action has a *significant* impact, then

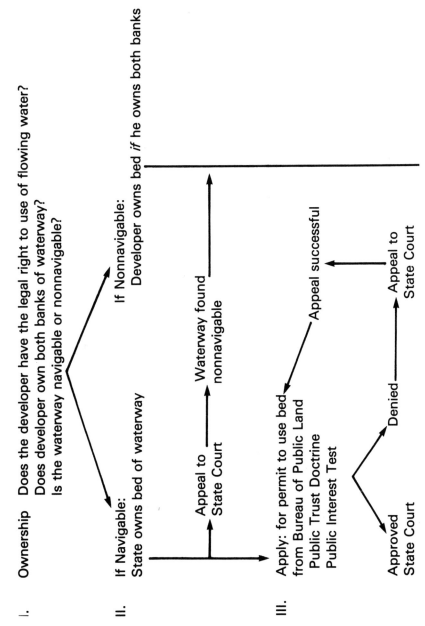

Project

I. Ownership   Does the developer have the legal right to use of flowing water?
Does developer own both banks of waterway?
Is the waterway navigable or nonnavigable?

If Navigable: If Nonnavigable:
State owns bed of waterway   Developer owns bed *if* he owns both banks

II.

Appeal to   Waterway found
State Court   nonnavigable

III. Apply: for permit to use bed
from Bureau of Public Land
Public Trust Doctrine
Public Interest Test

Appeal successful

Approved   Denied   Appeal to
State Court   State Court

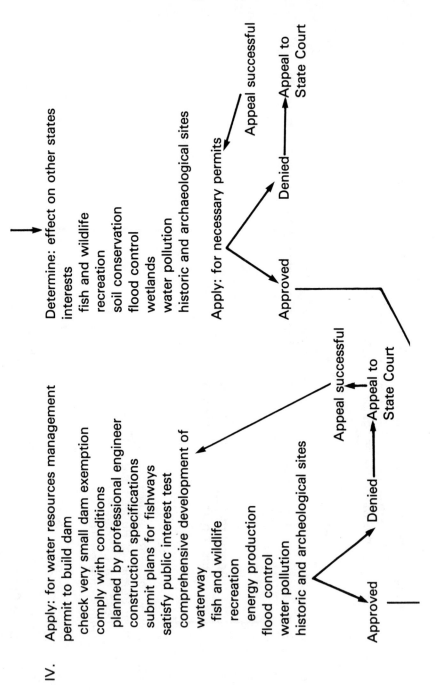

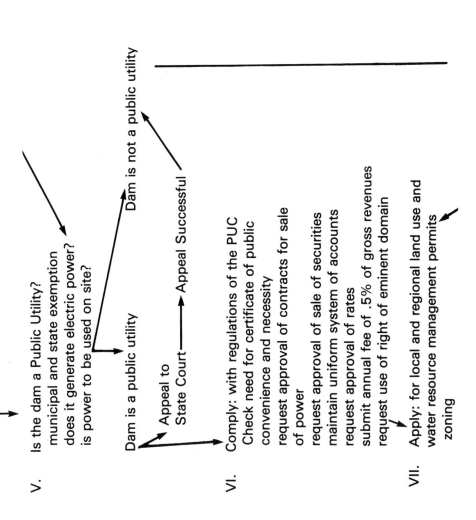

V. Is the dam a Public Utility?
municipal and state exemption
does it generate electric power?
is power to be used on site?

Dam is a public utility

Dam is not a public utility

Appeal to State Court ⟶ Appeal Successful

VI. Comply: with regulations of the PUC
Check need for certificate of public convenience and necessity
request approval of contracts for sale of power
request approval of sale of securities
maintain uniform system of accounts
request approval of rates
submit annual fee of .5% of gross revenues
request use of right of eminent domain

VII. Apply: for local and regional land use and water resource management permits zoning

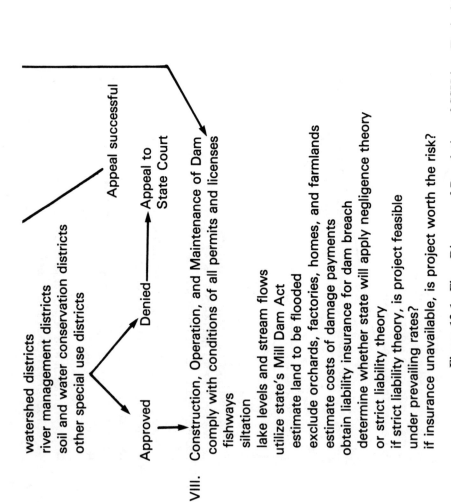

Figure 13-1. Flow Diagram of Regulation of SSH in a Typical State

a lengthy environmental impact statement (EIS) must be prepared. If the impact is not significant, then an EIS need not be prepared. In practice, the renovation of existing sites and the construction of new small projects (less than 1.5 megawatts) are usually held by the FERC not to require an EIS. This policy saves the small developer considerable expense and delay. The preparation, circulation, and evaluation of an EIS adds at least a year to the delay in project approval and can cost the developer hundreds of thousands of dollars.

If an EIS must be prepared on a project, the National Environmental Policy Act (NEPA) requires evaluation of the environmental impact of the proposed project; unavoidable adverse environmental impacts of the project; alternatives which might achieve the same result; the relationship between the short-term use of the project environment and the maintenance and enhancement of long-term productivity; and, finally, any irreversible and irretrievable commitments of resources involved in the project. It is worth noting that one out of every ten environmental impact statements prepared pursuant to NEPA has resulted in litigation. The FERC implements NEPA by assembling an EIS task force from the staff of appropriate FERC offices for the purpose of preparing a draft environmental impact statement (DEIS) based on both the application and comments from other federal agencies. The DEIS is circulated for comment to federal, state, and local agencies, as well as to interested parties and experts. Upon receipt of comments, the task force reviews the EIS to produce the final environmental impact statement (FEIS). If issues remain unresolved in the FEIS, an administrative law judge will decide the issues after the FERC staff and public intervenors file briefs and submit evidence. The FERC must specifically accept or reject the findings of the judge on points contested in the EIS. Any person with standing may intervene on the basis of the EIS.

If an EIS is not required, the FERC must prepare a "negative determination" showing that the commission took a hard look at the environmental impact of the project and convincingly demonstrated that the impact of the project was not significant. This determination may be appealed, and will be closely scrutinized by reviewing courts.

2. *Water quality*. The Environmental Protection Agency (EPA) is charged with the protection and enhancement of the quality of the nation's waters, primarily through the Clean Water Act, formerly known as the Federal Water Pollution Control Act. Because of the structure of the Act, the EPA may have no authority over the construction or operation of dams. Section 401 of the Act requires states to establish effluent limitations and standards for discharges into navigable water. An applicant for a FERC license must provide certification from the state that his or her activity is in

compliance with those standards. If a state's standards have not been approved as satisfactory by the EPA, the applicant will be required to demonstrate compliance with the standards of EPA. Thus, only in states whose clean water standards have not met EPA guidelines will EPA have a role in dam licensing. The FERC requires that the 401 certificate be acquired prior to filing a license application with FERC. The Section 401 certificate is an obstacle to SSH only where states have adopted a "seven-day minimum flow" standard, which impairs the operation of the dam. The seven-day minimum flow standard represents the level attained by the waterway during the seven days of lowest flow in a ten-year period. Clearly, if flow drops below this level, the dam must release water to raise the flow. This may be a particular problem with dams used to produce peaking power.

EPA may also gain jurisdiction over SSH pursuant to Section 402 of the act. Section 402 establishes the National Pollution Discharge Elimination System (NPDES), which requires a permit for the discharge of any pollutant into navigable waters. Although EPA has previously held in separate letters of opinion that dams are not point sources subject to NPDES regulation, a procedural victory won by the South Carolina Wildlife Federation in a suit to enjoin construction of an Army Corps dam and a petition for rule making filed with the EPA by the National Wildlife Federation have raised the possibility that dams will be subject to NPDES regulation. The plaintiffs and petitioners in these controversies allege that dams add trace metals and oxygen-deficient water to downstream waters. The corps and the Utility Water Action Group deny that dams add pollutants to water and contend that any trace minerals are absorbed from the bottomland of reservoirs. If SSH is subjected to NPDES regulation, a significant obstacle to the development of SSH will have been raised. This obstacle arises because of the difficulty in assessing the environmental factors and the attendant high costs of making such an assessment.

3. *The protection of fish, wildlife, and endangered species.* One of the more significant obstacles to SSH development is the governmental authority to protect and enhance our nations fish, wildlife, and endangered species. Although this authority is primarily the responsibility of the Department of Interior, due to various federal statutes the Department of Commerce and the FERC can also be involved.

Section 18 of the Federal Power Act mandates that the FERC shall require licenses to construct and operate such fishways as are prescribed by the U.S. Fish and Wildlife Service and the National Marine Fisheries Service. Although these agencies view their powers as advisory rather than as mandatory, the power of the FERC to require fishways makes them a significant obstacle to new dams and a somewhat smaller obstacle to the retrofitting of old dams. Generally fishways will be required when the particular dam is the furthest downstream barrier to the fish passage. If there are other water barriers between a dam and the ocean, the FERC will defer requiring the construction of fishways until either the barriers are removed or they are equipped with fishways of their own.

Under the Anadromous Fish Conservation Act and the Fish Restoration and Management Projects Act, the Secretary of Interior is authorized to expend funds for certain purposes, which purposes have been construed by some to include the construction of fishways. However, the obstacles to implementing such a program include a lack of funds and a contrary policy adopted by the officials involved.

The Corps of Engineers is authorized to construct fishways or river and harbor improvements in navigable waterways pursuant to the Rivers and Harbors Act of 1888.

The Endangered Species Act vests the Secretaries of Interior and Commerce with authority to protect species in danger of extinction or likely to become in danger of extinction. Any threatened species may be added to the Endangered Species List and regulations may be issued by the Secretary of Interior to protect the species. The regulations may include the designation of a species range or critical habitat in which commercial activity may not take place without permission of the secretary. However, the ground for permission is economic hardship, and exemptions for small dams are unlikely. Congress enacted an additional procedure to obtain exemptions from the act in 1978, but these procedures are designed principally for large projects, such as the Tellico Dam. It is doubtful whether the two review panels created by Congress would exempt a small dam from the strictures of the act. Thus the act serves as an insurmountable obstacle if a small dam threatens a listed species. Developers must check the lists of protected species published regularly in the Federal Register and the Code of Federal Regulations.

4. *The preservation of historic places, archaeological sites, and natural areas.* The preservation of historic places, archaeological sites, and natural areas presents unique problems to the SSH developer because the areas and places protected, like endangered species, have no common outward characteristics.

Projects affecting historic or archaeological sites on federally owned or controlled lands must obtain a permit from the Secretary of Interior, through the National Park Service.

Before the FERC can license a project which will pond more than forty acres of water, or which may have some effect on historic or archaeological materials, the project must be brought to the attention of the Secretary of Interior. The secretary may relocate such materials, using public funds from project appropriations if necessary.

The National Register, a list of sites nominated for their historic significance by government agencies concerned with historic preservation, may pose the most significant obstacles to SSH of the several federal institutions created to protect historic and archaeological sites. Listing of property in the Register has no effect on private owners, but does require federal licensing agencies to consider the effect of the project on properties listed or *eligible for listing* in the Register. A complex procedure, established by regulation, requires the FERC to evaluate the effect of a project on a site and negotiate agreements on methods of impact avoidance or mitigation with the executive director of the Advisory Council on Historic Preservation and the State Historic Preservation Offices. The FERC will give much weight to the policies of the Advisory Council on Historic Preservation in considering license applications, in part because of the demands of NEPA and the FERC's own regulations. The time and expense of assessing the historic or archaeological values affected by a project can be a significant obstacle to SSH, as can the process of negotiating and mitigating adverse effects.

Created by Congress in 1967, the National Wilderness Preservation System permits the designation for protection purposes of wilderness areas on federal lands. Although commercial activity is generally prohibited in these areas, dams may be built and operated in wilderness areas if the president finds that such use is in the public interest. The president may attach conditions to any permit. The effect of the system is to remove authority from the FERC to dedicate designated lands to power production.

The Wild and Scenic Rivers Act is the most significant obstacle to SSH of the several federal statutes which protect natural areas. Under the act, wild and free flowing rivers are designated by Congress as waterways worthy of protection. Rivers may be designated as wild, scenic, or recreational. If a river is so designated, the issuance of a FERC license for a project on that river is prohibited. In addition, the FERC may not issue a license for a project on any river included as a potential addition to the list until such time after 1981 when three years have elapsed since Congress added the last river to the list of potential additions.

The National Wildlife Refuge System is a consolidation of the various areas administered by the Department of Interior for the conservation of fish and wildlife. The Secretary of Interior may permit any use of a wildlife refuge which does not conflict with the purpose for which the area was established. U.S. Fish and Wildlife Service regulations provide for permits for the construction of transmission lines and generating units in wildlife refuges.

Since a significant portion of the nation's SSH potential lies on federal lands, federal land management policy is important to the small developer.

The Federal Power Act vests the FERC with authority to designate and reserve most federal lands for hydroelectric production. Once reserved, only Congress or the FERC may lift the reservation on lands. However, because of the passage of the Federal Land Policy Management Act (FLPMA), questions have been raised concerning FERC's authority to grant rights of way within the National Forest and National Park System. The FERC has commented on the joint regulations proposed to implement FLPMA. Regulation of the interagency dispute may not be effected until FLPMA's regulations have been finalized and tested in court. FERC's power to reserve federal lands is a significant incentive to SSH. Erosion of this power would create another obstacle to SSH.

For a graphic depiction of the federal licensing process and its interaction with environmental regulation, see figure 13-2.

Power Marketing

Because small scale hydroelectric power projects will produce electric power, there are a number of problems involving the relationship of these small scale hydroelectric projects to integrated electric utility systems. In those instances where the integrated electric utility systems develop the small scale hydroelectric power projects, these projects will be integrated into the system as are other generating facilities.

With respect to those small-scale hydroelectric projects which are developed by persons or companies which are not controlled or owned by integrated electric utility systems, the developer has typically had difficulty obtaining an adequate price for the sale of his or her energy due to the monopsony (single buyer) power with which he or she is confronted.

Although the scope and interpretation of the Public Utility Regulatory Policies Act of 1978 (PURPA) is not completely known at this time, PURPA addresses the marketing of power by small producers to integrated utilities and seeks to remedy the unequal market power of the utilities. The act provides for the establishment of rules that will require the utility in question to purchase power from qualifying small power producers who so request. The maximum capacity limitation for qualifying small power producers is eighty megawatts. The act prescribes that the rates to be set for required purchases are to be just and reasonable to the utility's ratepayers and nondiscriminatory to the qualifying facilities. PURPA further prescribes that the rates should not exceed the incremental cost of the purchasing utility's alternative energy. While the technical issues of rate setting are not germane to this description of the regulatory process, it is important to note that Congress, in enacting PURPA, explicitly recognized the burdens of the regulatory process and stated that rate setting, under PURPA, should not be the usual utility-type regulation. FERC recognized that the administrative costs to the small producer of a standard rate filing could easily outweigh the profits of the project.

In addition to the above, PURPA permits the FERC to order intercon-

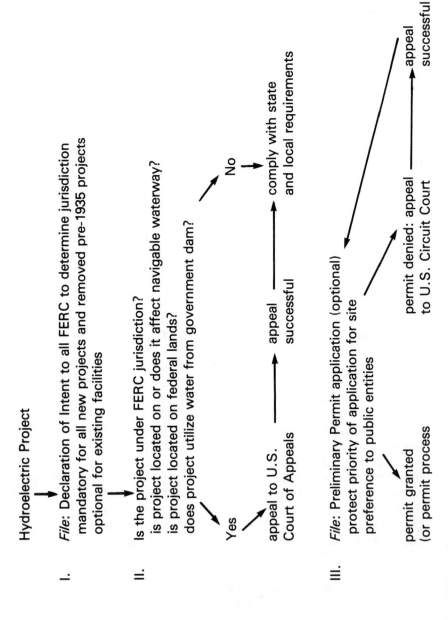

Hydroelectric Project

I. *File*: Declaration of Intent to all FERC to determine jurisdiction mandatory for all new projects and removed pre-1935 projects optional for existing facilities

II. Is the project under FERC jurisdiction?
is project located on or does it affect navigable waterway?
is project located on federal lands?
does project utilize water from government dam?

Yes

No

appeal to U.S. Court of Appeals

appeal successful

comply with state and local requirements

III. *File*: Preliminary Permit application (optional) protect priority of application for site preference to public entities

permit granted (or permit process

permit denied: appeal to U.S. Circuit Court

appeal successful

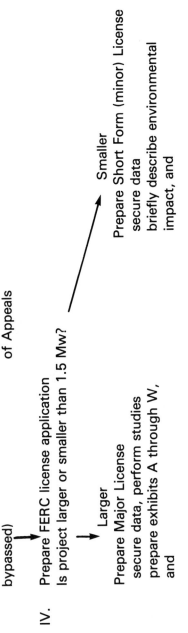

bypassed)

of Appeals

IV. Prepare FERC license application
Is project larger or smaller than 1.5 Mw?

Larger

Prepare Major License
secure data, perform studies
prepare exhibits A through W,
and

Smaller

Prepare Short Form (minor) License
secure data
briefly describe environmental
impact, and

acquire land, water rights
sign contract for sale of power
consult with fish and wildlife agencies
consult with historic and archaeological
preservation agencies
consult list of endangered species
consult Wild and Scenic Rivers
designations
consult National Trail System
obtain S 404 dredge and fill permit
obtain S 401 state water quality
certification and other state permits

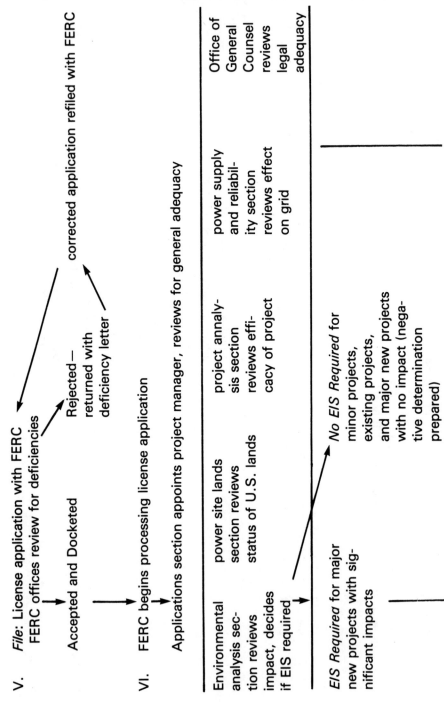

V. *File*: License application with FERC
FERC offices review for deficiencies

Accepted and Docketed

Rejected—returned with deficiency letter

corrected application refiled with FERC

VI. FERC begins processing license application

Applications section appoints project manager, reviews for general adequacy

Environmental analysis section reviews impact, decides if EIS required

power site lands section reviews status of U.S. lands

project annalysis section reviews efficacy of project

power supply and reliability section reviews effect on grid

Office of General Counsel reviews legal adequacy

EIS Required for major new projects with significant impacts

No EIS Required for minor projects, existing projects, and major new projects with no impact (negative determination prepared)

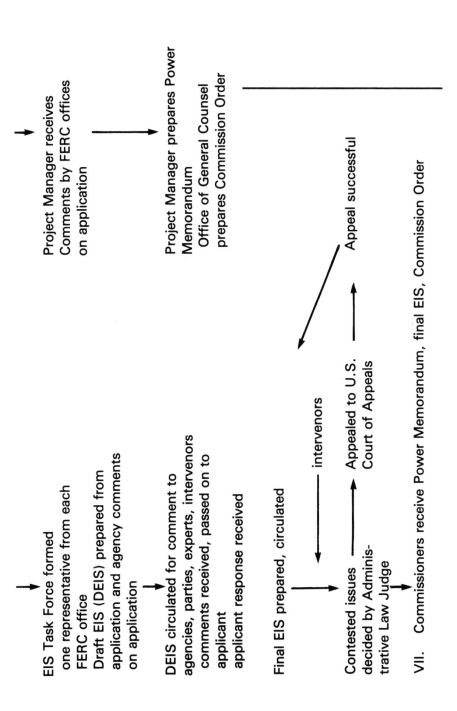

EIS Task Force formed
one representative from each
FERC office
Draft EIS (DEIS) prepared from
application and agency comments
on application

DEIS circulated for comment to
agencies, parties, experts, intervenors
comments received, passed on to
applicant
applicant response received

Final EIS prepared, circulated

Contested issues
decided by Adminis-
trative Law Judge

intervenors

Appealed to U.S.
Court of Appeals

Appeal successful

Project Manager receives
Comments by FERC offices
on application

Project Manager prepares Power
Memorandum
Office of General Counsel
prepares Commission Order

VII. Commissioners receive Power Memorandum, final EIS, Commission Order

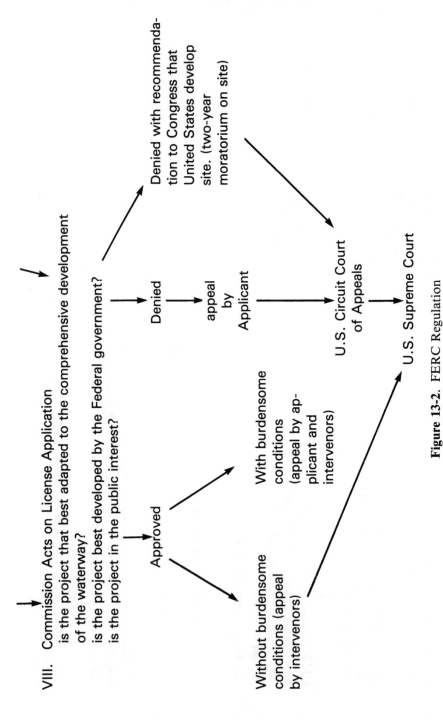

Figure 13-2. FERC Regulation

nection of the small power producer with the integrated electric utility system under certain conditions. Similarly, the act may permit small producers, under narrowly limited circumstances, to have their power wheeled over the transmission lines of an electric utility.

Of major importance in PURPA are the definitional provisions. Only those small-scale hydroelectric projects which meet the FERC's "qualifying" criteria will be protected by the rate setting provisions of PURPA. One of the more important elements of qualifying status is that only those SSH projects principally owned by private individuals or corporations which are not otherwise engaged in the business of selling electricity are eligible for PURPA's benefits. Accordingly, municipalities and rural electric cooperatives, as well as investor-owned utilities, are excluded.

To assure that qualifying SSH projects and other qualifying renewable energy facilities are given complete protection from burdensome regulation, the FERC under PURPA has the power, by rule, to exempt a qualifying small power producer having a capacity of thirty megawatts or less from all public utility regulations of the state, the federal Public Utility Holding Company Act, and certain administrative requirements of the Federal Power Act.

On July 3, 1979, the FERC promulgated proposed rules to implement the definitional provisions of PURPA and issued a discussion paper on the rate and exemption provisions of section 210. Final regulations on these provisions were issued in November 1979. As noted previously, municipalities and rural electric cooperatives do not "qualify" under PURPA and hence are not given the rate making protection which private developers will receive from PURPA. In some respects this leaves these groups subject to the market power of the integrated electric system. (This market structure will be much more significant in the Northeast, where integrated systems are almost exclusively privately owned, than in the West and the Far West.)

There are two other provisions in PURPA which are of significance to municpal and rural electric cooperative developers of SSH projects. PURPA contains provisions which would permit municipal and rural co-op systems to have power *wheeled* to customers at wholesale. Under the wheeling provisions of PURPA, one municipal, which has available capacity at small dams, could require, through the FERC, that the grid transport energy from the SSH to another municipal system or rural co-op which is short on capacity. Despite such attractive possibilities for "wheeling," there are a large number of conditions in PURPA which must be satisfied before the FERC will order wheeling. The conditions may be so restrictive as to make wheeling an ineffective marketing mechanism for municipal and rural co-op developers. However, as with most of PURPA, much remains in the hands of the FERC, which, at this writing, has not finally spoken on these issues.

Tax Policies and Subsidies

Of immediate assistance to SSH developers are low-interest loans provided by the Department of Energy to underwrite the costs of feasibility studies and license application activities. These loans are provided under Title IV of PURPA for rehabilitation of existing dams of fifteen megawatts or less which are not presently generating electricity. Up to 90 percent of the feasibility study or licensing activity costs may be underwritten. Loans will be forgiven if the project is unfeasible. New regulations have been proposed (May 1979) to implement this program. Ten million dollars were appropriated for this program during fiscal year 1979.

The Department of Energy funded fifty-four feasibility studies in 1978 and has the authorization to fund as many as 300 more. While such subsidies are obvious incentives to the potential developers receiving the grants, there are mixed blessings in the package for national hydro development. The prices paid to the engineering firm contracted to perform a subsidized project's engineering and economic assessment may have increased the market price for the minimal studies needed in nonsubsidized projects. Thus an obstacle has been created by the creation of an incentive.

In addition, President Carter has announced a Rural Initiatives Program which includes a strong emphasis on hydroelectric power development. Under this program the corps, the FERC, and the Bureau of Reclamation are to survey those sites which appear economically feasible. Once an array of sites has been selected, DOE, the Farmers Home Administration, the Rural Electrification Administration, the Economic Development Administration, and the Community Services Administration, among other agencies, are to provide assistance through their existing programs to eligible SSH developers. Three hundred million dollars is earmarked for this effort, with a target of 100 Mw under construction by 1980.

With respect to tax policy, it is important to note that hydroelectric projects and attendant equipment were not included for the energy tax credit under the Energy Tax Act of 1978. The Energy Tax Act was passed as part of the National Energy Act in the fall of 1978. It should be noted that most other alternative energy resources were recognized in the Energy Tax Act as qualifying for the additional 10 percent investment tax credit. Presently pending before Congress are several bills which would change this omission.

At the state level, tax policy obviously plays an important role in the development of small-scale hydroelectric power. It should be noted that many state laws exempt either wholly or in part certain forms of pollution abatement equipment from taxation. Although, under most state taxing laws and regulations, low-head hydroelectric equipment does not qualify as pollution abatement equipment, there is at least one instance in which a state, Massachusetts, has ruled to the contrary.

Finally, there is also legislation encouraging economic development in almost every state. Economic development legislation takes the form of the establishment of an economic development agency or public corporations which assist in financing various projects which will attract industry to a state and improve the economic situation of certain economically depressed areas. Unless the entity to which the proceeds of a bond issue will inure is tax exempt, the interest on those bonds will be taxable.

The incentives, loan programs, and tax policies previously described result in a crazy-quilt of incentives and conflicting tax policies. It is not known at this time whether or not any of the loan programs are operating successfully, nor is it known what the precise impact of tax policy will be on small scale hydroelectric development. However, it is known that low-interest loans and favorable tax subsidies increase the profitability of an SSH site. As with many government incentives, the actual impact will depend on the ability of the beneficiaries, in this case the developers, to utilize the proposed financial benefits of the program. It seems reasonable to assume that, should there be any successful and effective loan program, stimulating tax policy, or other subsidy, the rate of development of small scale hydroelectric power should increase. In other words, there should be a realized return on the government's investment in tax policy, loan programs, and other subsidies encouraging the development of small-scale hydroelectric power.

Conclusion

SSH at existing dams is an environmentally benign, technologically stable, and increasingly profitable energy resource of some abundance in this country. Its revival should play an important role in the nation's energy future. Of the renewable energy sources, SSH is the one which can be most easily and rapidly developed. However, construction has been initiated at only a relatively small number of sites when compared to the nation's potential.

Stringent regulations can often impose significant barriers. An important example of this is the case of the fish ladder requirement, the cost of which can run as high as one-half of the construction costs of an SSH project. It may be most reasonable for society to require certain dams to have these fish passages. But it does not follow that the power developer should be held financially responsible since it is the existing dam, and not the new electric generation equipment, that incurs the need for a fish passage. In this case the problem with the regulations is that the penalty for blocking the passage of fish is imposed on the most accessible party, the owner, as opposed to the party responsible for the social cost, the original builder.

While the physical and economic requirements of the regulations affecting SSH can provide signifiant disincentives, the sheer number and complexity of the regulations may constitute an even greater obstacle viewed in relation to resources available for developing a small power project. The matrix of regulations can impose a very large fixed administrative cost. In one instance, the development of a thirty Mw hydro site by a Wisconsin investor-owned utility, compliance with these administrative regulations has been estimated as costing over $1 million. The nature of the regulatory process has traditionally presumed a legal sophistication which a developer is unlikely to have attained concurrent with his or her first effort. The description of the regulations given in Section II outlines the array of potential problems confronting a small developer, the effects of which he or she is usually poorly equipped to judge.

An investment in SSH is similar to other business ventures in that it carries business risks commensurate with its returns. The regulatory risk is merely one part of that overall risk. Given the goals of regulation, a part of that regulatory risk is necessary. However, inefficiency in the regulatory process often imposes costs on the developer without correlative benefits accruing to society. The multitude of applicable rules affecting SSH almost guarantees such inefficiency. This has produced a situation in which many potential developers view the regulatory agencies as being a priori opposed to development. This situation is obviously inimical to the development of the nation's SSH potential. However, at this writing serious attempts at the federal and state levels, some of which have been noted in the text, have been and are being undertaken to decrease the regulatory burden on small hydroelectric projects without sacrificing the objectives of the regulations.

The success of the regulatory institutions in adapting the process to meet the needs of diverse groups of developers will determine to a large extent how important SSH will be in our nation's energy future. Regulatory flexibility which is stimulated by interest in this mature technology may flow well beyond the banks of the rivers and streams whose power it so efficiently and cleanly harnesses.

Notes

1. See "Estimate of National Hydroelectric Power Potential at Existing Dams," U.S. Army Corps of Engineers, Institute for Water Resources (Fort Belvoir, Virginia, July 20, 1977).

2. See "Interim Report on Inventory of Existing Dams in New England," New England River Basins Commission (Boston, December 12, 1978).

14 Public Participation in Power Plant Siting Decisions: The Case of the Mid-Atlantic Region

Janet B. Johnson and
Richard T. Sylves

During the past ten years and particularly since the oil embargo of 1973, many states have enacted legislation regulating energy facility siting. Such laws typically cite the need to provide for adequate supplies of energy and the need to protect the environment, two objectives which have often come into conflict with one another. Energy facilities in this chapter are defined as any public or investor-owned electric generating facilities large enough to come under the jurisdiction of energy facility siting law. Such facilities can be fueled by coal, residual oil, natural gas, or nuclear energy.

It has been a frequent claim of citizens' groups and local government officials that energy facility siting seems to proceed without adequate consideration of the more localized environmental and economic impacts of energy facilities. Yet, citizens opposed to construction of various energy facilities often have been successful in either delaying or completely blocking construction of new power plants. Fragmented permitting processes with numerous veto points furnished these interests with an opportunity for protracted debate concerning energy facility development issues. On the other hand, the traditional permitting process limited careful consideration of all issues. That is, regional energy priorities were forced to defer to local environmental or economic considerations. Furthermore, a considerable amount of time and money has been invested by both utilities and regulatory authorities before the permit stage is reached. The permitting stage follows an energy planning stage and a site selection stage. As a result, if a project is blocked at the permitting stage it may come as a serious and expensive blow to the utility and to various regulatory bodies.

New state energy laws address these problems by mandating increased state government involvement in the energy facility siting process. In many instances studies and hearings concerning the need for additional energy facilities and a proposed facility's environmental, economic, and social impact are moved forward and considered in the planning and site selection stages. Correspondingly, the permitting is streamlined so that fewer obstacles are likely to be encountered at this stage. As a result of these changes, the need for a particular facility and a "suitable" site for its construction are both determined by means of a state-level policy process which

215

is preemptive of local government authority. Local governments and local interests in the vicinity of the site are thus not permitted to "obstruct" power plant construction.

How much have these changes in the facility siting process restricted either the access or influence of citizen and local interests in the review and approval of new power plants? This chapter explores this question by analyzing power plant siting policies in the mid-Atlantic states of New York, New Jersey, Pennsylvania, Delaware, and Maryland. Issues concerning need, environmental protection, local economic impact, and state-local relations are carefully examined; and federal government decisions which affect facility siting are discussed.

State Involvement in Energy Facility Siting

The process of energy facility siting may be divided into three phases. The first is the planning phase and involves the determination of need for an energy facility. The second entails the selection of a suitable site, and the third, the permitting phase, involves the issuing of permits allowing construction and operation of the facility. The mid-Atlantic states vary in the extent to which they are actively involved in the three stages, although all states have been and continue to be involved in the permitting stage. All five states have some program or agency responsible for considering their long-range energy needs. The agencies are the Delaware State Energy Office, the Maryland Public Service Commission, the New Jersey Department of Energy, the New York State Energy Office, and the Pennsylvania Bureau of Conservation, Economics, and Energy Planning.

The Planning Phase

There are two main characteristics which distinguish state involvement in the planning phase for the mid-Atlantic states. In two states, and under consideration in a third, the state's determination of need is binding. This means that after the states certify that there is a need for an energy facility, the question of need may not be disputed in subsequent deliberations concerning site selection or the issuance of permits. It also means that unless need is confirmed by the state, an energy facility will not be built. In Maryland, electric utilities are required to submit annual long-range plans. The Public Service Commission assembles and evaluates these plans and uses them to devise a ten-year Master Plan specifying the energy needs to be met. New York State's Energy Master Plan formally identifies state energy needs for five-, ten-, and fifteen-year time intervals. Legislation has been proposed in Pennsylvania which would have the PUC determine the need for a power plant before the utility could proceed with site selection.[1] At present, Pennsylvania's Bureau of Conservation, Economics, and Energy Planning is responsible for long-range forecasting of energy needs, although it is not yet activated and its decisions would not be binding.

In New Jersey and Delaware, the state is involved in preparing long-range projections of energy need, but these are not binding. In New Jersey a ten-year Energy Master Plan, which is to be updated every three years, is being compiled. In Delaware, the State Energy Office is responsible for promulgating need and demand projections for energy. Delaware's energy needs are also addressed in the state's Coastal Management Plan (CMP), developed by the Office of Management, Budgeting, and Planning. Although the CMP prohibits construction of energy facilities in coastal and wetlands areas on the grounds that current energy need does not justify degradation of these areas, this imperative only carries the weight of a recommendation.

The second significant feature of state involvement in energy planning is that where the state's finding of need is binding, a time limit (typically eighteen months to two years) is imposed upon the project approval process. The time limit serves to break up delay-producing bottlenecks in the facility siting process and therefore adds an element of certainty which benefits both utilities and state planning bodies. Both New York and Maryland apply time limits to the facility siting process within their states.

Since state determination of facility need may be binding in some states, it is imperative that members of the public have an opportunity to participate in the planning phase which produces these binding decisions. Provisions insuring public participation in energy planning vary from state to state. In New York, public hearings are required at various steps in the planning process before the start of planning for public review of procedures and regulations, after the receipt of planning reports from the utilities, after the development of a draft Energy Master Plan (to be held in three geographical locations), and every other year to review the forecasts contained in the Master Plan.

New York is unique among the mid-Atlantic states because it furnishes grants of up to $200,000 to various public intervenor groups, enabling them to participate in the planning process. This money is made available to nonprofit organizations and municipalities for the purpose of retaining expert witnesses who will testify as public intervenors on behalf of their clients' interests. This provision does much to insure meaningful public participation in the planning process.

In Maryland there are no formal provisions for citizen participation in the review of a utility's projections of need. This seems odd given that the state's determination of need is binding. However, public participation is provided for in the next stage, site selection. In New Jersey, public hearings on the Energy Master Plan are required. In addition, there is an Advisory Council on Energy Planning and Conservation which has, as members, representatives of consumer and environmental interests. Nevertheless, the council is heavily weighted by producers and suppliers of various types of energy.

While state involvement in determining need moves the need question from the private to the public sphere, it remains to be seen whether increased state involvement in the planning phase actually leads to greater citizen input into the energy siting process. Separating the question of need from the question of site selection may reduce public interest, since citizens are likely to express the most concern during site selection. If state energy need decisions are binding, then local citizen influence in the energy facility siting process may be diminished. Discussion of trade-offs between need and costs associated with energy facility development are ruled out at later stages by the planning process. This is unfortunate when one considers that during the later stages of energy facility siting local costs and the affected public are more clearly identified.

Economic Conditions

The changing state role in determining need and its effects is also influenced by the changing economic conditions affecting the construction of generating facilities. Because state utility regulatory commissions are typically charged with the responsibility of assuring an abundant supply of economically available electric power, they find themselves in a position where they must make it easier for utilities to construct new generating facilities. Their legislative mandate requires that they urge utility executives to increase power generating capacity at a time when the utility may not find it economically advantageous to do so, given financing problems and high interest rates.

It is frequently assumed that great economies of scale can be realized in the production of electricity by erecting huge centralized generating facilities serving many thousands of residential, commercial, and industrial customers. The conventional thinking is that large turbines can generate electricity much more cheaply than small ones, despite the high costs and energy losses of transmission over many miles to many users. This line of reasoning contends that while the individual household or business could run its own generator, it can far more efficiently buy power from a central plant.[2]

Moreover, electric utilities should operate as natural monopolies in order to eliminate competition which would be duplicative and expensive for consumers. Captive electricity customers would be protected from the monopolistic practices of utilities by government regulation.

While there may be good reasons for continuing natural monopoly treatment of utilities, economies of scale are becoming increasingly difficult to realize under current economic conditions. A *Congressional Quarterly* report indicates that the cost of building new power plant capacity inflated so much over the last decade and a half that economies of scale may no longer be achievable. The report reveals that the cost of building new power plant capacity increased by 34 percent between 1960 and 1970. The cost jumped another 68 percent between 1970 and 1975.[3] These cost percentage increases far exceed the corresponding rate of inflation in the general Consumer Price Index for those periods. This means that building large new power plants is no longer as economically desirable as it once appeared.

There are a number of reasons for these extraordinary cost increases. First, as political pressure against higher utility rates grew, regulatory decisions (at the state level) lagged behind utility requests for higher rates and more money. This slowed construction of new plants and at the same time encouraged increased consumption of electricity due to artificially low rates. Second, environmental restrictions added to the costs of utility operation as well. Third, as earnings declined relative to costs, outside financing became difficult for utilities to obtain and utility bond credit ratings were devalued.

Nevertheless, consumer demand for electrical power has continued to increase despite dramatic rises in utility bills since 1970. This caused many experts to conclude that massive expansion of the U.S. utility industry would be necessary over the next ten years.[4]

As a result of these concerns, federal and state officials are beginning to remove obstacles in the path of new construction. One presumed impediment in the path of new construction is citizen involvement in the energy facility siting process.

The Site Selection Phase

During the site selection phase, the impacts of a proposed facility are evaluated and the suitability of a site is examined. Separation of the site selection phase from the permitting phase allows for more measured consideration of the impacts of energy development. It is here that the issues of environmental and local economic impacts are first addressed.

Involvement in the site selection phase varies from complete state control in the case of Maryland to little or no state control with no advanced assessment of sites in the cases of Pennsylvania and Delaware. Maryland's Power Plant Siting Program provides for the purchase by the state of up to eight sites to be held in inventory until the state's Energy Master Plan dictates their use. The suitability of any site must be determined within two years of the date it has been identified. The state may hold the site up to fifteen years before the original owner or the owner's heirs are given the opportunity to repurchase the land. In New York State, and potentially in Pennsylvania, site selection is reviewed by the state, although neither state plans to purchase sites.[5] Site selection procedures in these two states must be completed within a certain period of time (two years or less). New Jersey is in the process of promulgating facility siting regulations by type of facility. It is not clear at this time what these will entail. In Delaware, as mentioned previously, the Coastal Management Plan bans the siting of major energy facilities in coastal and wetlands areas of the state. The CMP sets out a procedure for assessing the appropriateness of specific sites should the prohibition be lifted. Sites are not selected ahead of time, because it is considered impossible to elicit serious public participation until an actual facility at a specific site is proposed.

Thus Maryland is the only state which asserts preemptive authority in site selection and actually purchases sites in advance of construction. Under these conditions, the provision for public participation and careful evaluation of energy facility impacts seems especially important. Originally the Maryland process contained no formal provisions for public participation, although public meetings were to be held late in the process once several sites in a service area were being compared. The current Maryland process requires one informational meeting and one public hearing in the affected county before a site is acquired; and a Power Plant Advisory Committee, which includes a representative from each county in which proposed inventory sites are located, advises the Secretary of Natural Resources.

Although New York State does not purchase sites, the state's determination of site suitability is binding, and provisions for participation in site selection are significant. A fund of $150,000 is created from applicant fees. The fund subsidizes the cost of retaining experts as witnesses at hearings. Half of the money is available to the affected municipalities and half goes to nongovernmental, nonprofit citizens' groups. A public hearing must be held in the area of the proposed power plant after an application is received. Other hearings may be held, although the number of hearings is not set. Finally, a resident of the judicial district in which the proposed project is located is appointed to a five-member siting board, which rules on site suitability.[6]

The need for careful analysis of environmental impacts of energy facilities generally is specified in detail in state energy facility siting legislation. In all states where authority for site selection resides with the state, the state environmental agencies are given primary responsibility for evaluating the environmental implications of plants at specific sites. In Maryland, an Environmental Trust Fund created from a surcharge placed on each kilowatt hour of electric energy generated in the state has been established.

The fund is used to support a power plant environmental research program within the Department of Natural Resources. New York State also has a power plant research program to investigate the environmental impacts of power plants. It appears that most of the mid-Atlantic states are prepared to give careful attention to environmental considerations. However, the local economic impact of project is given considerably less attention.

Local economic impact is an important concern in the site selection process. The presence of an electric generating facility can impose significant costs on a local area. In cases where states or regional authorities purchase land and then lease it to public utilities which in turn build and operate power plants on the site, a local government may sustain a loss in property tax revenue and a shrinkage of the local tax base. In some unusual instances, state governments compensate local governments for the property tax revenue loss. Yet the generating facility frequently imposes less obvious costs on adjacent municipalities, which are not sufficiently compensated by either the utility or the state. If the power facility stimulates population growth, the local government may be forced to expand public facilities and services to accommodate new residents. If the power facility is publicly perceived as a disamenity, property values in the vicinity of the plant may decline, again resulting in diminished property tax revenue.

As the state role in energy facility siting becomes more decisive, what happens to local economic concerns? In general, each state's needs for more electrical energy seems to take priority over local economic considerations. This allegation is based on the observation that, in states which have assumed a major role in facility siting (New York and Maryland), very little official mention is made of a project's local economic impact. Compensation to municipalities affected by new plants is rarely mentioned. However, in Maryland, provisions are made for property-tax reimbursement to affected local governments.

By contrast, legislation designed specifically to compensate local governments for the adverse economic impact of new energy facilities was proposed in the Pennsylvania legislature but never enacted into law (in the 1978 session).[7] The proposed legislation would have reimbursed affected municipalities and school districts for up to 75 percent of their expenses incurred in providing testimony pertinent to facility site selection. Limits of $350,000 per site and $2 million per year were suggested for reimbursement of local costs directly related to the construction of an energy facility. A fund of $7 million was to be established to reimburse municipalities which are required to construct and expand major capital projects. Finally, the Pennsylvania bill mandated property-tax relief for local taxing authorities. In Delaware, concern about a project's economic impact seems to be a major reason why local control over siting was retained.

Legislation such as that proposed in Pennsylvania would do much to alleviate local concerns about energy facility development. It would provide for a more equitable balancing of state energy needs and local economic considerations associated with power plant siting. The anticipated high costs to state government of this proposal may explain why Pennsylvania has not signed it into law. Other states might also be expected to look with disfavor on similar proposals. Increased state authority over site selection seems to be inversely related to concern for local economic impact of new energy plants.

The Permitting Phase

The final stage in the process is the permitting stage. Before a utility may begin construction, there are numerous permits to be obtained. Many people object to complicated permit procedures which exist in many states on the grounds that such procedures delay critically needed energy projects. The issuance of permits often involves public hearings. These hearings are frequently the scene of pitched battles between opponents and proponents of energy facility development. This may be attributed to the lack of meaningful citizen or local governmental involvement in the phases of planning and site selection. Sometimes it is only during the permit phase that important and controversial issues are discussed publicly.

As states have moved toward greater involvement in the planning and site selection stages, they have simplified the state permitting process. This simplification has had the effect of limiting local government participation in the permitting process. A frequent assumption of state officials is that state involvement in the early stages facilitates consideration of local issues and interests. For example, the Maryland Power Plant Siting Act states,

> In view of the safeguards provided by this subtitle through state units, and to assure the controlling effect of their determination, any property an electric company purchases or leases as provided in this subsection shall be used and operated for electric generating and associated transmission purposes without regard to any local zoning rule, regulation, law, or ordinance, and this use is not required to be submitted to or approved by any county or municipal governing board, authority or unit.[8]

In New York State, local laws may be overridden by the siting board if the board finds them to be "unreasonably restrictive."[9] Any municipality seeking to enforce any local ordinance affecting electrical generating plants must present evidence in support of the ordinance before the siting board at the certification hearing, or else the ordinance may not be enforced.

By comparison, the permitting process in Delaware has not yet been streamlined enough to allow for more complete participation of interested parties. County and municipal involvement in the permitting process has not been preempted by the state. This also seems to be the case in New Jersey, where state permitting activity has not preempted local laws affecting the siting of energy facilities.

It is important to note that federal government involvement in the facility siting process also influences state control over permitting and indirectly influences public participation in the process. The next section of the chapter addresses the issue of federal intervention in the facility siting process.

Federal Involvement in Energy Facility Siting

The extent of federal participation in the energy facility siting process is governed by the nature of the facility. Elaborate federal regulatory procedures exist which oversee the planning, construction, and operation of civilian nuclear power plants. In the recent past, for nonnuclear types of facilities, federal intervention has been concerned basically with environmental protection (under the National Environmental Policy Act [NEPA]) and market regulation. However, as concern about the country's energy problems increased, more and more federal legislation was enacted which affects energy facility siting.

Two federal agencies shoulder major responsibility in energy facility siting: the Department of Energy (DOE), through the Federal Energy Regulatory Commission (FERC), and the independent Nuclear Regulatory Commission (NRC). The federal Environmental Protection Agency under NEPA plays a more indirect role in the facility siting process.

The Federal Energy Regulatory Commission was created in 1977 and it embodies many of the powers and personnel of the now-defunct Federal Power Commission (FPC). FERC's Office of Electric Power Regulation has principal responsibility for regulating public utilities which produce and sell electricity on the interstate market. However, most activities of FERC and the former FPC involve setting the price of electricity rather than supervising facility siting.

Nevertheless, rate regulation can have some impact upon the construction of new power plants. One of the most controversial rate reform proposals involves whether authorities should allow a utility's costs for "construction work in progress" to be included in the utility's rate base. Industry spokesmen argue that allowance of construction work in progress in the rate base is an essential element in meeting the capital needs associated with growing electricity demand. But consumer advocates fear that permitting utilities to charge consumers for construction costs before new facilities are operating would encourage utilities to build even when new facilities may not be needed.[10] What this means in terms of energy facility siting issues is that federal and state authorities are likely to give more weight to the utility viewpoint in this argument as energy demand continues to escalate and as utilities face a capital-squeeze which inhibits new plant construction.

The Department of Energy does influence the energy facility siting process in a more direct way. For example, DOE officials can encourage executives of utilities to construct certain types of energy facilities at various locations best suited to availability of the plant's primary and secondary fuels. In 1977 about 44 percent of U.S. power plants were coal fired, 30 percent were powered by oil and natural gas, 16 percent were hydroelectric, and the remaining 10 percent were nuclear powered.[11] Under one of the provisions of the National Energy Act of 1978, the secretary of DOE was authorized to intervene in state utility commission regulatory proceedings in order to argue for energy saving measures.[12]

President Carter's original energy plan called for strong federal intervention in the regulation of public utilities. Yet Congress argued that the states should continue to oversee the utilities and it refused to make the president's guidelines mandatory.[13] While much of the initial Carter proposal referred to rate reform issues, there was special attention given to the issue of coal conversion. Under the terms of the National Energy Act, new utility plants were required to be built to use coal or a fuel other than oil or gas. Those plants already in operation which used oil or gas were to switch to other fuels by 1990. The energy secretary could order some industries on a case-by-case basis to switch fuels.[14]

DOE efforts to promote coal conversion may be expected to encounter resistance from people living in the vicinity of the proposed plant. As relatively clean-burning supplies of natural gas and residual oil become harder to obtain and more expensive, DOE officials are likely to call for the substitution of U.S. coal. By promoting increased use of coal DOE may also encounter opposition from the Environmental Protection Agency. EPA will seek to insure that new coal-burning facilities comply with clean air statutes.

State energy planning processes are affected by federal government pressure to establish integrated superregional power supply systems. This in turn has some affect on state government provision for public participation in energy facility siting.

From 1935 until the creation of the federal Department of Energy in 1977, the Federal Power Commission had urged local and regional interconnections of utility grid systems on the grounds that this would increase the efficiency and reliability of power delivery. By pooling generating capacity, the burden of meeting peak loads could be distributed among a number of utilities. Through pooling arrangements smaller systems, often municipal or rural cooperative electric utilities, were permitted access to large hydroelectric facilities. Coordination over a wide geographic area seemed to minimize operating costs and capital expenditures for plant construction. Building a few very large facilities enabled the facility siting process to produce the required amount of power with minimum adverse environmental impact.[15]

In the Federal Power Act of 1935, FPC was charged with rooting out unconsionable business practices of privately owned utilities. Yet the law (16 USC sec. 824) also directed the FPC to

> . . . divide the country into regional districts for the *voluntary* interconnection and coordination of facilities for the generation, transmission, and sale of electrical energy.[16]

It was not until 1960 that FPC began an ambitious effort to study the need for increased coordination in the industry. In its National Power Survey in 1964, the FPC proposed the goal of complete integration of all electrical power systems.[17] Even after the northeast blackout of 1965, the FPC called for "acceleration of the present trend toward . . . stronger interconnections between systems."[18]

Conforming to FPC directives, northeastern utilities were the first to form a regional coordinating council (1966). The purpose of the council was to set up regional planning entities, to formulate minimum reliability standards, to review construction plans for extra-high-voltage transmission lines and generating facilities, and to encourage interconnections between bulk power suppliers.

Following another major blackout on the Pennsylvania-New Jersey-Maryland interconnection in 1967, the FPC stepped up its pressure upon utilities, encouraging them to form regional councils. These councils are voluntary associations of utilities held together by mutual determination of participants who are free to end their membership on stipulated terms.[19] There are no formal sanctions for use against council members and the councils seem to facilitate exchange of information on plans for additions to regional grids.

While only about 13 percent of U.S. electrical energy is generated by civilian nuclear power plants, the federal role in the energy facility siting process for nuclear plants is extensive. This is logical given that atomic energy technology, from its inception, was initiated and actively guided through its development by the federal government rather than through private enterprise. The chief federal agency charged with supervision of civilian nuclear power is the Nuclear Regulatory Commission (NRC).

Due primarily to several Supreme Court decisions, opportunities for public participation in AEC/NRC administrative decision-making have been expanded. The public's right to participate in administrative decision-making is widely accepted. Federal energy agencies are obligated by their own regulations to insure public participation. The problem which remains to be resolved is the extent and scope of that participation.[20] In the past the public has played an important role in AEC regulatory proceedings. It has served as a check on the adequacy of safety and environmental reviews by government regulators.[21]

The NRC, like the former AEC, has a specific statutory requirement that a hearing be granted upon the request of any person whose interests may be affected by the proceedings.[22] The NRC, and the AEC before it, have been the main targets for challenges by environmentalists. Environmental intervenors have attempted to turn each licensing proceeding into a broader discussion of social policy. The AEC and NRC have responded to this problem by imposing more specific requirements before intervention will be granted.[23] The requirements force intervenors to confine their arguments to specific and pertinent facts directly relevant to their interests. Citizen participation is tolerated if addressed to technical aspects of the project, such as reactor safety, but this has limited the scope of licensing hearings. The hearings are structured so as to avoid discussion of broad policy questions involving the conflicting needs of energy production and environmental protection.[24] By focusing the hearings on highly technical questions which are often beyond the comprehension of the general public, meaningful public participation in the hearings is precluded.

The AEC/NRC decision to license a generating station represents a decision that a designated area will be exposed to an unquantified task. Local residents in the vicinity of the plant are forced to absorb most of the environmental and safety risks, while electricity consumers over a huge service area enjoy the benefits. Benefits also accrue to owners of the new facility.

The question of whether the benefits of a particular nuclear power plant are worth the safety and environmental risks must be answered by federal administrators. As a direct result of the March 1979 Harrisburg-Three Mile Island nuclear power plant incident, increased agency and congressional scrutiny is being given to review of proposed nuclear facilities.

However, the history of the Three Mile Island facility itself discloses that local opposition to nuclear power plants can be neutralized by furnishing economic benefits to the affected communities. Economic compensation for a new facility was made by the utility to the affected municipality. Indeed, the town located closest to the TMI nuclear plant (Goldsboro) receives all of its property tax revenue from Metropolitan Edison, which owns and operates the Three Mile Island nuclear complex.[25]

While provisions for some form of public participation in nuclear plant siting decision are maintained, much of that participation appears to be procedural rather than substantive. Federal nuclear power regulation contains few extraordinary opportunities or resources to make possible increased public participation in the licensing process. However, dramatic changes in the federal role in energy facility siting can be anticipated as a result of the Three Mile Island incident.

The increasing interconnection of utility grids, the establishment of regional councils of power producers, the ongoing effort of federal agencies to promote integration of utility power supply systems, and continued federal regulation of civilian nuclear power plants all signify a centralization of decision-making power which puts local citizens at a disadvantage in the energy facility planning process. The degree of interconnection and coordination appears to be particularly advanced in the case of the mid-Atlantic states.

Conclusions

In recent years states have found themselves in a position in which they must become more involved in the energy facility siting process. This is due to concern for a secure and adequate supply of energy as well as to dissatisfaction with an energy facility siting process which did not accommodate meaningful public determination and discussion of important issues. Most of the five mid-Atlantic states studied have especially become involved in determining long-term energy needs and evaluating the environmental impact of energy facilities. However, they generally are less concerned with the issue of local economic impact. Due to increased state involvement, opportunities for public participation in energy facility siting have changed. In general as states have assumed greater authority in the energy facility siting process, greater opportunities have been provided in the process of statewide public discussion of the question of need and environmental, economic, and social issues. At the same time, the influence of local interests has been curtailed.

Among the mid-Atlantic states examined, local governments and citizens are permitted to influence siting decisions to varying degrees. Because New York and Maryland have assumed greater authority for determining the need for new energy facilities and the suitability of sites, well in advance of actual power plant construction, the influence of local interests has been most diminished in these states. In the past, municipalities and citizens' groups which felt aggrieved by a proposed facility could count on blocking the project in the final permitting phase of the energy facility siting process. As state governments have assumed more powers in determining need and site selection for new facilities, the permitting phase has been modified. New York and Maryland have streamlined the permitting process by better coordinating permitting at the state level and by curtailing the issuance of local permits. This has reduced the number of veto points available to citizens' groups and municipal officials. At the opposite extreme, the states of Delaware and New Jersey have not curtailed the local role in energy facility siting, although both states do evaluate state energy needs and power plant environmental impact. Delaware is the most explicit in its policy of retaining local authority in siting decisions, which state officials justify in terms of the magnitude of environmental and economic impacts of energy facilities on local communities. The small size and population of the state affords it the advantage of conveniently melding state and local interests, interests which often coincide.

The dynamics of federal intervention in the facility siting process have contributed toward the trend of increased state influence. FPC efforts to promote interconnections of utility power grids, to spur the creation of regional councils of utilities, and to "scale up" projects to furnish power to larger interstate service areas all have encouraged the states to assume more responsibility in the energy facility siting process. DOE efforts to get utilities to convert to coal-burning plants have involved pressure upon state energy agencies to approve coal-burning facilities. Despite presidential proposals to increase federal supervision of utilities, Congress has chosen to allow key desion-making power to remain with state regulatory bodies. Federal supervision continues to be most pronounced in the case of nuclear power facilities. Yet citizen participation is increasingly constrained in the case of licensing nuclear facilities.

These conclusions suggest that the public's need for energy will take precedence over local environmental and economic concerns and that local affected publics will be less able to promote their interests independently in the energy facility siting process. This may signify a diminishing ability of citizens to influence important decisions affecting them. Where energy facility decisions have been made without active state government and public involvement prior to the permitting stage, citizens' interests were also inadequately protected. It remains to be seen whether provisions for public participation in comprehensive state energy facility siting processes will be a definite improvement.

Notes

1. The General Assembly of Pennsylvania, Senate Bill No. 781, as amended June 5, 1978.

2. David Howard Davis, *Energy Politics*, 2nd edition (New York: St. Martin's Press, 1978), p. 143.

3. Bob Rankin, "Electric Rate Reform: A Tricky Issue," *Congressional Quarterly* 35:13 (1977):544-554.

4. Ibid., p. 546.

5. Pennsylvania Senate Bill No. 781, as amended June 5, 1978. New York's site selection process is for steam electric generating plants.

6. Public Service Law, McKinney's Consolidated Laws of New York Annotated, sections 140-142.

7. Pennsylvania Senate Bill No. 781, April 26, 1977.

8. Annotated Code of Maryland, Natural Resources Article, sec. 3-306.1.

9. Public Service Law, sec. 146(d).

10. Rankin, "Electric Rate Reform," p. 549.

11. Ibid., p. 545.

12. Ann Pelham, "Energy Bill: The End of an Odyssey," *Congressional Quarterly* 36:42 (1978):3041.

13. Ibid.

14. Ibid., pp. 3040-3041.

15. Michael S. Hamilton, "Bulk Power Supply Reliability and Proposals for a National Grid: Roadsigns in What Direction?" *Policy Studies Journal* 7:1 (1978):96-112.

16. Ibid.

17. Davis, *Energy Politics*, p. 167.

18. Federal Power Commission, *Northeast Power Failure, November 9 and 10, 1965* (Washington, D.C.: Government Printing Office, 1965), pp. 7-8.

19. Hamilton, "Bulk Power," p. 99.

20. E. Dennis Muchicki, "The Proper Role of the Public in Nuclear Power Plant Licensing Decisions," *Atomic Energy Law Journal* 15 (Spring 1973):34-59. For the case, see *Calvert Cliffs Coordinating Comm.* v. *AEC*, 449 F. 2d 1109 (D.C. Cir. 1971).

21. W. Thomas Jacks, "The Public and the Peaceful Atom: Participation in AEC Regulatory Proceedings," *Texas Law Review* 52 (March 1974):466-525.

22. Muchnicki, "The Proper Role of the Public," p. 40.

23. Ibid., p. 41.

24. Ibid., p. 43.

25. "CBS News," CBS telecast, March 29, 1979: "Report on Three Mile Island," narrated by Walter Cronkite.

15 Electricity: Toward a Regional Strategy

Kai N. Lee

Of all energy forms electricity is most deeply committed to a centralized, capital-intensive, high-technology system of supply—the "hard path."[1] Precisely for this reason, electric energy confronts technological, economic, and political challenges of broad scope and controversy, particularly in nuclear power. The changes being undertaken and debated in electric power supply are accordingly significant, not only in themselves, but because these shifts suggest the institutional frameworks and public policies that lie beyond the hard path.

This chapter considers electric power as a multi-state regional undertaking, using the recent experience of the Pacific Northwest (Idaho, Montana, Oregon, and Washington) as a test case.[2] Three conclusions are suggested. First, the large and complex differences among the existing power supply networks require that national energy policies be adapted to regional variations. Second, the legacy of regional coordination, led by the federal government in the Tennessee Valley and throughout the West, provides an important forum for intergovernmental cooperation. Third, the technological and economic intricacies of power supply put an extraordinary burden on policy implementation, and thus on public administration. In particular, governmental leadership at the regional level may hold the key to moving toward marketlike, incentive-oriented, decentralized policy—the best hope for moving away from the inflexibilities of the hard path at acceptable cost.

Shifting Policy Priorities: A Brief History of BPA

The transition now underway in the Pacific Northwest is instructive. Long the center of the nation's hydroelectric development, the Northwest still meets 80 percent of its electrical demand from water power. But the hydropower that has for four decades been the mainstay of the region is now largely developed. Further growth in demand will have to be supplied by conservation, coal, nuclear, and renewable and unconventional sources. The utilities forecast additions to the regional power supply of just under 26,000 megawatts of generating capacity by 1998.[3] At today's prices this

The author acknowledges helpful conversations with Martin Marts, Donna Klemka, Hayward Alker, David Olson, Stuart Scheingold, Sterling Munro, and Randall Hardy.

would be a capital investment of over $30 billion. These additions, largely of coal and nuclear generation—referred to as thermal sources—would somewhat more than double the average power available in the region. But the increment is expensive. For comparison, the Bonneville Power Administration (BPA) of the U.S. Department of Energy anticipates that investment in the federal hydro system in 1998 will amount to only $8.5 billion.[4] Thermal power will dwarf the existing system in cost.

As these figures make plain, choices made in the next several years will commit the Northwest for at least a generation to major new sources of electricity and their environmental, economic, and social consequences. In this context, the need for regional management of energy and resources appears self-evident, although how responsibilities should be divided is far from clear. BPA, the existing regional agency, was chartered in 1937 to market federal hydropower; it has performed an indispensable mission. But growth, estimated in part by federal investments in the Pacific Northwest, has broadened the scope of public responsibility and made social choice complex and unwieldy. Bonneville is certain to retain a major role, though its mission and functions will change.

Yet there are important responsibilities that BPA cannot or should not bear alone in planning and managing the multiple considerations at stake in regional power development. For Bonneville occupies one corner of a traditional "iron triangle" or subgovernment long committed to development and expansion of power supply. At the other corners sit the Senate Energy Committee, chaired by Henry Jackson, Democrat of Washington; and the utilities and aluminum refiners of the Northwest, the main recipients of BPA power.

For a generation, BPA, the utilities, and their congressional patrons quietly developed national resources for the region's benefit. The principal policy shaping this investment program has been the "preference clause" of the Bonneville Project Act of 1937, which gave first call on federal hydropower to public power agencies—municipalities, public utility districts, and rural electric cooperatives. Despite the ideological baggage carried by "socialist" public power, there was no shortage of electricity in the early years. Public agencies, most dependent on BPA for all their electricity, flourished; there are 116 such preference customers of Bonneville today.

As the hydro capability of the region's rivers neared its limits, BPA and its utility clients moved toward thermal power. Thirteen thermal projects, nine nuclear and four coal-fired, are now on line, under construction, or in licensing to serve northwestern loads. Rapidly escalating costs and environmental opposition slowed, and then stalled, the thermal power program. Gradually, the continued rise of demand began to press on the once-abundant regional supply. In 1973 BPA halted sales of firm power to privately owned utilities; by 1975 it became clear that large industrial users which buy directly from Bonneville would not be able to contract for power beyond the 1980s; and in 1976 BPA issued Notices of Insufficiency to its public power customers, a move that legally released Bonneville from meeting these utilities' requirements after 1983.

As demand has grown beyond the capacity of the low-cost federal hydro pool, controversy and competition have been ignited among political and interest-group leaders. With the termination of firm federal hydro sales to privately owned utilities in 1973, retail rates in these companies' service areas began to rise. By the mid-1970s residential customers in Portland, Oregon, paid prices more than two and a half times as high as those charged consumers in Clark County, Washington, just across the Columbia River in a public power district. The Oregon legislature has enacted legislation declaring the whole state a public power agency, although no attempt has so far been made to claim a larger share of federal hydro under the preference policy.

These forces converged on Congress, beginning in 1977, seeking a major revision of the Bonneville Project Act of 1937, and with it a set of new—and somewhat conflicting—roles for BPA. In August 1979 the Senate passed a bill that charts new directions, though when, or whether, the House would follow suit remained in doubt.[5]

The Senate bill establishes four policies of relevance. First, future expansions of the regional power supply are to follow "soft path" priorities; first preference is given to conservation; second to renewable and high-efficiency resources (such as cogeneration); only then can "other" resources—a euphemism for nuclear and coal—be developed. In each case, alternative projects are compared in terms of their delivered cost to the consumer; the most cost-effective is selected, though conservation is permitted a 10 percent bonus.

Second, counterbalancing this commitment to the soft path, BPA is authorized to purchase on long-term contracts the capability of new sources of power. The term "capability" means that Bonneville—and the region's ratepayers—will pay, whether or not a power plant performs as expected. This open-ended commitment has been strongly lobbied for by the utility industry as a means to obtain the lowest-cost financing. Such a policy thus favors capital-intensive technologies.

Third, residential and agricultural consumers served by private utilities are granted lower wholesale costs, to ease the disparity in retail rates. The difference is made up by raising the rates of large industrial users.

Fourth, at the suggestion of the four northwestern governors, a five-member regional council has been established, with one gubernatorial appointee from each state and the Bonneville administrator. The council is responsible for formulating a regional power plan, regional forecasts, and model conservation standards.

The Political Issues

With rising and unequal utility rates, environmentalists calling for more conservation and "no nukes," and utilities anxious to proceed with any project that will produce kilowatts, electric power planning has become an arena filled with clashing interests. The administration of public organizations in this arena is accordingly a political task, one in which leadership is crucial.[6] This is the classic setting for Selznick's analysis of institutionalization, the process of clothing organizational entities with political values and social meaning.[7] Selznick discerned three essential ingredients shared by all successful institutions.[8] The first is a set of institutional objectives and purposes, sufficient to engage the loyalties of organization members—an institutional ideology. Second, the support of external constituencies, such as the utility and industrial support that undergirds the iron triangle of BPA. Third, successful institutions must endure, and they must accordingly make provision for recruiting new leadership as time passes.

It is crucial to institutional design that the public interests to be defined in the Northwest are numerous and mutually incompatible: short-run economic pressure for conservation. Therefore, more than one institutional voice is needed. That is, no single organization can control regional power affairs. Instead, a network of interdependent organizations is required to articulate publicly the competing views that need to be balanced and rebalanced in the task of regional governance.[9]

In particular, state governments are not about to surrender their authorities in energy facility siting, regulation of retail rates for electricity, or the police powers needed to enforce conservation policies to any multistate body. Many of the powers "needed" by a single regional energy authority are simply not available. Regional governance must involve shared—that is, intergovernmental—leadership and institutional redefinition.

A persistent theme of any new institutional structure will be the conflict which has plagued the existing one: competition between short-run economic interest and long-run objectives. The disparity between private and public utility rates has generated wide awareness that short-run interests are at stake in regional power planning—but without an accompanying sense of the long-term reverberations of those interests. This foreshortening of the intricacies of utility planning into the controversy over preferential hydro allocation can only make institutional maintenance itself precarious. Even if parochial economic interests remain primary, however, there will be considerable tension with less immediate objectives.[10] Despite the steep rise in electric power rates, energy conservation, environmental quality, and an enhanced sense of the social ends served by energy are all objectives which cannot be removed from the agenda or wholly sacrificed to short-run gain.

The challenge facing the leadership of regional institutions is to develop programs able to meet the challenge of these goals in a way that is politically compatible with the shared concern to protect vested economic interests. One should not underestimate the magnitude of the change involved. The iron triangle based upon short-run economic interests survived presidential changes in policy in the 1950s; the realignment suggested in figure 15-1 is at least as profound a change. Indeed, it is precisely for this reason that institutionalization is important—social forces larger than those available through reorganization must be mobilized. In particular, ties to interests and interest groups that have not been represented in the past need to be developed. The rising concern for energy in state and local governments is accordingly an important opportunity to be grasped.

Institutionalization of broad public values in the regional power program is the central element of managing the conflicts which lie ahead. Yet regional authority is at best a fragile idea in the American governmental tradition.[11] Moreover, the ideologically charged legacy of public power means that the very specification of which responsibilities are governmental and which private is continuingly contentious. Regional governance must

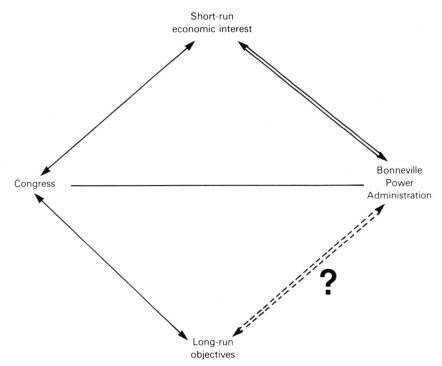

Figure 15-1. The Iron Triangle of Economic Interests

thus be grounded on that set of tasks which is generally regional, and focus upon responsibilities that are crucially public. Wise policy does not mean more government, nor does it necessarily mean a new layer of government at the regional level. Neither, in the late twentieth century, is likely to be workable.

The salience of power planning today, however, makes it possible to evolve a definition of the public interests to be nurtured, a definition reflecting broad democratic judgment.[12] Such a near-term definition of the "public cognizance" would comprise the core of the organizational ideology needed to achieve successful institutionalization of regional organizations, and thus flesh out the bare bones of new legislation.[13]

The Regional Council Approach

The regional council is similar to an interstate compact: a joint state-federal body with intergovernmental planning responsibilities. Its most striking feature is a limited but real assertion of federal supremacy: the Bonneville administrator, the federal member of the council, must vote with the majority on all major program decisions, including thermal power station investments. Beyond a regional power plan, forecasts, and model conservation standards, the Senate leaves to the council itself the definition of its missions and activities. Here I outline a set of functions which would promote institutionalizing public cognizance; this is a possible, if by no means certain, outcome of a new congressional mandate.

If evolution toward the soft path is to be sustained, the process of weaning the utilities away from their existing loyalty to thermal power must be backed by material resources and political support. The regional council can contribute to the latter by assuring that the informal and formal basis of regional actions reflects a far broader constituency and agenda than has been traditional. Six central questions of regional policy will be recurrently at issue: financing of new power supply and conservation investments; forecasts of future demand; siting and the rules by which power sources are selected; conservation standards, which must be tailored to geography and use category; environmental protection; and, most controversially, allocation of low cost federal hydropower.

The council is to develop a plan addressing these matters and, with the administrator, a public record on regional power decisions. The administrator must in turn state his reasons for departing from the regional plan. In a sense, the regional council is the analogue of the military Joint Chiefs of Staff, representing those affected by regional power policy yet not exercising decisional authority, which remains largely with BPA.

Funding independent of Bonneville's control, through a surcharge of up to 0.02 mills/KWH, providing an annual budget of up to $2 million, is sufficient to provide a small staff for studies, analyses, and staff support of council activities. A number of persons could be detailed to serve on the regional staff from state and local government agencies. Analysts from the Oregon Department of Energy, for instance, could give the council the benefit of that agency's experience in analyzing regional forecasts.

The functions to be served by the regional council are part of the larger institutional structure of regional power operations and policy. The council serves many of the purposes of a regional energy legislature, but with only limited authority to enact policy. Its legislative function reflects the continuing important divisions in the region about the ends which should be pursued by electric power. The compromises endorsed by the council are subject to an indirect electoral test, since the members serve at the pleasure of elected statewide public officials.

The Bonneville administrator is a regional executive, with decision-making authority that is, in principle, broader than that of any other single agent. In practice, however, the "legislative" powers assigned to the council provide checks and balances of considerable strength—if the council develops and exercises its potential influence.

Yet structural redesign by itself cannot solve the problems of regional power policy. The political environment of a public agency tends to outweigh both its organizational structure and official mandate as a determinant of its behavior.[14] The key to the existing political environment is the set of material interests linking together the utility establishment. If there were a way to tie precarious values such as long-range planning, energy conservation, and environmental quality to decisions concerning electric power, informal patterns of influence might develop which would institutionalize these values.

The Senate bill goes partway down this path in its requirement that cost-effective conservation and renewable resources be developed before thermal resources. This framework ties precarious values to BPA purchase authority. Whether this three-stage set of congressional priorities will be heeded by Bonneville remains to be seen, especially in light of the enormous pressure from utilities to use regional purchase to spread the costs of nuclear plants already planned. Moreover, the vaguely defined regional resource plan and model conservation standards invite technocratic misapplication. Both these provisions can easily be turned into symbolic defenses of business as usual, thus encouraging cynicism and further opposition.[15]

It is thus worth trying to harness electric power to the cause of institutionalization more directly. This is the purpose of the proposal discussed next.

Revising the Policy of Public Preference

Since 1906 federal law has provided that publicly owned utilies should enjoy preferential access to electricity developed at federal projects.[16] With the rising rates experienced by customers of privately owned utilities in the Northwest, there has been pressure to reallocate the economic benefits of low-cost federal hydro. The Senate bill provides the residential consumers of investor-owned utilities a wholesale power rate equal to that of public agencies. The question of preference has thus been framed this way: should the benefits of federal hydropower continue to be allocated to public power agencies, or should it be shifted to residential consumers no matter who delivers their power? Both visions of preference are too narrow, for neither set of claimants has bothered to reexamine the ends to be served by the public investment embodied in federal hydro.

The historical right of public bodies and cooperatives to federally developed power is clear. The New Deal Congress and President Franklin D. Roosevelt saw that multiple-purpose dams would provide broad, continuing economic and social benefits to large regions of the nation. The Tennessee and Columbia valleys have been the principal beneficiaries of that vision. Basic to this strategy of multi-purpose development was the extension of electric power to rural areas and to the public agencies that were then expanding to meet urban demand.

Since the 1950s, however, the publics have drifted away from their commitment to social progress. This is apparent in the quiet reluctance of northwestern public agencies to assist in the formation of new public entities, now that federal hydro is in short supply.[17] Moreover, the participation of the region's public agencies in large central-station projects has drawn public utilities away from the decentralized, responsive relationship to their ratepayers that constituted the historic strength of public power. In addition, the purposes supported by public power are often parochial and not in the broader regional interest. Local irrigation development has been promoted, for instance, at the expense of fisheries and downstream power generation.

If the claim of the public systems is tarnished, that of residential consumers promises at least to be durable. But if public preference is simply replaced by a residential preference policy, the economic discontent of residential consumers served by private utilities would be stilled, and with it the reviving interest in public power. This would be a sad and important loss. However weakened its conscience, public power remains a useful, sometimes influential counterweight to investor-owned companies. Diversity and competition—the so-called "yardstick" of public power, which provides a measure of private companies' efficiency—has served the Northwest and the nation well.[18] It is possible to modernize the yardstick without discarding it.

Federal hydropower can provide an invaluable incentive for public utilities to serve both their ratepayers and the region as a whole. But the permanent subsidy embodied in the preference clause needs reinterpretation if this incentive is to be harnessed. This can be accomplished through periodic reexamination of the ways in which publicly owned utilities advance the public interest. Where the long-term interests of the Pacific Northwest are well served by a utility and its associated local government, the agency's allocation of federal hydropower must be protected. Where a utility does not serve the public interest, its allocation should be phased down gradually. This would provide a strong but not abrupt signal that broad public values need attention.

The ends to be served by federal resources have become both complex and dynamic. While growth was once an unquestioned good, it must now be complemented by conservation. Where costs of production once fell before the advance of technology, rising rates now further dispossess the poor; and where industrialization, irrigation, and suburbanization once were the hallmarks of improving quality of life, the agenda of progress now requires informed judgments of new subtlety and balance.

The enormously valuable legacy of federal hydropower can contribute vitally to the search for this more complex, richer public interest—if the benefits of federal hydro are not permanently assigned to either a class of utilities or a class of ultimate consumers. In place of a preference policy, then, consider an incentive policy: the assignment of federal hydropower to a Pacific Northwest Public Incentive Pool (PIP).

At the outset, PIP resources would be assigned as they are now, to publicly owned utilities and cooperatives. Every three years, however, each utility receiving PIP would be required to justify its access to the benefits of federal hydro. Utilities would submit reports to an allocation committee responsible to the regional council; the committee's membership should by statute include representatives of the utilities, and consumer and environmental groups.

Reports to the committee would describe the ends served by PIP in the preceding three-year period. Among the broad public purposes that should be specified by Congress or the regional council are energy conservation, social justice, protection of natural resources, and business development that improves equality and employment. In addition, a utility might use Public Incentive resources to advance a regional or national policy objective, such as petroleum conservation through electrically assisted solar space and water heating. These reports would be subject to critiques by citizens and business and governmental organizations.

If in the judgment of the allocation committee a utility's use of Public Incentive resources met the evolving standards of the public interest, that utility would retain its allocation. If not, the committee would recommend to the BPA administrator that 15 percent of the utility's initial grant of PIP power be withdrawn: the utility would be given access, on a three-year contract, to wholesale power at the prevailing rate. The difference between the prevailing cost of power and PIP prices would be used to lower the prices of all classes of Bonneville customers. Withdrawal of PIP resources is equivalent to a surcharge on 15 percent of the allocation. The magnitude of the surcharge is set by the prevailing cost of nonfederal power. After another three years, a utility that had lost part of its PIP allocation could apply for reinstatement by submitting a report describing how the utility, its ratepayers, and its local government had utilized their total electric power sales in support of the public interest.

The recertification procedure resembles that required of holders of broadcast licenses from the Federal Communications Commission. To be sure, the FCC has often been criticized for insufficient vigilance in its regulatory undertakings; this is, by analogy, a potential weakness in the reallocation proposal. It is an acceptable one, however, since mere inaction by the allocation committee would result in preservation of allocations defined initially by congressional policy.

By requiring review every three years, the large number of utilities in the Northwest could be divided into three manageable pools, one pool to be reviewed each year. More than 2,000 megawatts of low-cost resources would be available for reallocation each year—a significant incentive in its own right for consumers seeking to scrutinize the reports of utilities under review.

The judgments of the allocation committee would, over time, form a body of "case law," serving to define the moving target of the public interest. As this judicial language suggests, precedent should influence the allocation committee heavily, so as to provide stability for utility planning. A utility that ignored the regional interest so defined would receive a gradual but strong economic signal. Over a twenty-year period, a utility consistently pursuing a selfish course would lose all PIP benefits. Examples of "selfish" behavior include acquiescence in new commercial or industrial customers without compensating conservation programs; soliciting of new commercial or industrial customers without accompanying attempts to ensure that service-area residents gain additional employment; or refusal to consider rising tailblock rates.

At the same time, the regional council acquires "legislative oversight" functions through PIP review, with the 15 percent withdrawal playing the role of a cut in appropriations by Congress. Such authority would strengthen the regional council dramatically by vesting it with the material leverage of economic sanctions. Without such significant power, the council would be hard pressed to prevail against the technocratic elite that dominates the utility establishment. The tendency of democratic participation, Selznick warned, is to dwindle to mere administrative involvement.[19]

Material interests, regularly scrutinized in public, provide a real—if imperfect—means to resist this tendency.

The definition of the public interest may seem perilously vague, indeed, naive, in a proposal by a social scientist. Moreover, the call to subject an allocation of public resources to political pressures seems idealistic at best, especially in a complex issue area such as regional electric power.[20] Even if the subjectivity inherent in estimates of the public interst can be tolerated, is it a proper use of public authority to attempt to manipulate the behavior of people in four states?[21]

These are substantial and serious challenges: can the regional council guide millions of consumers' judgments deftly enough to avoid the resistance that environmental regulation has engendered? And if it can, will the public interests to be pursued be at once clear enough to implement while flexible enough to adapt to uncertainties ahead?

Note first that this proposal affects the prices paid for power. The PIP process thus utilizes economic signals to "inform" consumers of the public purposes to be served by federal power. I put "inform" in quotation marks to emphasize that prices cannot transmit subtle messages. At the same time, the effectiveness of price signals depends on their simplicity. PIP is thus similar to the effluent charge, a means of charging for the right to dump pollutants into the environment.[22] More broadly, PIP belongs to a set of policy instruments that use market mechanisms to allocate scarce "public goods"[23] which cannot be sold efficiently through the free market.[24]

Second, it is worth pointing out that there are straightforward means of establishing criteria in each of the areas recommended for inclusion in the regional public interest. For example:

1. *Cost-effective conservation* as defined in the Senate bill.
2. *Social justice* through conservation subsidies to the poor.
3. *Conservation of natural resources* by protecting Columbia River salmon through minimization of peak-load power demands on the hydro-power system.[25]
4. *Sensible business development* that provides more jobs per kilowatt hour than the regional average.

These are not the only criteria that could be established by the council. But they are clear, quantifiable, and subject to independent examination and verification at reasonable or even minimal cost.

Cost-effective conservation is probably the most immediately important of these regional objectives. In 1978 David Bardin, Economic Regulatory Administrator of the U.S. Department of Energy, stated before the House subcommittee on Energy and Power, "The Administrator of the Bonneville Power Administration should be specifically authorized to require, as a condition of wholesale contracts, that distribution utilities institute comprehensive conservation programs, in cooperation with state and local governments."[26] This recommendation provides an explicit implementing mechanism through federal wholesale power sales. Employing the regional council as a forum to weigh the merits of utilities' conservation programs reinforces regional priorities in the decisions of the BPA administrator.

So profound a revision of the historic policy of public preference clearly raises a host of legal and administrative questions. But the highest barrier by far is political acceptability. The utilities, both public and private, resist any policy which impairs the predictability of their organizational environments.[27] At least until BPA gains confidence in its ability to meet its new mandates under congressional legislation the agency's leaders want the hot potato of federal hydro allocation to be handled by Congress. And the region's governors have little desire to acquire a regulatory authority with few electoral benefits—and many hazards.

Were it enacted, however, a Public Incentive allocation procedure would reinvigorate the public power movement. At the same time, the competition for the economic benefits of PIP resources would serve as a powerful incentive to all utilities to align their practices with the broad interests of the region.

Implications

The Pacific Northwest case has been explored in some detail to bring out the challenges—and the often-complex opportunities—of a regional approach to national energy policy. It is time now to explore these broader implications: the viability of a regional approach; possibilities for regional leadership such as the Bonneville Power Administration can provide in the Northwest; and the prospects of significant inclusion of the soft path in the future of electric power.

Historically, electric power networks have developed on a local basis. Although the Pacific Northwest industry structure of more than 120 utilities represents an extreme case of fragmentation, regulation and management of electricity production is concentrated at spatial scales smaller than the state. Multi-state power pools have been formed on a voluntary basis—with some federal prodding—and the large power stations of the hard path have been a major economic force pressing for regional integration.[28]

The historical diversity of the regional power pools constitutes the strongest argument for region-specific federal policies.[29] For example, the hydro-electric resource in the Pacific Northwest provides a peaking source of enormous size and value. The region's utilties have accordingly stressed baseload power in their planning. The heavy commitment to nuclear energy in New England, the greater Chicago area, and the Tennessee Valley illustrates the complementary situation: the greatest conservation savings in these areas is likely to come from peak-load management policies such as time-of-day pricing. Not only do existing generating technologies vary across the nation, but the projected large cost increases in all forms of power production will inevitably slow growth in demand and foster emphasis on cost-minimizing options such as cogeneration; these forces will increase the differences among regional supply systems.

In addition to technological diversity there are important organizational differences. More than three-fourths of the nation's electricity is marketed by investor-owned utilities. Accordingly, the strong position of public power in the Northwest is a regionally significant characteristic—one exploited in the Public Incentive proposal. Elsewhere, as in Texas, privately owned utilities often pace development of public policy.[30] Multi-utility consortia such as those that have sponsored New England's Yankee nuclear projects are also playing a major role in financing hard path options in some regions.

Several years ago Berlin, Cicchetti, and Gillen suggested that reorganization of the electric power industry would bring consumer and regulatory benefits.[31] The deepening financial and policy problems of the industry have made some of their proposals seem overoptimistic.[32] But their basic observation remains sound: for the foreseeable future, electric power is naturally organized at the regional level.

For all their variation, however, one common shortcoming affects all the regions except the TVA service area: regional leadership remains to be developed.[33] Indeed, a common complaint against federal policy has been the unrealized potential for regionally diverse leadership by the Federal Power Commission and its successor, the Federal Energy Regulatory Commission.[34] Regional marketing agents such as Bonneville have been recommended as centers of leadership, though there has been no detailed examination of the institutionalization problems since Selznick's pioneering work on TVA during the Second World War.

Aside from federally sponsored regional coordinators there are several other categories of plausible candidates. Vigorous state public utility commissions such as Wisconsin's can become regional leaders of policy innovation. State energy agencies like those in New York[35] or Oregon have also become involved in regional electrical policy, often through conservation and renewable resource programs. Investor-owned utilities operating in several contiguous states, such as Pacific Power and Light in the Northwest, or multi-utility power plant consortia like the Washington Public Power Supply System, can also assert regional leadership, though their business objectives will embody the public cognizance imperfectly and intermittently.

Thus, the mere presence of an organizational vessel for leadership hardly ensures institutionalization of the soft path. The complexity of electric power supply, together with the uncertainties of planning facilities that take a dozen years to build and then last a generation, shifts much of the burden of public policymaking onto the implementing agencies. A decade's harsh critiques of social policy that fail in implementation tradition suggest that the challenge facing regional power leadership is a sizable one.[36]

If the Senate mandate to pursue cost-effective conservation in the Northwest becomes law, a critical implementing step will be the interpretation of the term "cost-effective" in regulations and subsequent investment decisions. Reorganization of Bonneville to undertake its expanded missions will pose another important hurdle. Long dominated by its division of power management and a large engineering staff dedicated to expanding power supply, BPA has much of the institutional momentum of the utility organization that it is. Conservation activities have been buried, organizationally, within power management and current plans call for conservation to be elevated to branch status, commensurate with—but not superior to—other supplies of power. Creating a divisional-level assistant administrator for conservation and renewable resources would help advance the cause of these unfamiliar elements of the agency's mission.

More generally, intergovernmental cooperation needs to overcome a disjointed but pervasive preoccupation with transferring federal resources to lower levels of government. Federalism in the postwar era has been largely distributive, despite recurrent complaints about federal interference with local prerogatives. As the sometimes unhappy history of environmental policy demonstrates, however, regulatory federalism has yet to develop a satisfactory political and administrative rubric.[37]

The thread that runs through the problems of implementation, reorganization, and intergovernmental relations is administrative complexity. As the Public Incentive proposal suggests, the principal systematic approach to simplifying administrative complexity is reliance on marketlike signals—prices and other decentralized incentives that can lead to self-enforcing changes in behavior. The case of the Northwest illustrates how detailed and securely institutionalized even self-enforcing policies must be: if anything, the exceedingly narrow signaling capacity of prices dictates a region-specific "rifle shot" approach to policy design, instead of nationwide "shotgun" rules. The diversity of regional power pools offers a variety of incentive mechanisms—such as time-of-day pricing to manage peak loads—paralleling the Public Incentive Pool.

But the doubtful political feasibility of the PIP proposal underscores the fact that marketlike policies commonly encounter great resistance. In part the reluctance to use incentives derives from a tradition-bound moral sensibility: incentives to induce people to refrain from activities that are wrong is, in a sense, bribery. Resistance is compounded by the "public goods" character of the gains to be won by regulatory public policies, irrespective of implementing mechanism. The conservation gains resulting from PIP accrue at best to a utility service area, and individual consumers have little interest in risking higher prices for the sake of a chance to advance a diffuse common good.

Conclusions

The difference between hard and soft energy paths, Lovins observed, lies not in how much energy is used, but in the technical and sociopolitical *structure* of the energy system.[38] The regionally diverse structure of electric power supply in the United States limits the reach of both national and local utility policy: national conservation strategies run afoul of differences in geography and generating technology; and efforts by individual utilities to slow demand growth may lead perversely to higher short-run costs when the power supply is partly or wholly regional.

But a regional strategy for electricity must overcome large obstacles, even in areas, such as the Northwest, that already possess a region-scale institutional structure. The intertwined challenges of regional leadership and institutionalization of soft path values are at once unfamiliar and elusive in a society grown cynical about would-be leaders and puzzling over the long-run significance of our maddeningly slow-ripening crisis in energy. The responses now being implemented and debated in the Pacific Northwest and elsewhere manifest the dissaray, and the promise, of our search for feasible answers to the protean questions of energy.

Notes

1. Amory B. Lovins, "Energy Strategy: The Road Not Taken?" *Foreign Affairs* 55 (Fall 1976):65-96.

2. The Northwest case is drawn from Kai N. Lee and Donna L. Klemka, with Marion E. Marts, *Electric Power and the Future of the Pacific Northwest* (Seattle: Univ. of Washington Press, 1980), esp. chapters 5-7.

3. Pacific Northwest River Basins Commission, Power Planning Committee, *Review of Power Planning in the Pacific Northwest, Calendar Year 1977* (Vancouver, Wash., 1978), pp. 68-69.

4. Bonneville Power Administration, *1978 Annual Report* (Portland: BPA, 1979), p. 38.

5. U.S. Senate, "A BILL to assist the electrical consumers of the

Pacific Northwest," S. 885 (April 5, 1979), 96th Cong., 1st Sess. Reported by the Committee on Energy and National Resources and passed by the Senate on August 3, 1979; see Senate Report No. 96-272, "Pacific Northwest Electric Power Planning and Conservation Act." Two companion House bills are under consideration as this is written: H.R. 3508, the "establishment" version paralleling the Senate-passed bill, and H.R. 4159, an antinuclear, pro-soft path bill introduced by Representative James Weaver, Democrat of Oregon.

6. Ernst B. Haas, *Beyond the Nation-State* (Stanford, Calif.: Stanford Univ. Press, 1964), p. 88.

7. Philip Selznick, *Leadership in Administration* (New York: Harper and Row, 1957).

8. Ibid., pp. 14-17.

9. For a helpful typology of governance structures see John Gerard Ruggie, "International Responses to Technology: Concepts and Trends," *International Organization* 29 (1975):557-583; I promise here a "regime" form, in which no single organization monopolizes authority, resources, or power.

10. See Haas, p. 459.

11. Alan A. Altschuler and Robert W. Curry, "The Changing Environment of Urban Development Policy—Shared Power or Shared Impotence?" *Urban Law Annual* 10 (1975):3-41.

12. A similar idea is argued in Anthony Downs, "Up and Down with Ecology—the Issue-Attention Cycle," *Public Interest* 28 (Summer 1972):38-50.

13. The term "public cognizance" was coined by John Kenneth Galbraith, *Economics and the Public Purpose* (New York: New American Library, 1973), chapter 24. The notion of institutionalizing the public interest should be compared with legislative declarations of public purposes; see Theodore J. Lowi, *The End of Liberalism* (New York: Norton, 1969), chapters 5, 10, and compare Galbraith, *Economics*, chapter 29. Lowi sharply criticizes legislative policymaking, while Galbraith defends the ability of Congress to articulate the ever-elusive public interest.

14. Francis E. Rourke, *Bureaucracy, Politics, and Public Policy* (Boston: Little, Brown, 1969) p. 24.

15. Compare Murray Edelman, *The Symbolic Uses of Politics* (Urbana: Univ. of Illinois Press, 1964), chapters 1, 4, 5.

16. The Bonneville Project Act declares that "the administrator shall at all times . . . give preference and priority to public bodies and cooperatives. 16 U.S. Code 832c(a).

17. *Personal Interview*, BPA Official, February 1978.

18. The ability of public power agencies to induce lower cost service among neighboring investor-owned utilities is still controversial. See Martin

T. Farris and Roy Sampson, *Public Utilities: Regulation, Management, and Ownership* (Boston: Houghton Mifflin, 1973), p. 293; and Richard Hellman, *Government Competition in the Electric Utility Industry* (New York: Praeger, 1972), chapter 2 and p. 228.

19. Philip Selznick, *TVA and the Grass Roots* (Berkeley: Univ. of California Press, 1949), pp. 265-266.

20. Bruce J. Ackerman, Susan Rose-Ackerman, James W. Sawyer, Jr., and Dale W. Henderson, *The Uncertain Search for Environmental Quality* (New York: The Free Press, 1974), p. 220.

21. Charles L. Schultze, *The Public Use of Private Interest* (Washington, D.C.: Brookings Institution, 1977), p. 12.

22. A Myrick Freeman III, Robert H. Haveman, and Allen V. Knesse, *The Economics of Environmental Policy* (New York: Wiley, 1973), chapter 5.

23. An influential discussion of public goods is Mancur Olson, *The Logic of Collective Action* (Cambridge, Mass.: Harvard Univ. Press, 1965).

24. See Schultze, *Public Use.*

25. See Lee, Klemka, and Marts, *Electric Power*, chapter 4.

26. David J. Bardin, statement in *Pacific Northwest Electric Power Issues*, hearings before the Subcommittee on Energy and Power, Committee on Interstate and Foreign Commerce, House of Representatives, 95th Cong., 2nd Sess., Serial No. 95-193 (Washington, D.C.: Committee Print, 1979), p. 43. Emphasis added.

27. See Lee, Klemka, and Marts, *Electric Power*, chapter 3, and the theory of the "technostructure" developed in John Kenneth Galbraith, *The New Industrial State* (New York: New America Library, 1967), chapters 2-8.

28. See the analysis in Stephen Breyer and Paul W. MacAvoy, "The Federal Power Commission and the Coordination Problem in the Electrical Power Industry," *Southern California Law Review* 46 (1973):661-712.

29. Douglas Bauer and Alan S. Hirshberg, "Improving the Efficiency of Electricity Generation and Usage," *Energy Conservation and Public Policy*, ed. John C. Sawhill (Englewood Cliffs, N.J.: Prentice-Hall, 1979), p. 145.

30. John Walsh, "Texas Power Companies Converting from Natural Gas to Coal, Lignite," *Science* 198 (1977):471-474; and "Texas Is Testing Ground for Impact of Coal Use on Economic Growth," ibid., 586-588.

31. Edward Berlin, Charles J. Cicchetti, and William J. Gillen, *Perspective on Power* (Cambridge, Mass.: Ballinger, 1974), chapters 5, 6.

32. Kai N. Lee, "Energy Politics vs. Energy Policies," *Public Administration Review* 36 (1976):114-115.

33. On TVA see Deborah Shapley, "TVA Today: Former Reformers in an Era of Expensive Electricity," *Science* 194 (1976):814-818.

34. See Breyer and MacAvoy, "The Federal Power Commission," and Berlin, Cicchetti, and Gillen, *Perspective*, chapter 5.

35. Luther J. Carter, "New York Puts Together Its Own Intrastate Energy Policy and Plan," *Science* 199 (1978):864-868.

36. Eugene Bardach, *The Implementation Game* (Cambridge, Mass.: MIT Press, 1977).

37. See Ackerman et al., *Uncertain Search*, and Robert D. Thomas, "Intergovernmental Coordination in the Implementation of National Air and Water Pollution Policies," *Public Policy Making in a Federal System*, ed. Charles O. Jones and R.D. Thomas (Beverly Hills: Sage, 1976), chapter 6.

38. Lovins, "Strategy," p. 77.

16 State Commission Response to Implementing the Energy Act: Intergovernmental Relations Revisited

Douglas N. Jones

Occasionally there comes along a major piece of federal legislation which in its enactment, implementation, and playing out includes all the ingredients for a lively time in intergovernmental—and indeed intragovernmental—relations, state and federal. In racial relations the Civil Rights Act was clearly such a piece; so was the Revenue Sharing Act for fiscal relations. I believe the recently passed National Energy Act (NEA) is another such piece in the case of regulatory relations.

Accordingly, my remarks treat the legislative philosophy and central provisions of the NEA against the backdrop of four recurring themes in intergovernmental and intragovernmental relations. These themes are what seem to me the traditional ones of Diversity and Uniformity; Decentralization and Recentralization; Pluralism and Policy Determination; and Carrots and Sticks. First, however, a sketch of the NEA legislation itself.

The National Energy Act in Four Parts

In November 1978 President Carter signed into law five separate pieces of energy legislation after eighteen months of congressional debate and deliberation. These were the Public Utility Regulatory policies Act (PURPA; P.L. 95-617); the National Energy Conservation Policy Act (NECPA; P.L. 95-619); the Powerplant and Industrial Fuel Use Act (FUA; P.L. 95-620); the Natural Gas Policy Act (NGPA; P.L. 95-621); and the Energy Tax Act (ETA; P.L. 95-618). Of these acts, all but the last one (ETA) will have a direct and substantial impact on the responsibilities and agendas of state public utility commissions (PUCs). And, as will be mentioned later, even this (federal) tax legislation has an important indirect bearing on one aspect of state commission regulation. The first one listed (PURPA) is the focus of this chapter; the second one (NECPA) is of next

The views presented are those of the author and do not necessarily reflect the views or opinions of the National Regulatory Research Institute or the Ohio State University.

importance to this story; and the third and fourth (FUA and NGPA) are of passing reference in these remarks.

Public Utility Regulatory Policies Act

Briefly put, the Public Utility Regulatory Policies Act has as its goals (1) the conservation of energy supplied by electric and gas utilities; (2) optimally efficient use of utility resources (fuel) and facilities (plant); and (3) equitable rates to electric and gas users. To achieve these several goals six ratemaking standards were established; for example, rates that "track costs"; a presumption against traditional declining block rates (as consumption increases); a presumption in favor of rates that vary with time (time-of-day rates and seasonal rates); and encouragement of special capacity-saving arrangements with customers like offering interruptible rates and load control devices. In addition, five more standards are offered having to do with discouraging master metering in new buildings; constraining the use of automatic adjustment clauses; prohibiting the use of promotional or political advertising by utilities (except if paid for by stockholders); and relations of the utility to customers.

Now, with respect to the six ratemaking standards, the requirement of PURPA is that the state commissions "consider" them. There is no obligation for *adoption* unless state law requires adoption where the evidence is persuasive or, said another way, where to not adopt the standard would be "arbitrary and capricious." For this last reason PUC decisions on these standards must be reached in public, in writing, and be reviewable in state court. With respect to the other five policy standards, on the other hand, there is a legal obligation to adopt if the consideration process determines them to be appropriate and consistent with state law.

So while PURPA is mostly not mandatory as to the *outcome* of state PUC deliberations on these eleven matters, it is mandatory as to *what must be considered*. Further, the act does impose certain mandatory requirements on state commissions. For example, each state commission must

Officially acknowledge to DOE its ratemaking authority with respect to the utilities listed by DOE as being covered by the act.

Complete its consideration process for the ratemaking standards within three years, and for the additional regulatory standards within two years.

Include public notice and public hearing(s) in its consideration process, and allow consumer and federal participation.

Render a written determination which is based both upon its findings and the evidence presented at the hearing(s), and which is made available to the public.

Determine, to the maximum extent practicable, cost-of-service on the basis of a method that identifies cost differences by both time-of-use and major cost category (in prescribing such a method, the commission must take marginal costs into account).

Report annually to DOE, in such manner as DOE may prescribe, on its progress in carrying out the act, including its rationale for "grandfathering" any prior proceedings.

National Energy Conservation Policy Act—NECPA

A second part of the NEA establishes federal policy regarding residential energy conservation. Large electric and gas utilities—and therefore state commissions—are required to play a central role in carrying out this policy. Electric utilities selling more than 750 million kilowatt hours annually (other than for resale) and gas utilities selling more than 10 billion cubic feet annually to residential customers are covered by this act.

Each covered utility is required by NECPA to

Inform all its residential customers of suggested conservation measures, including costs and savings.

Distribute a list of qualified suppliers, installers, and financers.

Offer to conduct an on-site home energy audit.

Offer to arrange the installation and financing of conservation measures selected by the customer.

Offer to allow repayment of the conservation loan through its regular periodic billing procedures.

The conservation measures that must be covered by this "residential conservation service" include pretty mundane things like caulking and weather-stripping, insulation, storm doors, and clock thermostats. Although the legal requirement to offer this conservation service is imposed directly upon the covered utilities, the governor of each state is given the option of developing and administering a statewide program, subject to rules prescribed by DOE. All covered regulated utilities must be included in such a state plan and "nonregulated utilities" (public and cooperative systems not subjected to state or TVA ratemaking authority) may be included, in the interest of a unified effort.

For purposes of our story, the designation of a "lead" state agency—-whether the PUC or the Energy Office—to manage this conservation program directly affects the PUCs, since all costs incurred by regulated utilities in complying with this conservation program are subject to PUC approval.

Finally, NECPA requires DOE to directly assume responsibility for the conservation programs of all covered regulated utilities in a state, if a state does not have an approved state plan, or inadequately carries out an approved plan, or decides not to participate.

FUA, NGPA, and ETA

The Fuel Use Act prohibits the use of natural gas or oil in new electric power plants, as well as the use of natural gas in existing power plants. While there are numerous grounds for exemptions from these prohibitions, each exemption (both temporary and permanent) must be specifically requested by the utility and approved by DOE. Any exemptions granted to an electric utility by DOE may be conditioned upon the use of such "fuel conservation measures" as will reduce the amount of prohibited fuel consumed as a result of the exemption. In general, FUA will not have a direct impact on state utility regulation, except that the costs incurred by regulated utilities in complying with the act and subject to PUC review and approval.

The Natural Gas Policy Act extends federal regulation of natural gas pricing to the intrastate market, previously subject only to state regulation. The act also gradually removes all federal price regulation, with price controls to be entirely lifted by 1985.

The act further requires that distribution company (state determined) rates for ultimate consumers be fully consistent with the incremental pricing aspects of the (federally determined) pipeline price. While it is assumed that incremental pricing for pipeline transactions can be handled within the prevailing institutional arrangements (that is, among the pipeline, the distribution company, and the federal government participants), the pass-through provision requires a federal role in an area previously reserved to the states—establishing distribution company rates for ultimate consumers. Here the act authorizes the U.S. attorney general to enforce the pass-through provision.

This new federal role in gas distribution ratemaking obviously affects state utility commissions. Commissions may also be affected by the secretary of energy's authority to prohibit certain pipeline curtailments, and by the president's emergency authority to allocate gas supplies and allow extraordinary gas purchases.

The Energy Tax Act includes among its provisions encouraging certain kinds of fuel use and avoidance of others in power generation through several tax preference and tax penalty features. For our purposes here, the additions to the Investment Tax Credit for utilities are worth noting.

Themes and Issues in Implementing NEA

While it is, of course, still early, the outlines of the states' response to NEA and the public administration implications of that implementation are becoming clearer.

So that you may apply whatever discount factor you think appropriate to what follows, I would mention that my vantage point is one of having worked indirectly on the legislation during 1976 and 1977 as a public utility economist in the Congressional Research Service, Library of Congress, and directly on implementing the legislation in my present position as director of the National Regulatory Research Institute. In this latter capacity we held five NEA conferences in five different cities around the country in January 1979 with the specific purpose of assisting the state PUCs and energy offices in knowing just what finally was contained in the act, what it meant for them, and how federal guidelines for implementation could be made minimally disruptive in their promulgation. The Economic Regulatory Administration of the Department of Energy funded these five off-the-record conferences, and the only invitees were sitting commissioners and senior commission staff (and, of course, certain DOE officials). A total of some 300 people attended from every state but two.

While these experiences don't confer special insight, they do at least allow some impressions of the intergovernmental and intragovernmental issues that attend the implementation of this major legislation.

Diversity and Uniformity

There is little question that members of Congress—more specifically the staffs of the legislating committees handling the five elements of what became the NEA—were motivated by the usual federal quest for uniformity and standardization. While this is characteristic and probably even inherent in national lawmaking, it can have the effect of ignoring and maybe destroying diversity.

To take an easy one, federal tax laws obviously must apply uniformly, and hence the ETA portion of the NEA may not be too troublesome on this score. But even here, the provision of still more access by the utilities to additional investment tax credits (ITCs), with a requirement that accounting treatment of the ITCs by the state commissions leave the money so derived with the companies, may serve to exacerbate the state/federal quarrel over prescribing accounting methodologies. What I refer to here is the flow-through versus normalization accounting methods that give rise to the issue of so-called "phantom taxes." This is currently being litigated in Califor-nia, and other commissions are watching the outcome with great in-terest—as are the power and telecommunications utilities, the Internal Revenue Service, and the Treasury Department. Of course, if a credit is really to have the chance of influencing plant conversions and investment behavior, it only makes sense to leave the benefits with the utility. On the other hand, artificial devices of this sort are not traditionally thought to be the basis on which plant expansions in the utility sector should be made. Moreover, some state commissions are not keen on the idea that IRS can prescribe an accounting procedure for use with utilities under *state* commis-sion regulation. There arises also the further question of whether the already diminished federal tax liability of power and communication com-panies should be still further reduced.

To take a somewhat tougher one, FUA mandates converting power plants from oil and gas generation to coal and nuclear, and may well be sensible national policy. To certain states like Texas, however, a very sizable prob-lem is thus presented to the PUC—how to handle the federally decreed changeover in an accounting and financial sense. That is, who should pay for making plants obsolete which are otherwise fully serviceable, and should it be done through further accelerated depreciation or some other method with different burden-sharing?

In the case of NGPA, there may be a perceived need to allow federal regulation of natural gas in interstate commerce to reach through into regulation certain intrastate gas on grounds of national policy, but this surely erodes away traditional ratemaking authority for the state PUCs if they end up with having to pass through to consumers any federally sanc-tioned incremental price change.

By contrast, NECPA foists on state PUCs a batch of duties and respon-sibilities neither sought nor desired. Again, it is probably true that conserva-tion nationally requires nationwide prescription, but getting the state PUCs into overseeing and/or accounting for the utility companies' costs of com-plying with the weatherization and insulation programs of NECPA is of major consequence indeed.

In the first place, it could be argued that commission regulation has only recently gotten the utilities out of ancillary businesses, like selling lamps and stoves and other appliances, and concentrating on their central task—providing reliable power at the lowest possible cost. Now to en-courage or require them to get into the insulation and banking business and again "clutter up" regulation is a step backwards.

In the second place, such activities may allow at worst a commingling of assets and expenses such that accounting mischief is likely between the separate operations of providing power and offering weatherization programs. At best it will require commission decisions as to who shall pay, only the users of the program or all ratepayers collectively. Note that these difficulties will be faced by a PUC *whether or not* the governor names that agency or the state energy office as the lead agency under NECPA.

Finally, a consideration of PURPA in the context of a federal quest for uniformity and standardization presents perhaps the toughest case of all for intergovernmental relations in the aftermath of NEA passage. Behind its passage was a heavy dose of skepticism by the Congress—particularly the House—that, left to themselves, the state commissions could not be counted on to introduce rate reforms in electric utility pricing pointed toward conserving capital and energy. In part this was based on the view that most of the state PUCs had neither the staff resources nor the will to substantially alter the old ways of doing things in rate design, for example, keeping promotional rates like volume discounts and not acknowledging that system costs vary with time, hence pricing according to time variant burdens. In part it was based on the view that the state PUCs could not be expected to act on subjects outside their traditional jurisdictions (and thus purview) like elaborating interstate power pooling and interconnections. In part it was based on the likelihood that individual state commissions would be reluctant to be "out front" in radical rate design changes in the face of arguments about inducing a "flight of industry" from such an innovative state to a neighboring one of traditional rate design. In fact, this last theme has recurred in testimony before state PUCs when time-of-day pricing and alternate rate design issues have come up for debate. The Congress felt it was alleviating the who-goes-first problem by its national prescription.

From the vantage point of the state PUCs, PURPA was viewed by some as woefully outdated in that they had "already done most of what was called for;" viewed by others as not recognizing the diversity of circumstance of the individual commissions in either capacity to respond or interest in the subject matter; viewed by a few as a wholesale encroachment on state regulatory prerogatives exercised for ninety years; and viewed by all as an enormous levy on state PUC time and resources.

Decentralization and Recentralization

Closely related to the theme of diversity and uniformity is the theme of Decentralization and Recentralization. Whether or not the conventional wisdom is correct in saying that there is an almost inexorable movement toward centralization in government, there are at least cyclical episodes within that movement from centralization to decentralization. My own view is that these turns are taken as one or the other swing has proved ineffective in solving problems—or even making programs work. I believe the forces for decentralization over the last ten years have about run their course and the swing toward recentralization is perhaps beginning. It is in this context that the national energy policy—such as it is—and the NEA should be viewed.

At the time of passage of NEA and for the first few months thereafter, it was widely believed that with respect to the important Public Utility Regulatory Policies Act anyway "the House had lost and the Senate had won." This handy but erroneous conclusion had to do with the degree of mandatoriness of PURPA with most of the state PUCs having lobbied for a nonmandatory arrangement and most of the congressional staff and executive branch agencies lobbying for mandatory features.

Now it is true that in the conference committee the Senate's position prevailed toward emphasizing state laws and state PUC participation and not prescribing an outcome. However, the degree of specificity of just what must be considered by the states and the PUCs and the measures of compliance with PURPA "standards" are very much the House's doings and are not at all voluntary. Thus, whether a state adopts any of the prescribed guidelines or standards appears to be voluntary, but the *process* for consideration is not, and there is even a clear presumption in favor of adoption as PURPA is written. Applicable state law is cited throughout as the guiding beacon in all this, but DOE intervention is provided for and almost promised. In fact, the Intervention Office of the Economic Regulatory Administration just last month announced that it would be intervening in cases before the PUCs in Connecticut, Arkansas, Delaware, and Virginia.

Utility rates, the Congress said in PURPA, are to "track costs" in all cases—except where so-called lifeline rates are concerned. The utilities are to provide to the federal government cost data in a manner and a level of detailed not heretofore generally available, but the state PUCs must decide who pays for the gathering and assembling of these data. The cost-of-service standard is made the underlying factual determination in all the ratemaking changes, but PURPA requires that a marginal cost methodology for establishing the cost of providing electric service be at least considered.

Most of these actions must take place within a specified time and none over more than three years. Grandfathering of certain state PUC actions regarding the eleven standards is provided for, but no one yet really knows how difficult or easy it will be to get the records certified that this or that PUC is in compliance on some particular standard it treated in a recent (or current) rate case. In the extreme this could mean that each PUC would have to hold eleven evidentiary hearings in a three-year period to meet the requirements of PURPA: as a practical matter, some will take them up in the course of "normal" rate cases that come before the commissions and others will hold "generic hearings" to consider them. As might be imagined, the state PUCs are now in varying stages of noncompliance with PURPA, with the greatest concern of most of them being whether they have the staff and money resources to carry out the act in the time required.

Pluralism and Policy Determination

It is pretty clear that the present pluralism in regulation, that is, the expansion of the number of parties participating—governors' offices, energy offices, attorneys general, consumers' offices and advocates, federal counterpart offices—is a new force in regulation making for more sunshine and more democracy in the process. It is not yet clear that it makes for better policy.

Further, recalling the history of regulation, it is interesting to note that we have in some degree come full circle, as legislatures (state and federal) once again are inserting themselves in very particular ways—prescribing (for example) that lifeline rates will be allowed or that fuel adjustment clauses will not. If earlier periods of regulation have been labeled the "legal phase" and the "engineering phase" and the "accounting phase," I think the current phase is best described as the "political economy of commission regulation."

Thus the *intragovernmental* relations that the NEA touches and sometimes occasions include the relative roles of the states' energy agencies (broadly defined); the state legislatures to their executive branch; the governor to both. In the case of the federal government, the main intragovernmental relationships on these matters may be the Economic Regulatory Administration (in DOE) to the old Federal Power Commission (now FERC), part in and part out of DOE. Secondary intragovernmental relationships to watch may be between ERA and FERC together and other federal agencies who may have differing motivations in, say, rate design innovations. Here I have in mind the Government Services Administration and the Department of Defense, who routinely intervene in state PUC proceedings if they have issues at stake. Add to this, perhaps, the Justice Department and the Antitrust Division and the intragovernmental stage is still further filled with players. Issues of *intergovernmental* relations have already been set out.

One disturbing result of the new pluralism surrounding state commission regulation is the erosion of the original concept of PUCs as "quasi-judicial, independent regulatory bodies." The quest now is for "responsiveness," which seems to translate into the political science view that all decision-making is a matter of pressure and counterpressure with the outcome a matter of how many battalions the winning side can muster. From this comes the revival of proposals like making state PUC membership elective instead of appointive and even the emergence of consumer advocate offices in state government. While my own inclinations are certainly proratepayer, the advent of formally providing consumer representation before PUCs may have the unintended effect of inclining public utility commissioners to abdicate their responsibilities to the public—responsibilities which inhere in their office.

After all, it is a great perversion of the original intent of commission regulation to pretend that the role of a commission is to be entirely neutral, sitting as impartial arbiter midway between the public and the companies to be regulated. It is true, of course, that unhealthy financial conditions in a utility are not in the best interest of the public. But it is also true that in the unequal contending between the interests of the unorganized many and those of the organized few, a regulatory commission should tilt toward the side of the public.

Carrots and Sticks

Not surprisingly, in the passage of such a wide-ranging act as PURPA the Congress *authorized* some $60 million in "implementation assistance" of various kinds to encourage and aid state agencies in complying with the legislation. This breaks down into $40 million in grants; $8 million for innovative pilot projects in, say, rate design alternatives; $10 million for consumer offices; and $2 million for the National Regulatory Research Institute.

With half of FY 1979 gone by and the First Supplemental Appropriation for 1979 still before the Congress, the Economic Regulatory Administration's Division of Regulatory Assistance turned to using funds already appropriated under other legislation to finance state implementation of PURPA. Through September 30, 1979, these totaled about $18.6 million ($10 million in Implementation Grants, $5.6 million in Pilot Projects, $2 million for Consumer Offices, and $1 million for NRRI). The FY 1980 appropriation included funding for such assistance so that Department of Energy coffers were replenished at this dollar level by November 1979.

The writing of rules for the processing and awarding of these assistance monies (see table 16-1 for the schedule), closely followed the Conference Committee Report which contained the general direction of these rules. There is a presumption against the states using these funds "primarily" for personnel salaries and related costs and a prohibition against substituting these funds for state monies that would otherwise have been spent by state regulatory authorities. None of the states can receive more than an equal share of the amount of implementation grant money appropriated (although states may receive less "at DOE's discretion"). Pilot funds and consumer

Table 16-1
Economic Regulatory Administration, Department of Energy Activities Planned for 1979 for Carrying out the National Energy Act of 1978

January
Conduct State commission workshops
Publish advance notice of proposed rulemaking for NECPA "utility program"
Publish proposed rules for FUA "new" facilities

February
Issue request for proposal on gas rate study
Publish proposed rules for NECPA "utility program"
Publish proposed rules on FUA gas light ban
Publish proposed rules on PURPA cost-of-service reporting
Publish final rules on NGPA gas pricing
Conduct public hearings on FUA rules

March
Publish proposed rules on PURPA grants
Conduct public hearings on FUA gas light ban
Publish any changes in list of covered utilities
Publish final FUA rules for "transitional" facilities

April
Award gas rate study contract
Publish proposed PURPA reporting rules
Conduct public hearings on NECPA "utility program" rules

May
Conduct public hearings on PURPA grant and reporting rules
Publish final rules on FUA gas light ban
Publish final rules on PURPA cost-of-service reports
Publish final FUA rules for both "new" and "old" facilities

June
Publish final rules on PURPA grants
Award "utility regulatory institute" grant

July
Publish final PURPA reporting rules
Publish proposed rules on NGPA incremental pricing pass-through

August
Publish final rules for NECPA "utility program"

September
Award PURPA grants

October
Conduct public hearings on draft PURPA guidelines

November
Publish final rules on NGPA incremental pricing pass-through

December
Circulate draft gas rate study for comment
Publish 1980 list of covered utilities

Note: Activities announced by Howard Perry, Director of Regulatory Assistance, Office of Utility Systems, Economic Regulatory Administration, U.S. Department of Energy.

funds will be awarded on a competitive basis with no preset floor or ceiling. Rules for awarding these grants are to be only those necessary to carry out the act and in no way can be devised so as to allow the secretary of energy "to influence the outcome of deliberations in the states concerning these standards." Grants to NRRI were to be matched 20-80 in nonfederal funds the first year (FY 1979) and 40-60 the second year of the two-year authorization.

While there are several reasons why it is in everyone's interest to strengthen and improve state regulation of the electric and gas industries, the most pressing current one is the orderly and timely implementation of the National Energy Act, which (as mentioned) levies so many new responsibilities on the state commissions. Simply put, to enjoin the states to smoothly implement the five acts that make up the NEA while withholding funds to assist that implementation seems a poor bargain indeed—especially where so much of the act's intended success depends on good-faith efforts by all parties.

Of course, not all states want the carrot of regulatory assistance monies. Several New England PUCs, a few southern ones, and one western PUC have spoken against the idea on grounds of apprehensions about "strings attached." Still others—including some of the strongest commissions—may abstain from participating on the grounds that to do otherwise would serve to hasten the preemption of traditional state PUC regulation in the utility field by federal officials.

Prospects

For all of the recitation of real and imagined difficulties outlined above, it is likely that the implementation of the NEA legislation will go fairly smoothly. This is because (1) the legislation itself (particularly PURPA) is pretty sensible; (2) the actual content of the legislation is fairly technical and thus a businesslike approach with a good level of expertise is emphasized and called for; and (3) there is a good deal of good will around the state regulatory community toward rationalizing most of the issues the legislation raises. If the federal agencies are reasonably sensitive to the diversity of state agency circumstances and clientele and cognizant of their varied resources and substantial histories in this field, and if the Congress is understanding and patient in its oversight activities on this legislation, it all could work out quite well.

And, whether it does or not, it is the wise participant who gears up now for the next round in all this when the Congress turns to prescribing guidelines and standards for the *gas* utility sector—almost entirely finessed in the PURPA portion of the National Energy Act. At that time we will be revisiting the revisitation.

Part IV
Constraints and
Opportunities

Throughout this book we have attempted, above all, to provide pragmatic perspectives on what U.S. energy policies can and should be. This final part, offered in the same spirit of pragmatism, attempts to illustrate the very real constraints which limit the development of effective energy policies. Chapter 17, by Hanna J. Cortner, describes a number of the political, institutional, and organizational realities which constitute the environment of energy policymaking in the United States and which must be overcome before our energy future can be properly charted. Chapter 18, by David J. Rosen, uses survey data on public attitudes in New Jersey to illustrate the unwillingness of the public to accept that there really is an energy problem or to accept the sacrifices which may be required to ameliorate it.

The last selection, by John E. Carroll, emphasizes the importance of making use of all energy resources, soft path and hard path alike, and argues that an ideological commitment to the soft path may cause us to forego the advantage of resources which can be utilized effectively only on a relatively large-scale basis. Specifically, he describes the potential benefits to the eastern Canadian provinces and the northeastern United States from making use of Canada's abundant resources of megascale hydroelectric power and fossil fuels.

17 Developing Energy Policy within New Sociopolitical Realities

Hanna J. Cortner

There has been much debate recently within the energy policy community about the choices the nation should make regarding its energy future. Frequently, these choices are framed in terms of mutually exclusive options: either embark upon a journey down a soft energy path or a journey down a hard energy path.

The soft energy path, as described by its principal advocate, Amory Lovins, entails a commitment to the efficient use of energy and the rapid development of renewable energy sources. Large-scale electrical generating plants, no matter what the power source (nuclear, coal, or solar), are to be eschewed; they are to be replaced by many diverse units relying on appropriate, small-scale technologies—individual solar units, fluidized-bed boilers, home or community windmills. A crucial benchmark along the soft energy path is the elimination of the world's dependency on nuclear technologies.[1] The hard energy path, which is an extension of recent federal policy goals and research and development programs, relies upon the development of large-scale, high-technology and centralized solutions such as nuclear fission and fusion, coal gasification and liquefaction, and massive, interconnected electrical generating systems.

Advocates of soft energy technologies criticize the hard technology path because of its high capital costs, environmental risks, and the political, socioeconomic, and basic survival risks associated with nuclear proliferation.[2] Conversely, critics of the soft energy path question its economic and technical feasibility and the assumptions which are made regarding end-use. An important additional criticism is that the soft energy path is less an alternative energy strategy than an instrument for achieving social change;[3] and indeed, that does seem to be a central tenet espoused by Lovins.[4]

What critics of soft technology often fail to point out in return, however, is that any energy policy choice we make is going to provide the impetus for dramatic social and institutional change. We do not have a choice between a new and unknown sociopolitical structure or the present familiar situation. The two paths are not mutually exclusive. Both paths will inevitably lead us through a transition of a new societal mix, however different the principal advocates of each path perceive those future scenarios to be. While our current institutional and social fabric has been premised upon a set of economic and sociopolitical arrangements dependent upon cheap and available energy supplies, these can no longer be the assumptions upon which we operate. Energy price increases will inevitably change not only the allocation, distribution, and consumption of energy, but also the framework of social organizations which have emerged from past energy use patterns.[5]

Obviously, this relationship between our energy future and a changing social and political structure has not gone totally unrecognized. Numerous writers have, in fact, described the substantial changes in the scope and nature of governmental powers and in the relationship of the individual to the collective that are likely to occur as we attempt to handle our energy problems.[6] But the forecasts and analyses of these commentators have not yet been widely enough acknowledged or discussed as political leaders and decision-makers have sought to develop energy policy. And there appears to be virtually no recognition of this new reality among the general public. The failure to recognize publicly and to address openly and thoroughly this aspect of the energy dilemma is a major reason why our current record in energy policy development has been so dismal. Energy policy development is in a quagmire precisely because the choices and options we have developed and adopted have been based on assumptions, premises, and visions of the future that are no longer viable. We should be formulating policies to prepare citizens to live in a society where a high rate of energy consumption is no longer enviable, desirable, feasible, or affordable. Instead our energy policy actions have been attempting, albeit rather unsuccessfully, to return us to the more sublime state of an earlier era.

The discussion that follows briefly reviews some of the behavioral and organizational manifestations of this approach to energy decision-making. It indicates how this approach has thus far stymied energy policy development, and points to some of the sociopolitical issues that must be dealt with in the energy policy debate no matter what mix of energy paths we follow.

The "Except Me" Syndrome

Any group which is asked to sacrifice or perceives itself adversely impacted, particularly by energy conservation measures, wants an exemption. It will claim it is being made a scapegoat, that special circumstances impose an unacceptable economic burden, or that the potential for energy savings won't amount to much anyway. Government employees faced with the loss of free parking spaces, motel and resort operators fearing weekend gas station closings, and western impatience with the energy-conserving 55 mph speed limit are just three recent examples of this response. Moreover, while public opinion surveys show that 85 percent of the public reports engaging in a "fair amount" of conservation, conservation has not, in fact, been assiduously practiced. The most frequently mentioned conservation action, turning off lights, is relatively marginal. Reductions in driving are not a preferred conservation practice, and approximately 80 percent of the public remains opposed to raising gas prices or rationing as means to reduce consumption.[7] Energy conservation measures whose costs are indirect, distant, or minor tend to be supported and practiced, while the more stringent conservation proposals remain unpopular.[8] Everyone seems in favor of energy conservation, unless it necessitates a tangible sacrifice.

Minorities, the poor, and the elderly, who have been disproportionately impacted by recent energy shortages,[9] frequently oppose energy conservation as a solution to our energy problems. They believe that any future conservation strategies will not only inconvenience them the most, but will also continue to limit their opportunities to achieve a higher standard of living.[10]

Conservation, however, need not automatically mean sacrifice and hardship. Indeed, several studies have shown that the country can have a healthy, expanding economy while reducing energy usage.[11] Conservation, in other words, does not necessarily equate with a deterioration in life-style amenities. Unfortunately, such studies appear to have had only minimal impact upon policymakers. Few seem willing to dismiss the conventional wisdom that ties ever higher amounts of energy consumption to increased economic growth and improved standards of living.

One of the dominant political trends of the recent past has been the growth and increasing power and influence of special interest groups within the political process. It has become extremely difficult for policymakers to effect changes over the vocal, strident, and well-organized opposition of affected groups. Since so many groups are seeking exemption from any measure which they perceive—accurately or inaccurately—as entailing real sacrifice or demanding significant life-style adjustments, it is going to be quite some time before we see the widespread acceptance of a meaningful conservation ethic or the emergence of a significant proconservation constituency.

Distrust of the Energy Policy Community

Public trust of politicians has not quite recovered from the wounds inflicted by Vietnam and Watergate. Thus it is not surprising that despite President Carter's continued reaffirmations of the "realness" of our energy supply situation, and the emergence of the summer 1979 gasoline lines, still less than a majority of the American people (47 percent) consider the energy situation in the United States to be "very serious."[12] Many still believe that energy shortages are a hoax perpetuated by the oil companies and that political leaders seeking to convince the public otherwise are only dupes following the tune of the companies' Pied Piper.

The pervasive public distrust of politicians has already resulted in efforts to take energy decision-making out of the political arena, by establishing independent boards and commissions that are removed from political control. Proponents of such institutional arrangements argue that energy problems are unique, demanding specialized solutions and a decision-making milieu that is insulated from competitive politics. Yet we cannot afford much longer to postpone making some of the basic social and political decisions that our changed energy situation necessitates by simply taking the energy issue "out of politics." Our fundamental political system will be impacted by the choices that are made regarding our energy future, and only political decision-making can address those options. Energy in this sense is a highly political issue, and should remain so. Moves to take the energy issue out of politics are another manifestation of the inability to recognize the magnitude of what exactly is at stake.

Another important credibility gap has recently emerged which has seevere consequences for our ability to adapt to our new energy situation. This is the credibility gap between the scientific estate and the citizenry. If anything melted down at Three Mile Island it was the public's almost unquestioning faith in scientific expertise. More people began to regard the belief that scientific ingenuity and "good old American know-how" can soon find the technologies to lead us out of the energy quagmire as a great American myth.

Three Mile Island also raised public consciousness over the question of whether we should rush forward with dangerous nuclear technologies, or whether we should wait until more is known about such controversial and unresolved scientific issues as the health effects of low-level radiation and the problems of nuclear waste disposal and decontamination. Similar energy technologies that demand a commitment of faith that science will eventually solve disturbing unknowns about environmental and health and safety impacts are also likely to be more closely scrutinized and resisted in the future. There is a growing public skepticism of politicians and scientists who offer claims and promises of technical elixirs, and a greater recognition that the often hoped for technological fix may never occur, may be far off in the future, or may carry a very high economic and environmental price tag. But, just as technological fixes are apt to be distrusted, so too are politicians and scientists who promise that future economic prosperity and quality life-styles can be achieved with only minimal increases in the total amount of energy used.

The conflicting messages emanating from public officials and energy scientists over the severity of our energy supply situation and the debate over the efficacy of various soft path/hard path remedies have only deepened public confusion and bred more public mistrust. Public suspicion of the motives and alternatives offered by the entire energy policy community has become a salient political factor to be reckoned with.

Unwillingness to Take Political Risks

Public lack of recognition of the magnitude and severity of our energy situation and public distrust of just about everyone in the energy policy community have made deicsion-makers reluctant to take political risks. Political leadership flourishes when there is recognition of the need for action. It is difficult to lead when there is a high level of disagreement among groups as to the nature of the problem, considerable cleavage over what are legitimate courses of action, and a basic distrust of all those who could normally be expected to exert a leadership role.

Most policy proposals we have seen offered have been whittled down in the bargaining processes of policy formulation until they are minor and mostly cosmetic remedies. Rather innocuous policy departures are made to seem like major policy initiatives. Further, most of the agreed-upon policy initiatives make short-term adjustments, although there is often a conflict between the short- and long-term consequences of policy change. What seems feasible in the short term may actually be detrimental in the long run, contributing in fact to a worsening of the problem or precipitating exactly the opposite of desired results. Systems analysts term this the counterintuitive behavior of social systems.[13] But, for the vast majority of policymakers for whom a major motivating behavioral factor is the need to get reelected, responding to short-term contingencies is a political necessity. Opting for a long-term solution which may not show immediate results or which may impose a hardship in the near term requires too enormous a political risk. It is far easier politically to sell and profit from short-term promises and palliatives.

Decision-makers have also tended to abdicate their leadership responsibilities by passing on critical energy problems to the scientist. Technological solutions are preferred by decision-makers because they do not entail the political risks associated with decisions that regulate behavior or alter life-style patterns.[14] As a consequence, commitment of massive amounts of federal funds to research and development, especially in the area of large-scale energy technologies, has been the safer course. Take synthetic fuels, for example. Given impetus by the summer 1979 gasoline lines, a massive synfuels program is currently being pressed. Despite the knowledge that many environmental and technical problems have not been satisfactorily resolved, and that costs may far exceed benefits, the prevailing sentiment in Congress has been to do something even if it is wrong.[15] Thus political leadership is being demonstrated not by confronting directly the social and institutional meaning of declining energy availability, but by holding forth promises and visions of technological salvation.

Our elected and appointed decision-makers, however, cannot solely be blamed for inaction and political confusion. Most citizens lack fundamental information about energy. Many, for example, do not know that the U.S.

imports almost one-half of the oil we consume. Others are not convinced that the energy situation is as serious as inflation, unemployment, or crime.[16] Moreover, decision-makers are getting conflicting messages from constituents concerning important energy-related trade-offs. In the southwestern states, for example, citizens want more energy and are favorable to development of their plentiful energy resources. But they also want increased water allocations for agriculture and greater recognition of the significant environmental amenities the region has to offer. Yet water for both energy development and agricultural production will put too great a strain on the states' existing supplies, and energy development without some adverse environmental impacts is well nigh impossible. Thus we find decision-makers faced with the impossibility of satisfying incompatible and unrealistic public wants and demands, making symbolic statements, introducing legislation for symbolic purposes with no expectation for passage, or attempting to pass the buck to some other authority.[17] The general public, which fails to recognize the inconsistency of its policy preferences and which remains unconvinced that there is a real energy problem, is itself creating and nurturing the political conditions which make decision-makers reluctant to take political risks and exert political leadership.

Perception of a Temporary Crisis

There is a failure by many policymakers and most certainly the public to recognize the permanency of the whole new set of energy circumstances to which we must now respond. There still appears to be a belief that the "crisis" eventually will be ameliorated and somehow go away. Perhaps by equating our energy dilemma to the "moral equivalent of war" we have reinforced this belief. People may be thinking that using less and paying more is a temporary wartime exigency that can be removed once the war is won. Crisis rhetoric and crisis experiences may promote energy conservation.[18] But it is far easier to sacrifice or endure the hardships and inconveniences that energy conservation creates if they are perceived as temporary, crisis-relief measures and not as permanent modifications. It is considerably harder to come to grips with the inevitable prospect that even if we do improve our energy supply picture we still will not be able to return to the political and socioeconomic equilibrium upon which we previously depended. The new reality is that, no matter what, we will be paying more for energy, a fact which makes return to an institutional mix based upon plentiful and cheap energy impossible.[19]

Organizational Characteristics

Present institutional arrangements for energy policy planning, administration, and coordination are grossly inadequate. They have been unable to anticipate adequately the emergence of many of our energy problems, or adjust to new decision-making conditions by initiating, supporting, or implementing the policy actions which now must be taken. The challenge for our governmental institutions is not only to formulate comprehensive and unified energy policies, but it is also to secure the organizational requisites for equitable and responsible energy policy administration. But have we seen our institutions respond to the changing circumstances of energy supply and demand and develop capabilities for effective energy management? In a word, no.

At the national level, we have two National Energy Plans (NEP I and NEP II) and a new Department of Energy (DOE), but we still do not have a comprehensive, national energy policy. NEP I, passed by Congress in October of 1978, really is not a comprehensive energy policy; rather it is a compendium of several separate energy bills permanently pockmarked by the scars of a year and a half of congressional battling over passage.[20] NEP II, presented to Congress during the spring of 1979, is facing a similar prospect for protracted congressional debate. While Congress and the administration muddle along, attempting to juggle regional and parochial interests, much of our national energy policy is being determined by nondecision and by the actions of a foreign oil cartel.

The Department of Energy, created in 1977, left much control over energy in other hands. One observer has noted that DOE is perhaps more significant for what it left out than what was incorporated under its jurisdiction.[21] Much control over energy remains in agencies other than DOE. In the area of energy supply, for instance, DOE is primarily responsible for research and regulation of part of the electrical power industry. It has virtually no responsibility for managing basic water and fossil fuel sources of energy, or for regulating nuclear energy.[22]

The still fragmented federal energy organization has also had difficulty dealing with basic policy interrelationships—particularly the relation of energy to inflation and energy to environmental quality. Energy-environment and energy-inflation are being played like zero sum games when in fact the larger policy situation may well be non-zero sum.[23] Decisions as to the cost and benefits of alternative energy strategies appear to be made in isolation from each other. The very fact that our energy future has often been couched in terms of mutually exclusive energy paths has hampered efforts to find a middle ground upon which consensus can be built and accommodations made. When the reality is that a mix of planned conservation and hard and soft technologies will be required,[24] the political debate has put the matter in either-or terms. As a result, consensus on national energy policy has yet to emerge.

State and local response to our changed energy circumstances has not been much better. There have been exceptions in some states and local communities, and indeed some would argue that the real innovations are occurring at these levels.[25] Nevertheless, the scope and magnitude of such innovations, especially in response to the need to improve state capabilities in administration, planning, and coordination, are far less than could be hoped for. Take Arizona, for example. In Arizona, energy programs and related activities are spread throughout government. Numerous administrative agencies are active in energy administration. These governmental arrangements, while concerned with many aspects of energy planning, production, and management, are not designed to respond to the overwhelming energy problems the state has faced since the initial, visible emergence of the "energy crisis." Each agency is characterized by a limited mandate and is generally oriented to a limited set of development interests and clientele. While coordination of programs may and undoubtedly does occur among agencies, the existing governmental structure does little to encourage it. There is no legislatively mandated comprehensive state energy policy to link the programs of the various agencies or to lend an overall direction to state efforts. Several critical functions are performed only sporadically through the existing structure, if they are performed at all. There is no coordinated program of new energy source development—a particularly salient condition in a state that is heavily dependent upon imported energy supplies. Resource research and development are simultaneously pursued by a number of agencies, all with a distinct mission. Each agency, not surprisingly, is likely to advocate the development of its own particular resource without having the mandated responsibility for considering the totality of the state's resource needs. There is no permanently established structure for developing state positions on national energy policies and actions, and no state agency which is mandated to do long-range planning or energy needs projections.[26]

While the situation in Arizona may be more severe than in other states, it is certainly not that much of an aberration. More people are looking to Washington to solve their energy problems than to their state and local governments. Given this situation, state and local governments have had insufficient incentives to take the initiative in many of the areas in which they could act. And often when they have wanted to act they have had insufficient administrative capability to implement fully and adequately those new initiatives. As a result, state and local governments are also looking to Washington for money, direction, and solutions; but Washington has yet to figure out its leadership role and to develop the appropriate policy planning and coordinative mechanisms.

Conclusions

Energy policy development has lagged far behind other policy areas. While the long-term consequences of a failure to act will certainly be more detrimental than if we had lost the race to be the first nation to put a man on the moon, we have seen the same kind of commitment given to energy policy development that was given to the space race. Fundamental political divisions have hindered the development and implementation of almost all energy proposals with any teeth. As a result, we have not really embarked on any definite path—soft or hard or balanced mix—to adapt to our changed energy situation. Resistance to action and change has prevailed. We have tried hard to maintain a social, organizational, and political equilibrium that is no longer viable. More importantly, we have failed to recognize and account, in our planning and decision-making, for the fact that many of our future energy choices will mandate basic changes in our long-established social and political structures. Until more recognition is given to this inevitability, and acceptance is made explicit in both behavior and organization, we will continue on our present confused and retreating course of policy development.

Notes

1. Amory Lovins, "Energy Strategy: The Road Not Taken?" *Foreign Affairs* 55 (October 1976):65-96.

2. Ibid.

3. See "Soft vs. Hard Energy Paths: A Series of Critical Essays on Amory Lovins' 'Energy Strategy: The Road Not Taken?'" *Electric Perspectives* 3:77 (1977).

4. Lovins, "Energy Strategy," p. 77.

5. Terry D. Edgmon, "Energy as a Disorganizing Concept in Policy and Administration," *Policy Studies Journal* 7 (Autumn 1978):58-67.

6. William Ophuls, *Ecology and the Politics of Scarcity* (San Francisco: W.H. Freeman, 1977); Stephen C. Halpern, "Environmental and Energy Reforms: The Hidden Agenda for Individual Liberties," paper presented at the 1979 Annual Meeting of the American Political Science Association, Washington, D.C., August 31-September 2, 1979; Gregory A. Daneke, "The Energy Management Morass: Intergovernmental and Inter-Agency Responses to the Energy Crisis," paper presented at the 1979 Annual Meeting of the American Society for Public Administration, Baltimore, Maryland, April 1-4, 1979; Ben C. Ball, Jr., "Energy: Policymaking in a New Reality," *Technology Review* 80 (October-November 1977):48-51; and Edgmon.

7. Barbara C. Farhar, Patricia Weis, Charles T. Unseld, and Barbara A. Burns, *Public Opinion About Energy: A Literature Review* (Golden, Colorado: U.S. Department of Energy, Solar Energy Research Institute, 1979).

8. David J. Rosen, "Public Attitudes and Alternative Energy Systems:

The End-User Perspective," paper presented at the 1979 Annual Meeting of the American Society for Public Administration, Baltimore, Maryland, April 1-4, 1979.

9. Farhar et al.; Lenneal Henderson, "Energy and Social Equity," in Robert M. Lawrence, ed., *New Dimensions to Energy Policy* (Lexington, Mass.: Lexington Books, D.C. Heath and Co., 1979).

10. Also, pure market approaches to energy conservation are more likely to impact the poor than is planned conservation. See Paul Allen Beck, "Factors in Household Conservation: The Implications for Energy Policy," paper presented at the 1979 Annual Meeting of the American Political Science Association, Washington, D.C., August 31-September 2, 1979.

11. Ford Foundation, Energy Policy Project, *A Time to Choose: America's Energy Future* (Cambridge, Mass.: Ballinger, 1974); and Council on Environmental Quality, *The Good News About Energy* (Washington, D.C.: Council on Environmental Quality, 1979).

12. George Gallup, "The Gallup Poll: Public Concern Is Growing over Energy Crisis," *Washington Post*, September 2, 1979.

13. Jay W. Forrester, "Counterintuitive Behavior of Social Systems," *Theory and Decision* 2 (1971):109-140.

14. Dean Schooler, Jr., *Science, Scientists, and Public Policy* (New York: The Free Press, 1971), p. 275.

15. National Wildlife Federation, "The Real Energy Crisis," *Conservation Report* No. 17, 96th Congress, 1st Session (July 13, 1979).

16. Farhar et al., *Public Opinion about Energy*.

17. Helen M. Ingram, "The Legislators' Dilemma: Responding to Voters' Preferences on Energy/Environment Issues," paper presented at the 1979 Annual Meeting of the Midwest Political Science Association, Chicago, April 20, 1979; and Helen M. Ingram and John R. McCain, "Distributive Politics Reconsidered: The Wisdom of the Western Water Ethic in the Contemporary Energy Context," *Policy Studies Journal* 7 (Autumn 1978):49-58.

18. Beck.

19. Ball.

20. Walter Goldstein, "The Politics of U.S. Energy Policy," *Energy Policy* 6 (September 1978):180-195.

21. Daniel M. Ogden, Jr., "Protecting Energy Turf: The Department of Energy Organization Act," *Natural Resources Journal* 18 (October 1978):845-857; see also: David Howard Davis, "Establishing the Department of Energy," paper presented at the Annual Meeting of the Western Political Science Association, Los Angeles, March 19, 1978.

22. Ogden.

23. James L. Regens, "Wilderness Preservation and the Energy-

Environment Tangle: Policy Implications of the U.S. Forest Service Rare II Process,'' paper presented at the 1979 Annual Meeting of the Midwest Political Science Association, Chicago, April 20, 1979.

24. Robert Stobaugh and Daniel Yergin, "After the Second Shock: Pragmatic Energy Strategies," *Foreign Affairs* 57 (Spring 1979):836-871; Sam Schurr et al., *Energy in America's Future: The Choices Before Us—A Study by the RFF Energy Strategies Staff* (Baltimore: The Johns Hopkins Press for Resources for the Future, 1979).

25. Patricia K. Freeman, "The States' Response to the Energy Crisis: An Evaluation of Innovation," in Robert M. Lawrence, ed., *New Dimensions to Energy Policy* (Lexington, Mass.: Lexington Books, D.C. Heath and Co., 1979), pp. 201-207; James L. Regens, "State Policy Responses to the Energy Issue: An Analysis of Innovation," paper presented at the 1979 Annual Meeting of the Southwestern Political Science Association, Fort Worth, Texas, March 28-31, 1979; and Ronald D. Brunner, "Energy Conservation and Renewable Resources: A Decentralized Approach" (Ann Arbor, Michigan: Institute of Public Policy Studies, University of Michigan Discussion Paper No. 135, December 1978).

26. Hanna J. Cortner, *Energy Policy Planning, Administration and Coordination in the Four Corners States*, Consultant's Report to the Four Corners Regional Commission, March 1977. This particular section relied heavily (with permission) on material first presented in Gloria Sandvik and Dennis Thompson, "Energy Programs in Arizona: A Preliminary Analysis of Structures and Functions," staff report (Phoenix: Office of Economic Planning and Development, January 1976), p. 3.

18

Public Attitudes and Alternative Energy Systems: The End-User Perspective

David J. Rosen

The post-1973 concern with the adequacy of energy supplies has focused attention on alternative energy systems. In some instances this has meant the rediscovery of energy technologies once abandoned in the development of high-technology energy systems. In other cases it has fostered the application of new technologies and materials to the harnessing of renewable energy sources. In addition to the obvious advantages of energy sources which are renewable and less harmful to the environment, the alternative systems appeal to some as a decentralized alternative to the increasing control of energy supply by a decreasing number of institutions and corporations.[1] While not all alternative energy systems are conducive to decentralized control (for example, massive orbiting solar collectors beaming microwaves to a system of ground stations[2]), many alternative energy technologies can be implemented by individuals or communities.

Regardless of the complex technical, economic, and ethical issues posed by the choice between high technology and alternative systems,[3] it is quite certain that public attitudes about the energy crisis and its appropriate solutions will impose distinct policy parameters on any shift to alternative energy systems.

The shift to alternative energy may be achieved through one of the three following modes: (1) increasing prices of conventional fuels will encourage individuals to seek out and utilize alternative systems; (2) governments, at various levels, could take actions which would encourage and accelerate the market choice which is operative in the first mode; (3) governments, at various levels, could mandate the switch.

Under the first mode the governmental role would be restricted to the reduction of obstacles to the switch (building codes, zoning, and so forth) and perhaps the licensing of alternative systems to ensure safety and reliability. In the second mode governments could provide tax benefits, low-

This chapter is based on a paper presented at the 1979 Annual Meeting of the American Society for Public Administration. The author wishes to thank Thomas M. O'Neill of the Center for the Analysis of Public Issues and Stephen A. Salmore and Cliff Zukin of the Eagleton Institute of Politics for their thoughtful comments on earlier drafts. They are, of course, not responsible for any of the shortcomings. The interpretations of the data and views expressed in this chapter are the author's and should not be regarded as reflecting the views of the New Jersey Department of Energy or the Eagleton Institute.

interest loans, grants for R&D and demonstration projects, and similar measures which would increase the costs of conventional fuels and decrease the effective costs of alternative systems. The third mode would require the most intrusive governmental role, with the establishment of regulations forbidding some behaviors or technologies and requiring others.

In order to ascertain the likelihood of any of these approaches being implemented a clearer understanding of relevant public attitudes is required. Public acceptance and support of these alternative systems and government intervention on their behalf will be a significant factor in their ultimate success. In addition, the second and third modes are likely to face opposition from politically powerful groups which presently dominate the high-technology energy systems. In order to overcome this influence a countervailing constituency must be created. While environmentalists, alternative technology system vendors, and those suspicious of big business (and perhaps big government) might form the core of such a constituency, a high level of general public support will also be required to overcome the current governmental bias for high-technology energy systems.

In seeking to gauge relevant public attitudes our primary data source is a public opinion survey of 1,006 New Jersey residents. The survey was conducted in September 1978 by the Eagleton Institute of Politics of Rutgers University for the New Jersey Department of Energy. Earlier Eagleton surveys and some national polls are used to supplement this data. The analysis focuses on three general interrelated questions: (1) what do New Jerseyans regard as the severity, significance, and cause of energy problems; (2) what governmental energy policies do New Jerseyans support; and (3) what actions are individuals taking in response to energy problems?

The Nature of the Problem

In the spring of 1977 President Jimmy Carter called on the American people to respond to the energy crisis with an effort which would be the "moral equivalent of war." In New Jersey the governor and legislative leaders tried to mobilize the local battalions. The once meager energy militia was given a field promotion to a cabinet-level department. Evidence from national and New Jersey public opinion surveys suggests that we will soon discover, in the words of the 1960s poster, "What happens when they call a war and no one comes?"

The public apparently does not share the sense of urgency about energy problems which is prevalent in some quarters in Washington and Trenton. Energy is seen as an important issue, but is not among the top priority concerns of the people. Energy problems achieve high prominence only when they have a direct and immediate impact on the population. This tends to produce erratic fluctuations in public concern about energy. The relatively low salience of energy is demonstrated by a CBS-*New York Times* national survey conducted several weeks after the president's 1977 energy message and at the height of media attention to the issue. A majority of those surveyed regarded crime, inflation, health, unemployment, and defense as more important issues than energy.[4] Eagleton Institute polls reveal a similar low priority for energy. From 1971 until the winter of 1974, respondents, when asked to name the two or three most important issues facing New Jersey, offered nearly 100 different issues, without naming energy.

In a poll conducted in January 1974, when the gasoline lines were longest, 44 percent named energy as the most important state issue and another 30 percent ranked it second or third. Once the shortage began to ease, however, public indifference returned and, in a March 1974 survey, again no one mentioned energy among the three most important issues. The lack of concern continued until April 1977, following a winter of natural gas shortages and immediately after the president's energy address. In that poll 12 percent listed energy as the most important issue facing New Jersey. A year later this had dropped to only 5 percent. A series of national polls conducted by Gallup shows a similar fluctuating concern about energy. After an April 1974 peak in which 46 percent of Americans regarded energy as the most important national issue, interest rapidly declined. Until a modest rise in April 1977 the percentages remained below 10 percent and often below 5.

Significantly, Americans are far more likely to view energy as a national rather than state or local issue. In the April 1977 Eagleton poll, 54 percent viewed energy as the most important national issue, while only 12 percent thought it the most important state issue, and no one named it the most important local issue. This finding is particularly important because New Jerseyans tend to be more concerned aout energy than residents of most other states. A Gallup national poll in November 1977 found that only 17 percent thought energy was the most important national issue,[5] less than one-third the rate in New Jersey. Thus, as future conditions raise the salience of energy throughout the country it seems likely that people will turn to Washington, rather than to their statehouses or city halls, for solutions.

While other issues may overshadow energy in times of noncrisis, when asked specifically about the energy problem, two of every five New Jerseyans regard it as very serious and four of five regard it as at least somewhat serious. As table 18-1 indicates, level of education affects perceptions of the seriousness of energy problems, with 49 percent of those with a post-high school education regarding the issue as very serious, compared to 36 percent among those with less education. It appears that the complexity and long-term implications of energy issues are best understood by those with more education.

Table 18-1
Attitudes on the Seriousness of the Energy Crisis
(percent)

	Very Serious	Somewhat Serious	Not Serious	Not a Problem	Don't Know	Total
Total sample	40	41	13	2	4	100
Education						
Less than H.S.	37	36	18	3	6	100
High school	36	47	13	1	4	101
More than H.S.	49	40	8	1	1	99

New Jerseyans appear unimpressed with recent efforts to cope with the energy problems and are generally pessimistic about improvement. By a margin of 43 percent to 27 percent they believe that the energy situation has worsened rather than improved during the past year. Further, nearly one-half believe that the situation will worsen during the next twelve months, while one-third think it will improve. This pessimism was expressed prior to the political turmoil in Iran, the 1979 round of OPEC price increases, the accident at Three Mile Island, and the gasoline lines of the summer of 1979. The data in table 18-2 indicate that the group most likely to consider the energy situation most serious—the better educated—are least likely to expect improvement in the next year. Only one-quarter of those with a postsecondary education believe that the situation will improve during the next twelve months, compared to 38 percent of those with less education. This is further illustrated by the fact that by a margin of 40 percent to 26 percent those believing that the problem is somewhat serious, as opposed to very serious, are more likely to expect improvement.

Table 18-2
Attitudes on Energy Problems during Next Year
(percent)

	Will Get Better	Will Get Worse	Will Not Change	Don't Know/ Depends	Total
Total sample	34	47	8	12	101
Education					
Less than H.S.	38	44	6	12	100
High school	38	44	7	12	101
More than H.S.	25	55	11	9	101
View of Energy Situation					
Very serious	26	57	5	13	101
Somewhat serious	40	42	9	9	100
Not serious	38	40	7	15	100

With the shortlived exceptions of the gasoline lines of 1974 and the natural gas shortage of 1977, energy price increases have been the most tangible and salient signs of energy problems. Yet fewer than one-half of all New Jerseyans believe that energy shortages have been a major cause of energy price increases in recent years, and one in four does not think shortages played any part in the increases. As shown in table 18-3, inflation; avarice by utilities, energy supply companies, and energy exporting nations; and energy waste by American consumers are mentioned more frequently as the major cause of energy price increases. Governmental regulation of the energy industry is seen as a lesser but still significant cause.

New Jerseyans clearly perceive energy waste as a serious matter. As noted above, two of every three think energy waste is a major cause of higher energy prices, and over 90 percent think it is at least a partial cause. When asked directly about energy waste, over three-quarters of those interviewed—77 percent—say Americans waste a lot of energy and another 17 percent perceive at least some waste. The blame for waste is directed most frequently at individuals (37 percent) rather than at business and industry (29 percent) or government (23 percent). However, these relative orderings should not obscure the lack of consensus on a single culprit primarily responsible for energy waste.

Similarly there is no consensus about who should lead in energy conservation efforts. New Jerseyans are divided between those saying individuals (38 percent) and those favoring government (35 percent). Significantly, among those under thirty, nearly one-half believe that individuals should lead, compared to one-quarter who favor government leadership. It is not clear from our data whether these opinions of the young reflect greater faith

Table 18-3
Attitudes on Causes of Recent Energy Price Increases: Is . . . a Major Cause, a Minor Cause, or not a Cause?
(percent)

	Major	Minor	Not a Cause	Don't Know	Total
Inflation	72	20	5	4	101
Higher profits for utility companies	69	20	6	5	100
Arab countries rising prices	68	21	6	5	100
Higher profits for energy supply companies	67	20	5	8	100
Energy waste by consumers	66	23	8	3	100
Energy shortage	41	32	22	5	100
Government regulations	39	34	12	15	100

in the effectiveness of voluntary individual efforts or lesser faith in the capability of government. Many national public opinion surveys, however, have documented a growth of cynicism about the capacity of government to handle contemporary problems.[6]

In order to ascertain general orientations to the energy situation and its implications for the future, respondents were presented with three statements about the seriousness of the situation and the degree of individual sacrifice necessary to cope with the problem. The statements among which respondents were asked to choose range from least to most severe:

1. The energy problem can be dealt with by cutting back on waste while maintaining current standards of living.
2. The energy problem can be dealt with by tightening belts and giving up some luxuries.
3. The energy problem can only be dealt with by accepting a major change in lifestyles and giving up some things that are now considered essentials.

Four New Jerseyans in ten believe that we can cope with the energy problem simply by reducing waste and thereby maintain current standards of living. The remaining 60 percent are about evenly split between those who feel that we will have to give up some luxuries and those who believe we will have to make major changes in life-style. Thus it appears that no general consensus has emerged from the energy debate about the seriousness of the problem or the severity of the remedy. While only 30 percent believe that major life-style changes are needed, twice that number believe that some sacrifices will be necessary. It should be noted that recognizing the need for "people" to make sacrifices and the willingness of specific individuals to make self-sacrifices are of course very different things. Individuals often feel that sacrifices should come from "others." The next two sections of this chapter will examine which policies people are willing to support and what sacrifices they are making or are willing to make.

Support for Energy Policies

Among New Jerseyans, support for energy policy options varies with the perception of the direct costs they will be required to bear. They tend to support measures whose costs are minor, indirect, or distant and oppose those policies which necessitate tangible sacrifices. Willingness to support those policies is greatest among those who perceive the energy situation as most serious. Table 18-4 presents the level of support for ten energy policy proposals and, when data are available, comparisons with support in prior

Table 18-4
Attitudes on Energy Policy Options, 1976-1978

Percent Who Favor	1978	1977	1976
Requiring annual servicing of furnaces	88	n.a.	n.a.
Strict enforcement of 55 mph limit	84	83	85
Requiring businesses to reduce energy use	76	n.a.	n.a.
Increase offshore oil drilling	75	73	66
Increase use of nuclear energy	60	66	74
Natural gas price deregulation	33	n.a.	n.a.
Relax enforcement of pollution controls	31	30	36
Gasoline rationing	22	34	24
Increase energy prices	15	n.a.	n.a.
Increase gasoline tax	13	20	17

Note: n.a. means question was not asked in given year.

years. Table 18-5 relates individuals' perceptions of the seriousness of the energy problem to their support for each of the proposals.

The two policy proposals which are each supported by over 80 percent of New Jerseyans—a requirement for annual servicing of furnaces and strict enforcement of the 55 mph speed limit—are relatively costless. Other data indicate that a large majority of New Jersey homeowners already have annual servicing of their furnaces and therefore would have no additional cost imposed by this proposal. While a drive on the New Jersey Turnpike may suggest that a majority of drivers do not adhere to the 55 mph speed limit, the limit has been in place for several years and the public apparently finds it tolerable. The reduced speed limit also has the nonenergy benefit of reducing the highway fatality rate, which may contribute to its popularity. Support for the limit has remained nearly constant since 1976.

Nearly three New Jerseyans in four favor a law which would require that businesses conserve energy by reducing their use of heating, air-conditioning, and lighting. The impact of such a law would affect most citizens only slightly or indirectly. Support for this proposal varies with the perceived seriousness of the energy problem, receiving support from 82 percent of those who believe the energy problem is very serious and only 63 percent of those who think it is not serious.

The only other policy options in the list of ten which are favored by a majority are measures to increase energy production. Support for offshore oil drilling has grown among New Jerseyans from two of every three in 1976

Table 18-5
Support for Energy Policies by Perceived Seriousness of the
Energy Problem

| | | Perception of Seriousness of "Energy Problem" | | |
Percent Who Favor	Total Sample	Very Serious	Somewhat Serious	Not Serious
Requiring annual servicing of furnaces	88	87	90	82
Strict enforcement of 55 mph limit	84	86	83	80
Requiring businesses to reduce energy use	76	82	76	63
Increase off-shore oil drilling	75	72	79	68
Increase use of nuclear energy	60	61	60	65
Natural gas price deregulation	33	33	35	29
Relax enforcement of pollution controls	31	30	29	35
Gasoline rationing	22	26	20	13
Increase energy prices	15	17	13	13
Increase gasoline taxes	13	18	10	9

Note: All entries are the percentages of those saying they favor the policy option listed in the rows.

to three of four in 1978, perhaps reflecting the media attention which has accompanied the start of exploration off the New Jersey coast. During this same period support for an increase in the use of nuclear power has dropped from 74 percent to 60 percent. This decline may be a reaction to the increasingly public debate about the benefits and risks of nuclear power in the nation and, to a lesser degree, in New Jersey. The erosion of support for nuclear power accelerated after the Three Mile Island accident. An Eagleton poll in April 1979 found that only 48 percent of New Jerseyans favor increased use of nuclear power. That survey also disclosed a strong ambivalence about nuclear power. While 60 percent agreed with the statement, "Although there are safety problems with nuclear power, we need to build more plants to meet our energy needs," 55 percent agreed that "all nuclear plants should be shut down until safety problems are eliminated." Support for these energy production measures is unrelated to perceived seriousness of energy problems, as those who think that energy does not constitute a serious problem are as likely to support increased production as those who do believe it is serious. It seems likely that support for increased production is related more directly to an individual's attitudes about growth, technology, and other matters.

Only one New Jerseyan in three supports the removal of price controls on natural gas, and this level of support was unaffected by the adoption of gradual decontrol in the Natural Gas Policy Act of 1978.[7] Based on responses to other questions, one suspects that if the proposal read: "removal of price controls leading to an increase in natural gas prices," the level of support might have been even lower. Again, level of support is unrelated to perceived seriousness of the energy problem.

A proposal to save energy by relaxing pollution control laws is favored by 31 percent, compared to a similar 36 percent who favored it two years ago. As is shown in table 18-6, support for an environmental rollback is greatest among people over fifty (39 percent), those who have not graduated from high school (40 percent) and those making less than $10,000 per year (43 percent). These findings are consistent with other studies which have found that environmental quality concerns are greatest among better-educated, more affluent, and younger citizens.[8] Support for the relaxation of pollution control laws appears to stem from attitudes about environmental quality (and its putative economic effects) rather than from concern about energy problems.

The two most stringent conservation proposals on the list—gasoline rationing and increasing gasoline taxes—are both unpopular. Rationing is supported by 22 percent and an increased gasoline tax by only 13 percent. Support for each has dropped slightly during the past two years, as the memories of 1974 fade. Support for each of these policies is modestly related to the perceived seriousness of energy problems, with those believing the problem to be very serious more likely to support the measures than

Table 18-6
Attitudes Toward Relaxing Pollution Control Laws

	Favor	Oppose	Other/ Don't Know	Total
Total sample	31	64	5	100
Age				
18-29	29	70	1	100
30-49	23	72	5	100
50 plus	39	55	7	101
Income				
Under $10,000	43	53	5	101
$10,000-$15,000	33	63	4	100
$15,000-$20,000	25	67	8	100
Over $20,000	20	76	3	99
Education				
Less than H.S.	40	51	7	99
High school	29	67	4	100
More than H.S.	22	73	4	99

those who feel it is not serious. It is worth noting, however, that even among those most concerned about the energy problems these conservation measures are quite unpopular.

Rationing and gas taxes can be viewed as alternative means to the same end—reduced gasoline consumption. While the president's original energy plan and most other governmental policy discussions favor the tax approach more New Jerseyans prefer rationing. In the 1977 Eagleton survey, people were asked which option they would prefer, if one or the other were necessary, and rationing was favored over the tax increase, 68 percent to 25 percent. A 1979 CBS-*New York Times* national survey found a similar preference for rationing.[9]

The general proposition that energy consumption should be reduced by increasing prices was supported by only 15 percent of New Jerseyans, reflecting opposition to a proposal which would have a direct cost for individuals. Again, it is striking that this approach, which is central to much energy policymaking, is so unpopular.

In addition to these ten proposals, respondents were asked about two other policy measures. Seven New Jerseyans in ten say they strongly favor a policy of tax credits for money spent to make residences more energy efficient, and another 17 percent express mild support. However, when those who support the idea are asked if they would approve a small tax increase to fund the credits, support drops dramatically, with less than one-half favoring the proposal. Thus, when energy conservation tax credits appear as free benefits, 87 percent are in favor, but when these benefits have a cost, support drops to 36 percent.

Another proposal which does not appear to have a direct cost—a requirement for adequate insulation before a house can be sold—receives support from three of every four New Jerseyans. When asked their opinion on a program that would prohibit the sale of houses that were not properly insulated until the necessary insulation work was done, 76 percent say they would favor such a program while 20 percent would oppose it and 4 percent offer no opinion.

One suspects that if they were asked if they would support this measure even though it would increase the purchase price of housing, the level of support would drop. As evidence of this, renters are more likely to support this plan (by an 83 to 13 percent margin) than are homeowners, who would be most directly effected by the plan (by a margin of 72 to 23 percent).

The data in this section indicate that public support is lacking for tough conservation laws and regulations. Support is forthcoming only for those measures which will not impinge greatly on individuals' lives. While our prior discussion indicates that many people take energy problems seriously, the problems are not viewed as sufficiently severe to justify real personal sacrifice. Even among those viewing energy as a very serious problem there is little willingness to endorse tough measures. Apparently support for such measures will emerge, if at all, only when the public is convinced not only of the seriousness of the problem, but of the absence of easy, low-cost alternative solutions.

Energy-Related Behaviors

While none of the 1,000 respondents had installed solar collectors, switched to a wood-burning stove, or erected a windmill, many have taken energy-conserving actions during the past two years. Almost everybody claims that they have been more aware of turning out lights when they leave a room, have set their thermostats at lower temperatures than they used to when sleeping, and have run appliances such as dishwashers and washing machines only when they have full loads. Nearly as many say they have added weather-stripping or taken other measures to seal windows and cracks in residences. Three out of four say that they have inspected their homes for energy efficiency and waste.

Individual economic calculations seem to be the primary motivating force for these conservation actions. As is shown in table 18-7, while homeowners and renters are about equally likely to turn off unneeded lights and use appliances more efficiently, homeowners are more likely to inspect their homes for waste, add weather-stripping, and turn down thermostats. Most of the renters in our survey pay for electricity (which is consumed by lights and appliances) but not for heat (which could be conserved by the other three measures).

A series of detailed questions about thermostat settings indicate that a majority of thermostats in New Jersey homes are never set above 68° F and that when people are not home or are asleep a majority are set at 65° or less. It is important to note that the conservation and thermostat data reflect individuals' reports of their own behavior rather than actual observations.

Table 18-7
Energy Conservation Measures Taken

Percent Saying They Have	Total Sample	Owners	Renters
Turn out unneeded lights	94	95	93
Turn down thermostats when sleeping	88	90	79
Run appliances when full	88	89	87
Add weather-stripping, seal cracks	81	85	70
Inspected home for energy waste	75	79	63
(n)	(1,011)	(706)	(305)

There may be a tendency for respondents to overstate their conservation efforts. However, the fact that some people may be inclined to exaggerate their conservation efforts would indicate that attitudes have been changed, even if behavioral change is lagging.

New Jersey homeowners seem convinced that home insulation has substantial benefits. Better than nine in ten believe that insulation reduces the number of cold spots in the house, makes a home more comfortable, and provides a more uniform temperature. Nearly as many believe that energy savings will pay for the cost of insulation and that an insulated home is better for health. Among those who have not insulated their homes the primary reason given is the cost. The issue of cost appears again in response to the question: would you insulate if you would be paid back in energy savings in seven years? Among those with incomes over $20,000 64 percent responded affirmatively, compared to only 39 percent of those with incomes below $10,000.

Based on the responses reported here, successful efforts to increase the use of insulation would have to be directed at overcoming the financial constraints perceived by many homeowners. They appear to understand the benefits of insulation; what remains is convincing them that they can afford to insulate.

Transportation is one of the primary energy-consuming sectors of the economy and our study of commuting patterns in New Jersey establishes the clear primacy of the least energy efficient mode of transportation—the private automobile with a single occupant. Not only is the use of public transportation relatively insignificant in the state, but attitudes expressed by respondents suggest that increasing the use of public transportation will be very difficult.

As table 18-8 shows, 83 percent of New Jersey workers drive to work, compared to only 11 percent who use mass transportation. Of those who

Table 18-8
Modes of Transportation to Work

	Drive Alone	Drive Carpool	Bus	Train	Walk	Other	Total
Total sample	70	13	7	4	4	1	100
Income							
Under $10,000	55	14	21	2	6	2	100
$10,000-$15,000	71	11	6	2	7	3	100
$15,000-$20,000	79	15	3	2	1	0	100
More than $20,000	74	13	5	4	4	0	100
Area							
Center city	59	19	13	6	3	1	101
City and older suburb	65	13	7	2	10	3	100
New suburb	75	12	7	4	2	0	100
Rural	70	16	3	2	4	5	100

drive, five of six do not use car pools. The bus is used more than the train, with the number of New Jerseyans using the latter no greater than the number who walk to work.

The dominance of the automobile holds for all demographic groupings, although there are some minor variations. Among those earning less than $10,000 and those living in central cities, automobile use is lower (although still dominant) and the use of buses is higher. This variation seems to be explained almost entirely by rates of automobile ownership. For instance, the commuting patterns of low-income people who own automobiles is almost identical to that of higher income groups. It appears that when people own automobiles they will use them to get to work, and 90 percent of New Jersey households own at least one motor vehicle, with 56 percent owning two or more.

Of those who drive to work, almost three-quarters claim that public transportation is not available between their home and workplaces. The availability of public transportation varies by location, with the greatest rates of reported availability in central cities and the more urbanized northern part of the state. However, even if public transportation were available everywhere, only 34 percent of those who now drive say they think they would use it. Their reasons for eschewing public transportation are summarized in table 18-9.

The reasons most frequently cited are the most difficult to remedy. The major drawbacks to public transportation according to respondents are that "it takes longer than driving"; "it doesn't fit [people's] schedules"; and "it's inconvenient." While the last problem might be partially remedied by

Table 18-9
Reasons for Not Using Public Transportation
(percent)

			Applicability		
			Not At	Don't	
Reason	Lot	Little	All	Know	Total
It takes longer than driving	66	14	15	4	99
It is inconvenient	51	19	25	6	101
It does not fit any schedule	45	23	28	5	101
I need my car at work	33	9	54	4	100
It is too crowded	32	19	41	8	100
It is not dependable	28	27	37	7	99
It is uncomfortable	24	29	45	3	101
It is too expensive	20	18	57	5	100
I don't like the people who use it	4	15	75	6	100
(n)					(145)

schedule changes, these objections are fundamental to most mass transit systems. New Jerseyans appear unwilling to forego the convenience of door-to-door transportation whenever they wish it. The dependability, comfort, and expense of public transportation, which could be affected by government subsidy, are not major causes of nonuse.

Voluntary car pooling does not appear to be an effective means for reducing the use of automobiles. When those who now drive to work alone are asked if they would call a designated telephone number to arrange for a car pool, only one in six indicated a willingness to try this system. The reasons cited for not forming car pools seem to be very similar to those for eschewing mass transit.

Achieving major conservation gains in commuting in New Jersey will be most difficult. The public's preference for the private automobile is strong and is not likely to be altered by minor improvements in public transportation. It would seem that in order to shift significant numbers to mass transportation, the carrot of improved (especially in terms of "convenience") or less expensive public transport will have to be coupled with the stick of disincentives for automobile use.

Implications for Alternative Energy Systems

Based on the responses analyzed the task confronting proponents of alternative energy systems is a most difficult one. Most individuals do not perceive a fundamental energy crisis which requires that they make tangible sacrifices. The public will support energy policies which do not have any direct adverse impacts on itself and they will conserve energy (and presumably use individual-level alternative energy systems) when it becomes economically necessary or attractive. There is little backing for strong governmental intervention to alter the relative economic attractiveness of differing energy options, because such intervention would necessarily require higher taxes, higher prices, and/or government regulations. In the absence of perceived necessity such actions would be most unpopular. It is significant to note, however, that, forced to choose between unpleasant alternatives, the public would prefer regulation or rationing to price or tax increases.

Faced with these public attitudes it would appear that the extent of a shift to alternative energy systems in the short run will be largely shaped by market conditions. If fuel prices continue to increase and home solar units come to be perceived as reliable, homeowners can be expected to embrace this latter technology. Under such circumstances government can play a minor but important role by eliminating obstacles, assisting in financing, and perhaps certifying solar energy systems. While many of these governmental actions could be pursued at the local or state level, rather than in Washington, this would require altering public expectations. As we noted above most people view energy problems as national, and the collective benefits derived from alternative energy systems would be national in scope. Further, with each municipality adopting its own programs and standards certain municipalities may feel that they are placing themselves at a competitive disadvantage by setting high energy efficiency standards or subsidizing alternative systems (through property tax incentives, for instance). Also, if alternative energy systems are to be mass produced, differing municipal standards may create marketing obstacles.

Clearly the most difficult area in which to bring about the shift to alternative systems is in transportation. As our prior argument suggests, a shift to greater reliance on mass transportation will not be achieved simply (and this has proven to be far from simple) by improving mass transit systems. The attraction of the private automobile is so great that strong disincentives for auto use will be necessary, and such measures are overwhelmingly unpopular. A city which raised tolls and eliminated on-street parking (as some may be forced to do to comply with clean air standards) would risk substantial economic losses and would be disadvantaged vis-à-vis municipalities without such measures.

A political climate conducive to strong and effective alternative energy policies requires a broad general consensus about the seriousness of the energy crisis. Not only is such a consensus currently lacking, but, short of an energy catastrophe, the prospects for its formation are poor. Owing to the complexity of the energy situation, it is always possible to perceive some culprit (the oil companies, the Arabs, the government) to blame or some technical fix in which to place one's faith. That each of the possible culprits is to some degree culpable and that some of the current lines of energy research may produce significant breakthroughs make it possible to avoid confronting current energy realities. It is far more pleasant to believe that energy problems can be resolved through reforms of someone else's (oil companies, Arabs, or government) behavior or the wonders of science than to face real and tangible personal sacrifices. Disabusing the public of easy answers and forging a constituency for difficult energy solutions will provide a test of the capacity and responsibility of American political leadership.

Notes

1. See, for example, Amory B. Lovins, *Soft Energy Paths* (Cambridge, Mass.: Ballinger, 1977) and Albert Fritsch and C.J. Swet, *Solar Energy: One Way to Citizen Control* (Washington, D.C.: Citizen's Energy Project, 1977).

2. G.K. O'Neill, *The High Frontier* (New York: Morrow, 1977); and G.K. O'Neill, "Space Colonies and Energy Supply to Earth," *Science* 190 (1975):943-947.

3. *Alternative Long-Range Energy Strategies*, Joint Hearings before the Select Committee on Small Business and the Committee on Interior and Insular Affairs, U.S. Senate, 94th Congress, 2nd Session, December 9, 1976, and *Additional Appendices—1977*. Interior Committee Serial No. (94-47) (92-137).

4. CBS News, Script for "CBS News Special Report, 'Energy: The Facts . . . The Fears . . .The Future,' " August 31, 1977, p. 2.

5. *The Gallup Opinion Index*, November 1977, p. 4.

6. *ABC News-Harris Survey*, Vol. 1, No. 27, March 5, 1979.

7. P.L. 95-621.

8. Frederick Buttel and William L. Flinn, "The Structure of Support for the Environmental Movement," *Rural Sociology* 41 (1974):382-390; Robert B. Ditton and Thomas L. Goodale, "Water Quality Perceptions and Attitudes," *Journal of Environmental Education* 6 (1974):21-27.

9. *CBS News-New York Times Poll*, "Oil Shortages? June, 1979, Part II," June 11, 1979, p. 3.

19 Energy and the Northeast: The Canadian Connection

John E. Carroll

Impassioned advocacy of an energy future charactertized by primary reliance on renewable resources, administered on a decentralized basis, and using more "human" technologies, for all its strong points, suffers from one serious disadvantage. The dismal predictions of the media notwithstanding, there are still resources of megascale hydroelectric power and fossil fuels from Canada, adequate to serve a significant portion of total northeastern U.S. demand within the foreseeable future and for a long time thereafter. Harnessing, converting, and distributing these energy resources will very probably require large capital investments and, therefore, administration which is considerably more centralized than is palatable to the soft path advocates. Considerations involved in the development of these energy resources will be rather more regional than local in scope, and will certainly lead to serious reservations about their social and environmental costs. Certainly these costs should be analyzed and minimized, but they should not be rejected as unacceptable out of hand, as some supporters of renewable resources are wont to do.

This chapter attempts to identify the real benefits that will be foregone in the northeastern United States and eastern Canadian provinces if we posit renewable resource strategies to the exclusion of more conventional energy development.

Eastern Canada and Northeastern United States: A Mutuality of Interests

The New England states and the eastern Canadian provinces (Quebec, New Brunswick, Nova Scotia, Prince Edward Island, and Newfoundland-Labrador) share two significant energy characteristics. They are both uniformly poor in fossil fuel resources and, being at the end of the pipelines in their respective countries, they are the last to receive the benefit of domestic reserves of oil and natural gas; and they are both heavily dependent on OPEC-controlled and therefore expensive imported oil for their very survival.

The overall northeastern U.S.-eastern Canadian region has no known petroleum reserves, with the potential exception of a probable small quantity on the outer continental shelf; no proven natural gas reserves, though gas is expected to be found offshore from Labrador, Nova Scotia, and perhaps on Georges Bank; limited coal reserves in Nova Scotia and, to a lesser extent, in New Brunswick; and no uranium, with the possible exceptions of northern Quebec and interior Labrador. One of the greatest potential energy resources in the region is in the conversion of such renewable resources as wood, peat, wind, and solar into more useful electrical or thermal energy. The region is well forested and contains substantial peat reserves. It also has high and steadily blowing offshore winds, and there does appear to be potential for wind development around the Gulf of St. Lawrence and on Prince Edward Island, as well as a number of other Canadian and New England sites. However, total quantities of useful energy derived from these sources, at least in the near-term future, are likely to be relatively small and to have local rather than region-wide significance.

The only energy source in abundance in this vast region is hydroelectric power, both developed and developable, and its variant, tidal energy, which is at present a long way from development. The region's great hydro resources, developed and potential, are almost exclusively Canadian, and center in Quebec (James Bay and the Manicougan-Outardes region on the north shore of the St. Lawrence) and Newfoundland-Labrador (Churchill Falls and Gull Island), with substantial existing capacity occurring elsewhere in Quebec and in New Brunswick.

Hence, the region is uniformly poor in fossil energy sources, and the hydro resources are almost exclusively Canadian. However, owing largely to the extension of the trans-Canada pipeline to Montreal and its planned extension to Halifax, there is great potential for the importation of some of Canada's abundant natural gas supply from Alberta and the Arctic to New England. In addition, Ontario has a large developed nuclear capacity as well as access to Appalachian and western Canadian coal which may ultimately find its way east in the form of electricity.

Of course, all exports of energy from Canada will require the approval of Canada's National Energy Board (NEB), which must by law consider Canada's actual and potential domestic needs, regardless of the willingness of Canadian utilities to sell the power or the availability of a market. However, given the commonality of the eastern Canada-northeastern U.S. region, both sides of the border react to their respective federal governments and national energy policies in a similar manner and increasingly identify with each other's similarly disadvantaged positions. There is a strong foundation here for energy cooperation which will benefit both sides of the border—New England and the Northeast by virtue of the need there for more electrical energy, especially in light of the new uncertainties associated with nuclear development plans, and Canada, by access to a sizable market for its surplus hydroelectric and nuclear power and natural gas. Certainly this mutuality of interest will be a major factor considered in the deliberations of Canada's National Energy Board.

Northeastern United States-Eastern Canada
Energy Exchange: A Brief History

In the 1950s and 1960s initial efforts were made to enable the exchange (in contrast to importation) of small quantities of electrical energy between utilities in or near border communities and resulted in specific exchange agreements involving utilities in New York-Ontario, New York-Quebec, Vermont-Quebec, and Maine-New Brunswick. In the late 1960s and early 1970s broader arrangements were put into effect after the integrated electrical grids were established in the northeastern United States, and Ontario and New Brunswick were tied in. Designed primarily to provide excess peaking capacity and emergency needs, these arrangements were still limited to exchange and sharing rather than importation, but involved larger geographical areas and greater quantities of power. Thus U.S. utilities were able to avoid building expensive excess-generating capacity by simply buying unneeded excess from neighboring Canadian grids. The Power Authority of the State of New York (PASNY) maintained such a relationship with Ontario Hydro through the Niagara Falls linkage, while Central Maine Power maintained a similar though smaller scale relationship with the New Brunswick Electric Power Commission.

By the early 1970s it was becoming obvious that these arrangements were becoming rather one-sided, with greater quantities of electricity moving from Canada to the United States than vice-versa. However, the total quantities were still small.

In this same period Hydro Quebec moved rapidly to develop one of the world's most ambitious hydro-power projects, at James Bay in northwestern Quebec, a megascale project ultimately designed to generate up to 16,000 Mw. What would Quebec do with this incredible amount of power? Several hundred miles to the south in the board rooms of Consolidated Edison Company of New York, one of America's largest utilities, attention was turning north to the possibility of importing summer peaking power and perhaps ultimately firm base-load power from Quebec's expected surplus. Hydro Quebec was quite interested in the New York market, and a historic agreement was approved in late 1976 enabling the Power Authority of the State of New York to buy 800 Mw of firm capacity from Hydro Quebec and resell it to Con Ed. Electricity began flowing in the spring of 1979 and will continue at least until 1997. This agreement was limited to summer peak load power and takes advantage of the fact that Quebec's peak demand is the winter heating season while New York peaks in the summer air-conditioning season. The linkage is made through the Beauharnois Dam on the St. Lawrence River and crosses to Utica, New York, via a new 765 Kv transmission line from the border to that city. This is the first significant net importation of Canadian electric power into the northeastern United States.

The way has now been paved for increased Hydro Quebec exports to New York, and perhaps Vermont and elsewhere in New England as James Bay begins to generate power in late 1979. Interest has also increased in Ontario Hydro to export electricity to New York and New England; and New Brunswick would like to export surplus to Maine when the Point Lepreau nuclear station goes on line in 1980. Even Newfoundland-Labrador, with its great developed generating capacity at Churchill Falls and with other major potentials in Labrador, has eyed the northeastern U.S. market.

Specific Canadian Energy Projects with Export Potential to the Northeastern United States

There are three areas of real potential for Canadian export of energy into the Northeast: James Bay Hydro, Churchill Falls-Labrador Hydro, and natural gas via pipeline and tanker.

James Bay and Quebec Exports

One of the earliest hints that the province of Quebec recognized the potential for substantial export of hydroelectric power to the northeastern United States was provided in 1969 in J. Lewis Robinson's book *Resources of the Canadian Shield*. Commenting on the advances in the technology of extra-high-voltage transmission Professor Robinson foresaw what we now know is already beginning to happen—the export of large quantities of electric power to New York and New England markets.[1]

It was this very breakthrough in long-distance electric transmission technology, as well as a recognition of untapped markets south of the border (particularly in New York) and need for the importation of foreign capital to develop the Quebec economy that spurred a young Quebec minister of natural resources named Réné Levesque and his fledgling crown utility, Hydro-Quebec, to look north toward the hydro-development possibilities of a series of large rivers flowing into James Bay in the northwestern part of the province. Today, with Réné Levesque as premier of the province, with Hydro-Quebec bigger and stronger than ever, and with the need for foreign (U.S.) capital and markets even greater if an economically marginal dream of independence for the province is to come to fruition, James Bay power must begin flowing southward that much sooner.

The James Bay hydroelectric project, as first announced by Liberal Premier Robert Bourassa in early 1971, was designed to divert all the major rivers along the eastern (Quebec) shore of James Bay (Nottaway, Broadback, Rupert, Eastmain, Opinaca, LaGrande) and one Hudson Bay tributary, the Great Whale River (since deleted from project plans). Power houses on these diverted rivers would have an installed capacity of 14,000 Mw, almost one-third of the total current hydroelectric production in Canada. The James Bay Energy Corporation was created as a crown (government) corporation, separate from but basically directed by Hydro-Quebec, to carry out the project, and in May 1972 the decision was made to proceed with Phase One of the project, the La Grande complex. Now almost complete, Phase One involved the construction of four generating stations along the LaGrande River producing 8,330 Mw, utilizing the entire flow of the LaGrande and significant percentages of several other rivers flowing into it. The entire James Bay Project is scheduled for completion in 1983.

Although it is sometimes said that James Bay is being developed to provide for the future power needs of Quebec, the evidence appears to be to the contrary. Indeed, six months before the project itself was launched, Premier Bourassa addressed the Canadian Club in New York City and indicated that power from Quebec would play a major role in supplying northeastern U.S. energy needs.[2] At the same time, spokesmen for Consolidated Edison Company of New York were indicating that company's willingness to buy as much Canadian power as is made available. Even more persuasive than these early statements is the construction by Hydro-Quebec of high-voltage transmission lines to the U.S. border and the negotiation of export sales to New York which will run under contract until 1996. Indeed, Quebec will soon be supplying 20 percent of the needs of the Power Authority of New York.

A PASNY official noted in correspondence to the author that his authority expected to import 800,000 kilowatts of firm hydroelectric power from Hydro Quebec during the seven warm-weather months each year, and that the firm Canadian power would be provided under a twenty-year contract between the two agencies. In addition, the Canadian National Energy Board authorized export to PASNY of a maximum of 1,360,000 kilowatts of interruptible power throughout the year.[3]

It is now known that Premier Levesque and other Quebec leaders are most eager to market Quebec electricity as early as possible in the New England states as well, and related negotiations are currently in progress between Governor Richard Snelling of Vermont and Premier Levesque. A consummated deal may involve as much as 7 percent of all Vermont's power needs. This marks the first time that the Quebec government has sought U.S. markets outside of New York for its electricity, and Governors Hugh Gallen of New Hampshire and J. Joseph Garrahy of Rhode Island are among other New England leaders who are showing tangible interest.

The most up-to-date data available on the expected output of Phase One of the LaGrande Complex of James Bay is dated September 1, 1978, and is as follows:[4]

Dam	No. of Generating Units	Installed Capacity (Mw)	Annual Output (billion Kwh)	Date of Service
LG2	16	5,328	35.8	Nov. 1979
LG3	12	2,304	12.3	Jul. 1982
LG4	9	2,637	14.1	Feb. 1984
Total	37	10,269	62.2	

Another 1978 Publication of Societe d'energie de la Baie James presented the following with respect to installed capacity and annual output:[5]

Dam	Installed Capacity	Annual Output
LG2	5,328,000 Kw	35,000,000,000 Kwh
LaGrande Complex	10,190,000 Kw	68,000,000,000 Kwh
Manic-Outardes Complex	5,500,000 Kw	30,000,000,000 Kwh
Churchill Falls	5,225,000 Kw	34,500,000,000 Kwh

This is without question a very significant amount of power, all hydrogenerated and all available within five years. The question which immediately arises, of course, is how much of this is surplus to the province's needs and therefore available for export. This is a highly speculative subject and much depends on the bias of any of the numerous promoters and critics of export. However, according to Hydro Quebec's own testimony in their October 1977 application for an export license, the amount of surplus energy available form Hydro-Quebec's combined reserve from June 1978 to December 1983 will be 59,000 Gwh, more than enough to satisfy the import demands of the Power Authority of the State of New York (PASNY).[6]

The figures broken down by year are:[7]

Period	Maximum Surplus Power (Gwh)	Average Surplus Power (Gwh)
June-December 1978	11,370	5,500
1979	17,500	6,500
1980	17,500	6,500
1981	17,400	6,360
1982	17,000	5,950
1983	17,000	5,950

The James Bay hydro-project is not without considerable social and environmental costs. The impact on the social structure of the Cree Indian population of the region has led to serious social problems and to court litigation of Indian rights claims. In addition, the ecological impact over many thousands of square miles of northern forest lake and river country, its fauna and flora, and on the James Bay-Hudson Bay estuarine ecosystems is substantial. An impact as serious as climatic change is considered possible. However, the decisions are made and the work is largely done, so these are all moot points as far as the project is concerned.[8]

Quebec's power production prospects are not by any means limited to James Bay. Considerable potential remains for further hydro-power development in eastern Quebec north of the St. Lawrence, a region closer to settled areas than James Bay, though not previously tapped. The development of the generating capacity of the St. Maurice River, at 1,500,000 Kw, was spread over sixty years, while the development of the Manicougan-Outardes Rivers, with four times that capacity, will require only a decade. Then this one large interconnected river system will provide the largest bloc of hydro power in Canada and produce more power than all of the hydro plants operating in British Columbia at that time.[9]

Then, of course, there is the other crown jewel of Quebec hydro production, a development technically outside of but in fact fully under the control of the province. This is, or course, the huge Churchill Falls hydro-power project in Labrador, which markets virtually all of its power through the Hydro-Quebec system under long-term contracts with that corporation and at rates most favorable to Quebec. Churchill Falls (formally known as Hamilton or Grand Falls) is one of the most spectacular and also most remote and least known of all the great cataracts of North America. With a total drop of 1,000 feet in sixteen miles, its potential power output has been estimated at 3 million to 5 million Kw, considerably more than could possibly be used locally.[10] However, the issue of Churchill Falls power is complicated by the fact that Canada and the province of Newfoundland both consider Labrador as officially part of the province of Newfoundland (or Newfoundland-Labrador, as it is called), while Quebec (or at least Premier Réné Levesque and the ruling Parti Quebecois) lay claim to all of Labrador as part of Quebec and depict it as such on all maps. The Quebec separatism issue makes the problem more perplexing, for with it the question arises whither Labrador if Quebec leaves the Confederation.

Churchill Falls-Labrador

Hydro Quebec signed a long-term forty-year contract with Churchill Falls (Labrador Corporation, Ltd., which would guarantee the Quebec government utility virtually all the power generated at Churchill Falls in southern Labrador, a generating station with a rated capacity of 5,225,000 Kw, except for a modest 300,000 Kw which may be recaptured by the Churchill Falls Corporation. This contract covers the period September 1, 1976, to September 1, 2016, and is automatically renewable for a further period of twenty-five years under already agreed upon terms. Quebec was able to negotiate a very favorable price for this great quantity of power, largely because the owners (Churchill Falls Corporation and the Newfoundland-Labrador government) had no alternative but to transmit it over Quebec territory to markets in the south. Given present technology and costs, it is not feasible to transmit it across the Labrador Sea to the island of Newfoundland (where there would be no large market in any event), and the power corporation and the province were largely forced to accept Hydro-Quebec's terms if it was to be marketed anywhere. At the time (late 1960s) the government of longtime Newfoundland Premier Joey Smallwood was grateful for any such opportunities at almost any price, and the agreement was consummated to the great satisfaction of Quebec, which not only received a significant new source of power at a low price but also became exclusive bargaining agent for the export of Labrador electricity to New Brunswick, and ultimately to the United States.

By the mid 1970s conditions had changed greatly. The value of electrical energy (as a replacement for suddenly expensive oil) soared, and Newfoundland-Labrador had experienced its first change of government since entering the Canadian Confederation in 1949. Incoming Premier Frank Moores and his cabinet were not as predisposed toward selling the province's resources at any cost, and thus, in September 1976, Churchill Falls Labrador Corporation, Ltd., and Hydro-Quebec were served with a summons by the attorney general of Newfoundland to appear before the provincial Supreme Court. The province claimed she was entitled to request 800,000 kilowatts of power generated from the waters of the Upper Churchill River watershed starting in October 1983, and that she would not be in default of her contract by doing so.[11]

Hydro-Quebec is contesting the jurisdiction of the Newfoundland Supreme Court, and the litigation is presently before the courts.

This dispute adds fuel to the previously noted fires of Quebec-Newfoundland disagreement as to which provincial jurisdiction rightly includes Labrador. Canada does not accept the Quebec territorial claim, however, and the outcome of the dispute remains to be seen. In my view, Labrador will likely remain with Newfoundland, though ultimate control over Labrador's vast hydroelectric, mineral, and fishery resources is not as clear, as Newfoundland has practical problems related to the marketing of these resources, especially hydro-power, without utilizing Quebec territory.

Currently, 5,200 Mw of installed capacity exists at Churchill Falls, and there is a potential to develop an additional 1,800 Mw at Gull Island on the lower Churchill River. Development of the Gull Island hydro project remains in limbo, however, pending outcome of the previously mentioned litigation. This site is much closer to the coast, and therefore to Newfoundland, and it is hoped that an eleven-mile tunnel and power cable under the Strait of Belle Isle would enable transmission of this power directly to

Newfoundland, thus avoiding Quebec territory and any necessity to market in that province.

In early 1978 agreement was reached by the province of Newfoundland-Labrador and the Canadian federal government to establish a Lower Churchill Development Corporation with financial support from both governments, with a primary objective " . . . to establish a basis for the development of the hydroelectric potential of Labrador, with the first emphasis being on the Gull Island project. . . . "[12]

The significance of this development to the northeastern United States is not simply the 1,800 Mw associated with the Gull Island project, but far more the enormous and as yet untapped hydroelectric power resources of Labrador, for which no market now exists in eastern Canada. Should this electricity resource be developed through significant federal-provincial collaboration and federal funding, it could well find its way into the integrated electricity grids of eastern Canada and thence *very possibly* into the northeastern United States. Being hydro, this energy is of course relatively inexpensive and completely renewable. Being of very great quantity it could very well be found surplus by Canada. Only time will tell.

Natural Gas

The New England region has traditionally been one of the least supplied regions in the United States vis-à-vis natural gas, and has one of the lowest natural gas pipeline densities of any region in the United States. The major natural gas pipelines from the gas fields of Louisiana, Texas, and Oklahoma have generally tended to terminate in New York State, with only a very few minor narrow-diameter lines being found in southern and central New England. With the advent of liquefied natural gas (LNG) and its importation from Algeria and elsewhere overseas, some additional gas has entered the region in recent years (specifically at LNG terminals in Everett, Massachusetts, and Portsmouth, New Hampshire), but, overall, natural gas has been a minor element in the New England fuel supply mix. Talk of national shortages and the once-believed inevitability of rapid depletion of conventional U.S. natural gas resources have only encouraged continued regional ignorance as to the possibilities for a gas as a viable New England and northeastern energy alternative.

Several events of the past few years have indicated, however, that the future role of natural gas in the region may be significantly greater than heretofore imagined. Among these events must be included the likelihood of some commercial reserves of natural gas in the Georges Bank and Baltimore Canyon outer continental shelf (OCS) areas (the likelihood of gas being greater than that of oil, according to most industry sources); the availability of significant quantities of Algerian LNG, provided the pipeline and port facilities of the region are constructed to receive it; the interest and ability of Tenneco, Inc., of Houston, Texas, to construct such necessary facilities to transport natural gas through (though not necessarily to) the region, using the port of Saint John, New Brunswick, and a cross-New England pipeline, an enterprise in which Tenneco has thus far been frustrated by U.S. energy policies; the advent of natural gas price deregulation by the mid-1980s, a change which should encourage more natural gas exploration and distribution activity; and, most important for this discussion, the availability of significant quantities of Canadian natural gas to the northeastern United States.

The bulk of Canada's conventional sources of both natural gas and oil are to be found in the province of Alberta, although additional quantities of natural gas may be found in British Columbia and to a lesser extent in Saskatchewan. Many years ago the Canadian government and private enterprise built a trans-Canada pipeline to carry oil and gas to the great petrochemical industrial complex at Sarnia, Ontario. A number of other lines were built from Alberta and British Columbia south into the western and midwestern United States. In the mid-1970s, for reasons of national security (specifically to free the Montreal area and Quebec from dependence on insecure sources of overseas supply), the line to Sarnia was extended east to Montreal.[13]

Today, Alberta Gas Trunk Line, Ltd. (AGTL), of Calgary, Alberta, one of Canada's largest and most successful natural gas and pipeline companies and 98 percent Canadian owned, has applied to the National Energy Board (NEB) in Ottawa to extend this trans-Canada pipeline east from Montreal to the Maritimes, terminating in Halifax, Nova Scotia, and with spur lines to various off-route points in Quebec, New Brunswick, Nova Scotia, and the United States. To do this, AGTL has joined with PETRO-CAN, the Canadian government's crown corporation in oil exploration and development, in forming Quebec and Maritime Pipelines, Ltd. (Q & M Pipelines, Ltd.), a subsidiary designed solely to carry out the extension of the pipeline to Halifax. (The ownership ratio is 60 percent AGTL and 40 percent PETROCAN.)

The Q & M plan is to construct and operate a natural gas pipeline system of 1,900 miles in length (760 miles of mainline and 1,140 miles of laterals) from Montreal through Quebec, New Brunswick, and Nova Scotia to Halifax. Construction is to begin in summer 1980, and November 1982 is the target date for operation of the entire system. Sources of gas for this system are initially conventional Alberta Foothills natural gas, supplemented later by Arctic Islands gas (by LNG tanker or Polar Pipeline down the western shore of Hudson's Bay), Western Arctic gas (via the Alaska Highway Gas Pipeline Project), Atlantic Coast OCS gas, and possibly new reserves yet to be confirmed in Quebec. Hence there are many different potential sources of supply, although the conventional discoveries in Alberta are alone believed to be sufficient to justify the project.

Specifically included in the Q & M permit application is the export of 91.3 billion cubic feet annually to the United States, delivered to St. Stephen, New Brunswick, on the Maine border and transferred to a new U.S. pipeline system to be constructed down the New England coast to Boston and beyond. Not specifically mentioned in the application is a possible U.S. connector to the Q & M lateral to Magog, Quebec, which would carry gas south via the Connecticut Valley to central New England. Also possible is a tie-in to the Tenneco pipeline proposal from Lorneville, New Brunswick, if the Tenneco line is ever built. Obviously, New England would benefit from this new energy supply, but so too would Canada. According to AGTL Vice President Robin Abercrombie,

> This Project would develop a useful new domestic market for natural gas by starting user familiarity which in the long range must help all those companies which are developing arctic island production and eastcoast offshore natural gas prospects.
>
> In the most immediate time frame, the Project would also provide a modest but immediate market for some of the extra Alberta gas production capability.
>
> The Project's favorable effect on Canada's balance of trade by reducing the crude oil import deficit, would be so collossal as to possibly recommend its prompt installation for that reason along. An improvement of some $50 billion over the next twenty years is indicated.
>
> With capacity to furnish some limited export to Maine and New Hampshire, the Project would widen the range of export markets to which Canadian gas could be delivered if found surplus in the future.[14]

In analyzing the AGTL-Q & M Pipeline proposal, it is especially important to note that (1) AGTL is 98 percent Canadian-owned, which makes it a very acceptable company to many Canadians who are concerned about foreign (that is, U.S.) ownership of Canadian industries and resources—hence, AGTL is politically acceptable where others might not be; (2) the total project would involve 90 percent Canadian content in employment, materials and financing, desirable for the reason noted above; (3) Quebec and Maritimes Pipelines, Ltd., is 40 percent owned by PETROCAN, which is a government of Canada crown corporation and obviously a major participant in the project; (4) AGTL has the expertise and capital necessary to carry out such a large project, or the means necessary to obtain it; (5) AGTL has or controls the natural gas necessary to both start up the project and keep it going for some years; (6) the quantity of gas proposed for export to New England, 91.3 billion cubic feet per year, is over one-third of the total current gas consumption in the six state New England region.

All of these points, and others, make this eastern Canadian natural gas pipeline project a serious and significant endeavor. Coupled with the clear AGTL-Q & M interest in supplying New England with natural gas, it is indeed a project which cannot be ignored, and may in fact change the entire New England energy picture and the energy supply and demand projections which have thus far been made for the region.

Interdependency

Concern always exists among U.S. utilities and public policymakers as to security of energy supply, given that Canada is a foreign source, and to the perceived perils of developing a dependency on such foreign sources. The U.S.-Canada situation, however, both continentally and regionally, is a two-way street and therefore a situation of interdependency rather than dependency exists. While the United States may need certain Canadian resources, such as energy, Canada also needs a market for those resources if she is to maintain a healthy economy, reduce unemployment, and support her already weakened dollar. In many resource areas, she lacks a domestic market, while the great U.S. market to the south is often the logical way to turn. The central question, therefore, is not whether Canada should export to that U.S. market, but whether she has enough of a given resource to satisfy her own needs first. This question can obviously only be answered by Canadians in their own domestic political arena.

With respect to its abundant hydropower resources, there is no question that the Levesque government in Quebec recognizes a potential for energy export and clearly desires the benefits of such export. In Quebec's recently released "white paper" on energy, *Insurance for the Future: An Energy Policy for Quebec*, Minister of Energy Guy Joron remarks:

> There is no doubt that, with the predicted increase in the Quebec network, much greater quantities will become available for export through the years, and this will help both Hydro-Quebec from the financial point of view and its partners from the supply point of view. . . . So, it is normal for Quebec to try and interest its neighbours in buying it and to profit financially from it. *These profits could become substantial* [emphasis added].[15]

Minister Joron further attempts to justify such export by stating:

> . . . High water levels play a role. Normal quantities of water can be collected in large reservoirs; but when Hydro-Quebec forsees an overflow, it is in its interest to increase its production if it can find purchasers. Otherwise, an overflow without production would mean a complete loss of energy.[16]

Hence there exists a feeling that talk of exports must (and can) be justified to the people of the province, even if some politicians charge that selling to the Americans at higher prices causes shortages or hardship within the province.

The energy minister (and, in effect, the government) goes a step further in suggesting that if there is a prolonged decline in predicted Quebec demand, the supply of basic (rather than surplus) energy would become so great that ". . . it would be logical to export this assured energy, *which would probably bring in a higher price than surplus energy and power*" (emphasis added).[17] (At present, Quebec exports no assured energy.)

In viewing the Quebec energy picture in broad perspective vis-a-vis U.S. exports, it must be remembered that the province produces no hydrocarbons or uranium and, in spite of all the interest in hydroelectricity export, is still highly dependent on energy imports per capita to maintain her large urban-industrial population. The exports prospects are essentially based on power yet to come on line, though it inevitably will. When it does, Quebec will become one of the last places in the world still capable of providing cheap power on a guaranteed basis. Again, the major question will be: how much should be made available to the United States?

In a recent report from the C.D. Howe Institute in Montreal, it was made clear that any U.S. optimism that great quantities of Quebec hydropower will be made available in New England may be premature. The dominant industries in Quebec, pulp and paper, aluminum and other metal refining, and petrochemicals, are highly energy intensive and have, in many cases, located or relocated in Quebec because of the relatively low energy prices that have prevailed there until only recently.[18] The energy cost advantage of locating or relocating in Quebec cannot be maintained unless hydropower from James Bay is made available there, thus reducing the percentage of this hydropower which would be available for export to the United States, at any price.

Without doubt, the Quebec government appears to be placing almost total domestic reliance on the province's hydro potential, and there is no question that Quebec's existing hydro sites will continue to provide relatively low-cost power and thus be of primary benefit to the province.

In this light, U.S. states and utilities would be well advised to be firm in their stand for long-term contracts in contrast to short-term spot contracts if they are not to be caught short when and if the province turns off the tap. (Actual U.S. sales in 1976 were .5 billion Kwh and $7,995,000, which was 10.2 percent more in volume and 18 percent more in revenue than the preceding year.)[19]

One other indirectly related Quebec energy issue which should at least be mentioned in passing is the subject of excess oil refining capacity in the oil refineries of the St. Lawrence Valley. (An excess refinery capacity problem also exists in the Maritimes and in Newfoundland, but it has been much more elevated as an issue in Quebec due to Premier Levesque's personal interest and public statements.)

At a meeting of the eastern Canadian premiers and New England governors at Whitefield, New Hampshire, in June 1978, Premier Levesque, in addition to his not surprising optimistic remarks on Quebec's great hydro resources and his hope for sale of extensive quantities of electricity to the United States, made reference to the fact that the province's oil refineries are now operating at only about three-fourths capacity, and he stated:

> . . . an increase of our shipments (of refined oil) to the New England States could be highly beneficial to all parties involved over the next few years. The insufficient capacity of American refining . . . is already felt . . . all over the Northeastern States.
>
> I realize that there are obstacles to the kind of increased North-South flow which is so logically indicated—obstacles which lie mainly in various lobbies and corporate policies.
>
> Yet, isn't there enough combined political weight represented here, so that, if it does make sense, we should at least give it a solid try with some confidence?
>
> The economic advantages could be just as important for all of us, as the cooperation in power exchanges which as I said before, could be made available by the enormous developments which will soon double and eventually triple our network's capacity.
>
> In the same spirit *would it not be logical to take advantage of the complimentary factor we find in our respective oil situations, in order to help resolve both the looming supply problems in New England and our own refinery problems in eastern Canada?* [emphasis added].[20]

These remarks have stirred considerable political interest in New England, particularly among the governors and within the New England Regional Commission, and will become a subject for inquiry and discussion on the agenda of the newly formed Northeastern International Committee on Energy, a joint U.S.-Canadian committee under the auspices of the New England Regional Commission and the Council of Maritime Premiers. And, it is quite possible that this excess oil refinery capacity issue may become directly linked to Quebec hydroelectric power sales to New England if Canadian governments decide to make long-term sales to the United States dependent on U.S. use of their excess refinery capacity. This remains to be seen.

In any event, once domestic needs are satisfied, however they are defined, it is in Canada's interests to export the surplus to the United States. Nationally, the United States and Canada have a relationship of interdependency in energy and in many other resources. In addition, Canada does not have the capital required or the borrowing power to carry out the development of the many megascale projects, mostly energy, in which she is involved. To date, she has been dependent on American investment capital for these projects, further strengthening the interdependent relationship.

Specifically with respect to energy development in the eastern region, Canada has a need to market her great off-peak surplus of electrical energy from such megaprojects as James Bay and Churchill Falls, and may ultimately have a need to export baseload firm power from these projects as well. She also has the need, at least temporarily, to market the current Ontario electricity surplus, in order to maintain payments on her capital investment in coal-fires and nuclear generating capacity. Finally, there is a growing realization in the Maritimes that, if the western Canadian natural gas pipeline is to be extended to Halifax and if the price of the gas is to be kept competitive, there must be a significant gas export to New England to provide economies of scale. The market in the Maritimes is simply too small to do this alone. Thus, if Maritime Canadians are to get natural gas, Americans must be available to buy it as well. Finally, Quebec, whether as part of Canada or as a separate entity, will grow dependent on the cash value of its exported electricity and may become even more dependent on the U.S. market than Americans on Quebec electricity.

This almost completely interdependent relationship should preclude fears in the United States as to the security of energy supply.

In recognition of the common problems of this eastern international region, the New England Governors and Eastern Canadian Premiers (Quebec to Newfoundland-Labrador) have established a new Northeast International Committee on Energy, under the auspices of the New England Regional Commission and the Council of Maritime Premiers, and based at Boston and Halifax. Initially, this committee will oversee a computerized energy information exchange program between the two regions and promote demonstration projects in renewable energy technologies. There is a call, however, for the committee to become involved in the solving of problems pertinent to all energy forms and issues in the region, and great likelihood exists that the committee will answer this call.

The possibilities for international energy cooperation in this region are endless and the potential rewards to this most energy deprived of all regions in North America are great indeed. Provided the will exists.

Notes

1. J. Lewis Robinson, *Resources of the Canadian Shield* (Agincourt, Ontario: Methuen Publications, Ltd., 1969), p. 78.

2. As quoted in Boyce Richardson, *Strangers Devour the Land* (New York: Alfred A. Knopf, 1975), p. 327.

3. PASNY Official, Power Authority of the State of New York, *personal correspondence*, September 1978.

4. Societe d'energie de la Baie James, *La Baie James d'hier a aujourd'hui* (Montreal, P.Q., 1978), p. 28.

5. Societe d'energie de la Baie James, LG2 (Montreal, P.Q., 1978), p. 7.

6. Hydro-Quebec, "Demande a L'Office National de L'Energie pour une Licence Visant L'Exportation de Puissance et D'Energie Convention D'Interconnexion Entre La Commission Hydro-Electrique de Quebec et Power Authority of the State of New York," Vol. I (Montreal: Hydro-Quebec, October 1977), p. 63.

7. Ibid.

8. For a summation of the principal social arguments against the project, see Boyce Richardson, *Strangers*. His subtitle, "A Chronicle of the Assault upon the Last Coherent Hunting Culture in North America, the Cree Indians of Quebec, and Their Vast Primeval Homelands," explains his positions rather succinctly.

9. Robinson, p. 77.

10. Ibid., p. 78.

11. Hydro-Quebec, *Annual Report—1977* (Montreal, P.Q., 1977), p. F13.

12. Energy, Mines and Resources Canada, *Energy Update—1977*, EM and R Report No. E1 78-2 (Ottawa, 1978), p. 33.

13. See J. Carroll and M. Valiante, "Energy and Canadian-American Relations," and "Of Oil and Gas: A Primer on the Role of Oil and Gas in Canadian-American Relations," *Journal of Natural Resource Management and Interdisciplinary Studies* 3:1 (1978) for further background.

14. Robin J. Abercrombie, Senior Vice President, AGTL, Press Release (Calgary, Alberta, October 23, 1978), p. 3.

15. Government of Quebec, *Insurance for the Future: An Energy Policy for Quebec* (Quebec City, P.Q.: Quebec Ministry of Energy, 1978), p. 50.

16. Ibid.

17. Ibid.

18. Carl E. Beigie and Judith Maxwell, "Quebec's Vulnerability in Energy," *Accent Quebec Series* (Montreal: C.D. Howe Research Institute, 1978), p. 15.

19. Hydro-Quebec, *Annual Report—1977*, p. 15.

20. Hon. Rene Levesque, Premier of Quebec, "Remarks on Energy" delivered at the Eastern Canadian Premiers-New England Governors Conference (Whitefield, New Hampshire, June 11-13, 1978).

Index

About the Contributors

Peter W. Brown is director of the Energy Law Institute and professor of law at the Franklin Pierce Law Center in Concord, New Hampshire. He received the B.A. from Bowdoin College and the J.D. from Columbia University Law School. Dr. Brown has been a Wall Street lawyer, the first deputy attorney general for the Commonwealth of Pennsylvania, and chief counsel to the Pennsylvania Public Utilities Commission. He has written and lectured widely on public-utility regulation and was instrumental in the formulation of Title IV of the Public Utility Regulatory Policies Act of 1978.

Ronald D. Brunner is a professor of political science and public policy at the University of Michigan. Dr. Brunner has taught previously at Yale University and has served as consultant to state, local, and federal governments on issues of resource and energy policy.

John E. Carroll is associate professor of environmental conservation at the Institute of Natural and Environmental Resources of the University of New Hampshire. He received the Ph.D. degree in resource development from Michigan State University. Dr. Carroll is a specialist in U.S./Canadian energy and environmental relations and has served as consultant on energy-related matters to the Brookhaven National Laboratory and the C.D. Howe Research Institute in Montreal. He is currently the New Hampshire representative to the Northeast International Committee on Energy and advisor to New Hampshire Governor Hugh Gallen on Canadian energy matters. He has written widely on energy and the environment, particularly as they influence U.S./Canadian relations.

Hanna J. Cortner received the B.A. degree (1967) in political science from the University of Washington and the M.A. (1969) and Ph.D. (1973) degrees in government from the University of Arizona. She is a research associate in the School of Renewable Natural Resources at the University of Arizona and a member of the Forest-Watershed and Landscape Architecture program faculties. During the 1979-1980 academic year she worked on an Intergovernmental Personnel Act (IPA) assignment in the Office of Policy Analysis, U.S. Forest Service, Washington, D.C. She has written a number of monographs and articles on energy policy development.

Henry V. Harman is chief of evaluation for the Department of Developmental Programs of the City of Richmond, Virginia, where he is responsible for the information system of the city's Community Development Block Grant Program and for evaluations of the Comprehensive

Employment and Training Act Program. He was previously the executive director of the York County (Pennsylvania) Community Progress Council for three and a half years. He received the B.S. from the U.S. Coast Guard Academy, the M.Div. from Yale University, the S.T.M. from Gettysburg Lutheran Theological Seminary, and the M.A. from the University of Northern Colorado. He has long had an interest in both energy and environmental matters and was a charter member of the Section on Natural Resources and Environmental Administration of the American Society for Public Administration.

Elaine Hussey is a geothermal energy specialist at the California Energy Commission and was formerly a senior engineer in the energy program at the Jet Propulsion Lab in Pasadena, California. She holds the M.A. in Public Policy from the University of California, Berkeley, and has done additional work in planning (at Berkeley) and environmental management (at the University of Southern California). Ms. Hussey was instrumental in the creation of the Section on Natural Resources and Environmental Administration of the American Society for Public Administration and served as that section's first elected chairperson in 1978-1979. She has lectured and taught on environmental processes and energy in California for the past seven years.

Janet B. Johnson received the Sc.B. in applied mathematics from Brown University in 1972 and the Ph.D. in government from Cornell University in 1979. Dr. Johnson is currently an assistant professor of political science at the University of Delaware, where she teaches in the areas of urban politics, environmental politics, and research methods. She is presently engaged in research on land-use politics in the suburban Philadelphia area. Other research interests include citizen participation and environmental politics.

Douglas N. Jones is director of the National Regulatory Research Institute and professor of regulatory economics at The Ohio State University, where he received the Ph.D. degree in economics in 1960. He has served as assistant chief, Economics Division, Congressional Research Service of the Library of Congress, legislative assistant to Senator Mike Gravel, special assistant to the secretary of commerce for regional development, and chief economist and research director for the President's Committee for Developing Alaska. He has also been consultant to the assistant secretary of defense, the assistant secretary of the air force, and the air force chief of staff. Dr. Jones's principal areas of interest are in regulatory economics, regional development, public finance, international economics, and the economics of national security. He has written and lectured widely in these fields.

Andy Lawrence received the B.A. degree from Amherst College and the M.A. degree in environmental systems from the Center for Technology Administration at The American University. He is presently employed as an analyst in the environmental-analysis division of MITRE/METREK Corporation, McLean, Virginia.

Kai N. Lee received the Ph.D. in physics from Princeton University and is an assistant professor of environmental studies and political science at the University of Washington. He has coauthored *Electric Power and the Future of the Pacific Northwest* (forthcoming in 1980).

Walter J. Mead is a professor of economics at the University of California at Santa Barbara. Professor Mead is widely recognized as one of the nation's leading scholars in the area of natural-resource economics. Professor Mead has provided testimony for Congress on energy issues and is a consultant for the American Enterprise Institute in Washington, D.C. He has published numerous works on energy economics.

Sumner Myers is director of the Technology and Transportation Group at the Institute of Public Administration in Washington, D.C. Dr. Myers has worked for several years in the areas of technology innovation and energy policy, particularly as they relate to public administration.

Lawrence W. Plitch received the B.A. from Rutgers University and the J.D. from the Franklin Pierce Law Center in 1978. Dr. Plitch served as staff attorney for the New England Regional Energy Project, a low-income advocacy group in Burlington, Vermont. He is currently senior research fellow at the Energy Law Institute of the Franklin Pierce Law Center and has been actively involved in the development of Federal Energy Regulatory Commission's proposed regulations under section 210 of the Public Utility Regulatory Policies Act of 1978. He is now undertaking a major study of optimal financing strategies for municipal developers of small-scale hydropower facilities.

Martin Ringo received the A.B. degree from Grinnell College and the M.A. degree in economics from Brown University, where he is currently a candidate for the Ph.D. degree. Mr. Ringo is staff economist at the Energy Law Institute of the Franklin Pierce Law Center. He is an econometrician and has taught economics at Miami University of Ohio.

David J. Rosen is an assistant professor in the Department of Human Ecology and Social Science, Cook College, Rutgers University, and the Department of Political Science, the Graduate School, Rutgers University. His research and teaching focus on energy and environmental policy in the

United States and internationally. He has lectured and published widely on various aspects of energy policy. He received the Ph.D. in political science from Rutgers University in 1975.

Marc Ross is professor of physics at the University of Michigan. He received the Ph.D. in theoretical nuclear physics from the University of Wisconsin in 1952. He worked in the theory of fundamental particles until 1970, when his interests shifted to energy and environmental problems. He codirected the Physical Society's study of efficient energy use in 1974 and worked with the Ford Foundation energy study. His research focuses on the technology of energy use.

Philip R. Sharp is a member of the U.S. House of Representatives from the State of Indiana. Congressman Sharp serves on the House Subcommittee on Energy and Power.

Richard T. Sylves is an assistant professor of political science at the University of Delaware. He received the B.A. and the M.A. degrees in political science from the State University of New York and the Ph.D. degree in political science from the University of Illinois at Urbana-Champaign. He has worked on the staff of the New York State Senate Finance Committee (1972) and has been an assistant professor at the University of Cincinnati (1975-1976). His published work is in the fields of environmental and energy policy.

Richard Worthington is assistant professor of political science at Rensselaer Polytechnic Institute, where he is also affiliated with the Center for the Study of Human Dimensions of Science and Technology. Prior to coming to Rensselaer he received undergraduate and advanced degrees in political science from the University of California, Berkeley, and the University of Oregon. His professional interests include environmental politics, energy policy, appropriate technology, and technology assessment. He is currently working as the lead author on a book of articles on socialism and ecology.

Jerry Yudelson was appointed director of the California Solar Business Office by Governor Jerry Brown on May 3, 1978. He received the B.S. in civil engineering from California Institute of Technology and the M.A. in engineering and economics from Harvard University. He has been a consultant on solar energy, environmental planning, alternative energy sources, and urban affairs since 1968 and was instrumental in setting up and staffing the Governor's Office of Appropriate Technology in 1976. He has lectured and written widely on ecosystem management.

About the Editors

Gregory A. Daneke teaches policy and administration in the School of Natural Resources at the University of Michigan. Dr. Daneke received the Ph.D. from the University of California and has taught previously at Oklahoma State University and Virginia Polytechnic Institute. During 1978-1979 he served as a faculty fellow with the Energy and Minerals Division of the U.S. General Accounting Office and taught energy assessment techniques at The American University in Washington, D.C. Dr. Daneke is the author of numerous articles on applied research in the energy field and two textbooks on planning and management methodologies. He has also served as a consultant to state and local governments.

George K. Lagassa teaches public policy, public administration, and energy resource management in the M.P.A. program and the political science department at the University of New Hampshire. Dr. Lagassa received the A.B. degree from Kenyon College and the Ph.D. degree from the State University of New York at Buffalo, where he was a Woodrow Wilson Fellow. He has worked on the staff of the New York State Senate Committee on Banks and he has written in the areas of consumer credit, electric-utility regulation, energy policy, and policy analysis. He has served as a consultant to state government and is currently doing research on the role of the states in energy resource management.